Rosa Luxemburg

Divided Poland in 1795 after the third partition   *(approximate)*

Rosa Luxemburg

A LIFE

Elżbieta Ettinger

HARRAP · London

First published by Beacon Press, 25 Beacon Street,
Boston, Massachusetts 02108,
United States of America, 1987

First published in Great Britain 1987 by
Harrap Limited, 19-23 Ludgate Hill,
London EC4M 7PD

ISBN 0 245-54539-5

Text design by Copenhaver Cumpston
Printed and bound in Great Britain by
Mackays of Chatham Limited

To my parents
Regina and Emmanuel Ettinger

Contents

Illustrations

Preface

THE LAST TWENTY YEARS have brought a curious revival of interest in Rosa Luxemburg and along with it an emergence of old and new controversies. In April 1983 the West German magazine *Der Spiegel* published some of the recently discovered letters Luxemburg wrote to her last lover, Paul Levi, one of the cofounders of the Communist Party of Germany; in the early 1970s a dispute flared in West Germany over the issuance of a postage stamp with Luxemburg's likeness—some people, outraged over the honor accorded to "the foreigner," burned the stamps; in the 1960s students in Cologne named the local university after her, whereas the government of the German Federal Republic declared her assassination in 1919 to have been in accordance with martial law, although there was no charge and no trial. The two-volume biography of Rosa Luxemburg by J. P. Nettl published in Great Britain in 1966 was the first comprehensive account of her life written since 1940, and Luxemburg's letters to her friends and collaborators have appeared in France, Poland, Japan, and other countries. Collections of her articles, pamphlets, and speeches have come out in countries as disparate as the United States and Sri Lanka, and her theories are being studied anew by Marxists and non-Marxists alike.

In her native Poland there is but a lightbulb factory bearing her name. The handful of students who show interest in her have difficulty sorting out contradictory information. Some Polish scholars maintain that as a Jew Luxemburg lacked sensitivity to Poland's needs and culture, others that her origin did not make her less a Pole. One of the most prominent socialist thinkers, Luxemburg is still awaiting a biographer in her own country.

It is symptomatic that in Poland Luxemburg is a Jew and in Germany, her adopted country, she is a foreigner. That many publications refer to her as a "German revolutionary"—notwithstanding her prominent role in Polish socialism—is perhaps not merely a sign of ignorance but of the confusion which surrounds her.

During her lifetime Rosa Luxemburg, though well known worldwide in the socialist movement, could not claim the fame many of her contemporaries enjoyed. Her reputation was far outdistanced by that of such theorists as August Bebel, Karl Kautsky, and Eduard Bernstein in Germany, Jean Jaurès in France, and Georgij Plekhanov in Russia. Yet these names are known today mainly by scholars, whereas hers attracts ever more interest. Why? In a world torn between two superpowers, neither of which has fulfilled humankind's yearning for social justice, Rosa Luxemburg has become for many the symbol of the yet unattained dream.

Then there is a strictly political reason both for Luxemburg's fading from view since the 1930s and for her recent comeback. In 1931 Stalin accused Luxemburg of turning Marx's concept of revolution into a "caricature." This verdict was tantamount to Luxemburg's exclusion from the canon of Marxist ideology East and West. Stalin's death and the subsequent reevaluation of Luxemburg's concept of socialism brought her works back to public attention.

Besides the renowned revolutionary, however, there is another Rosa Luxemburg, a largely unknown person thrice stigmatized: as a woman, as a Jew, and as a cripple. This biography is devoted primarily to the portrayal of that person. Once we come to know her dreams and her struggles, she becomes our contemporary—a woman who firmly believed that personal happiness can be achieved without sacrificing public life and whose fight for both a personal and a public life was hard, stubborn, and not always rewarding.

Luxemburg's personal life has been neglected for a variety of reasons. Her friends respected her intense need for privacy; her comrades were interested solely in her public activities; the lingering Victorian taboos, political expediency, and imposed or self-imposed censorship; and the inaccessibility of documents (some in private hands) contributed to the portrait of the one-dimensional woman that the world knows.

In many ways Luxemburg was representative of her generation, in others she was exceptional. Her passionate desire to have a child, a loving man, and a family and at the same time to be a leader in the international socialist movement was not common. Men had wives to take care of them, their children, household, and finances and to help them with their work. Women often sacrificed personal life to the cause. Not Luxemburg. She did not believe women necessarily had to make such choices; she believed they could and should have both.

Luxemburg's notion of a life "worth living," as she put it, determined her destiny. Love and work, inseparable, made for a fulfilled life. She was forty-seven years old, ravaged by illness and imprisonment, when she wrote to a friend: "For me too love always was (or is? . . .) more significant and more sacred than the object who stirs it. Because love turns the world around us into a glittering fairytale, and love releases in us what is most noble and most beautiful, it elevates and frames in diamonds the most trivial and petty, and it lets one live in rapture and in ecstasy."[1] Her work was the fight for social justice. Oppression stimulated that fight, and she continued it in the best tradition of her forebears, always maintaining her intellectual independence, respectful of spiritual aspirations, questioning any mortal authority.

She lived and loved, was exuberantly happy and infinitely un-happy, but always she was alive. She was torn by conflicting feelings, at one time determined to rid herself of the burden of her Jewish origin, at another filled with doubts and guilt. She wanted to be good to her parents, but their pathetic love and admiration embarrassed and irritated her. She wanted to be good to her lovers, but she was possessive and jealous. She wanted a revolution yet dreaded blood-shed. But she gallantly suffered the contradictions of her nature and her beliefs. Her mind soared far beyond the present while her own needs and tastes remained traditional. She was a woman of torrential passion, which made her personal and public life difficult. Yet she never lost hope in either realm. She carried on her lonely struggle determined to live in her own way and to realize her dreams and ideas.

Born in 1870 into a middle-class family, Rosa Luxemburg was raised and educated in Warsaw. It is a truism that Polish Jews were especially attracted to socialism, but what is largely ignored is that Polish socialism was socialism with a romantic tinge. Romantic poets, above all Adam Mickiewicz, promised deliverance to all oppressed peoples, among them the Jews, the most despised minority. To escape oppression and inspired by Mickiewicz, Rosa went to Switzerland at the age of nineteen. There she met a Russian revolutionary, Leo Jogiches, the great love of her life, with whom she lived in common-law marriage for fifteen years. Together they founded the first Polish Marxist workers' party, the Social Democracy of the Kingdom of Poland and Lithuania. In 1897 Rosa obtained a doctorate in law and political science at the University of Zurich, and the following year she moved to Germany. She became one of the leading figures in the German Social Democratic Party and in the Second International. She was assassinated in 1919 in Berlin.

The loss of sovereignty—Poland was divided among Russia, Prussia, and Austria in the partitions of 1772, 1793, and 1795—left the Poles with broken dreams of power and glory and a feeling of impotence that easily ignited fanatic nationalism. Rosa, the reluctant Jew and the enthralled disciple of Adam Mickiewicz, would come to regard nationalism as the greatest evil. Mickiewicz also inspired her faith in the wisdom and instinctive righteousness of the simple people, the workers. Later elaborated into the theory of spontaneous revolution, it was proved right by the revolutionary movements in Poland and Hungary in 1956, in Czechoslovakia in 1968, and again in Poland in 1980. No amount of arms, in any corner of the world, she believed, could stop people thirsty for justice and hungry for bread from rising up against those who corrupt them morally and exploit them economically.

The image of Rosa Luxemburg, the stalwart revolutionary who lived and died for "the cause," is not only one-sided but also distorted. The woman who emerges from letters written by her family in Warsaw and by her to the men she loved—Leo Jogiches, Konstatin Zetkin, and Paul Levi—is a person of flesh and blood, with strengths and weaknesses, triumphs and nightmares. Brilliant and courageous, she still was racked by doubts, insecurity, and disappointments inevitable in the life of a woman who transcended her time.

xiv

While it is possible to analyze Luxemburg's economic and political writings independent of her personal life, it is not possible to present her personal life and at the same time ignore her work. No attempt was made here, however, to give a comprehensive analysis of her writings; such analyses are easily accessible. Nor was an attempt made to write a definitive biography. There is no such thing as a "definitive biography." A biography is always a selection and therefore a biographer is always "biased." This is then a portrait with no glass and no frame.

Poland

I | *Zamość:*
The Native Town
1870–1873

IT IS POSSIBLE to imagine that certain characteristics of Zamość, where Rosa Luxemburg was born, were woven into her life. A town of disquieting charm crippled by geographical position, ambitious from inception but undermined by shifting political winds, it strove to link East with West but failed. It was a proud and resilient city. And, faced with adversity—bold and courageous.

Situated halfway between two big commercial areas, Lublin and Lwów, Zamość became in the sixteenth century an important international trade center lying on a transit route and at the crossroads of different cultures. Armenians, Turks, Greeks, Persians, and Jews, Germans, Scots, and Englishmen, all granted preferential treatment, found the town congenial. The local aristocracy developed a taste for learning and luxury. The Zamoyski Academy, established in 1595, further enhanced the town's cultural life.

The bloody Swedish invasion that swept Poland in the seventeenth century left the soundly fortified town unharmed, but its prosperity ended. No longer a safe place, plagued by epidemics, fires, and overcrowding from refugees, it was gradually abandoned by the foreigners.

In the eighteenth century sovereign Poland ceased to exist; it was divided in three consecutive partitions—in 1772, 1793, and 1795—

among Russia, Prussia, and Austria. The first partition put Zamość into Austrian hands, and the closure of the famous Academy in 1784 marked the end of the town's splendor. After the Russian-ruled Kingdom of Poland was created in 1815, Zamość, now in Russian hands, became a military outpost.* Few of the graceful Renaissance buildings escaped redecoration. The town hall and the Franciscan church were turned into barracks, the castle into a military hospital. Yet the town's heritage did not disappear completely. Zamość remained a cultural center for Poles and Jews (one-third of the 6,222 inhabitants in the mid-1800s were Jews), and trade and crafts flourished.

Zamość's growth into an important cultural and commercial center for Jews was due to a settlement privilege granted to Sephardic Jews in 1588 by Jan Zamoyski, Great Chancellor of the Crown. The town attracted doctors, apothecaries, international merchants, and highly skilled craftsmen who presented no economic threat to the local inhabitants. In the aftermath of the Swedish invasion, however, the Sephardic Jews fled while Ashkenazi Jews, unsophisticated and unskilled, flooded the town. The economic structure changed and so did social attitudes—Poles and Jews competed for their livelihood. Decrees were passed by the Zamoyskis aimed at "supporting the Christian commoners and craftsmen" and curtailing the rights of Jews in trading, housing, and ownership of property.[1] Restricted in occupation, excluded from guilds, hedged in by discriminatory laws, Jews became brokers, peddlers, money lenders, middlemen, and innkeepers, occupations that earned them the animosity of non-Jews and reputations as swindlers. The introduction of tsarist rule in the early nineteenth century did not improve their situation.

The Russians' interest in warcraft was matched only by their preoccupation with the appearance of the Jews. Jewish garb, headgear, and hairstyles generated meticulous orders that kept busy both the Russians who issued them and the Poles who had to enforce them. Wigs and shaven heads for women were outlawed, as were beards and earlocks for men. Elaborate distinctions were made between cutting, trimming, and shaving hair, the length and cut of coats, and the shape of hats. All this exasperated the Polish mayor of Zamość. "To take

*The Tsar held the title King of Poland; hence the term "Kingdom." Warsaw was the capital of the Kingdom of Poland.

them all to court means no less than incarcerating the whole city and that is simply impossible," he informed the authorities in the 1850s.[2] The passive resistance of the Jews brought about the abolition of a tax imposed on their clothing, but did not put an end to harassment—although neither the Austrian nor the Russian authorities ever developed a precise recipe for a proper-looking Jew.

According to family legend, the ancestor of the Polish Luksenburgs was a young landscape architect whom Count Andrzej Zamoyski met in Brussels in the eighteenth century and, favorably impressed, brought to his Zamość estate. However, the well-preserved Zamoyski archives contain no document to support that claim. Rosa's paternal grandfather was a prosperous timber merchant whose business extended to the West and to the East. Rather early, he fled the confines of Jewish Orthodox life, and his son, Elias, inherited both his business and his drive for assimilation. Rosa's mother, Lina Löwenstein, the daughter of Rabbi Itzakh Oser Löwenstein, was a descendant of seventeen generations of rabbis and Hebrew scholars, reaching back to a famed commentator on the Talmud, Rabbi Zerachya Halevi, in twelfth-century Spain.[3] Lina's brother, Rabbi Bernard Löwenstein, became a doctor of philosophy and theology; as adults the brother and sister maintained no contact, perhaps an indication that Lina's family disapproved of her marriage outside the Orthodox faith. Lina and Elias met in Zamość, where they settled because of Elias's business.

Rozalia (Róża) was born in Zamość on 5 March 1870, the youngest of the couple's five children. The oldest, Chana (Anna), was born in 1858, Natan (Mikołaj) in 1860, Maksymilian in 1866, and Józef in 1868. The family lived in a spacious two-story brick house in the main square. The language spoken at home was Polish, but Elias Luksenburg used Yiddish in business, which was often transacted at home. Lina Luksenburg faithfully observed Jewish holidays—feasts that brought the family together—even after her children grew up and left home.

Rosa spent the first three years of her life in tranquil and comfortable surroundings. The darling of her parents and her older siblings, she was a confident and cheerful girl. But her sunny childhood ended abruptly in 1873. Elias Luksenburg lacked his father's knack for business. His fortunes declined as his family's needs grew—particularly with respect to the children's education, to which both parents felt strongly committed. Elias decided to try his luck in the capital.

There may have been other reasons for the family's move to Warsaw. The Luksenburgs, it seems, formed no lasting friendships among the Zamość Jews, many of them Orthodox and Hasidim, who shunned the assimilationists. It is probable that the family moved to escape the ever-present anti-Jewish sentiment. A big city offered a measure of anonymity and better protection against overzealous bureaucrats. Although exempt from the persecution suffered by poor and Orthodox Jews, the assimilated Jews were not exempt from the stigma of the association. The 1863 Polish insurrection against Russia, which inflamed the Zamość region, brought Draconian repression of both the insurgents and their supporters, among them Jews who supplied soldiers, guides, uniforms, and arms. By then the Luksenburgs had two children, and though it took another ten years before they left Zamość, the move might already have been contemplated. At that time the Enlightenment (Haskalah), an intellectual movement geared toward secular education and culture, made serious inroads in the Jewish world. But in Zamość it was fiercely opposed by the Hasidim and the strong Orthodox rabbinical center. Lina Luksenburg's absorption in German and Polish literature and her keen efforts to bestow her interests on her children ran counter to the traditional Jewish values. In Zamość, Jews were faced with a multitude of conflicts unknown to their emancipated coreligionists in western Europe. Isolation, anti-Semitism, and economic necessity thus brought the Luksenburgs to Warsaw in 1873. Rosa was three years old.

2 | *Warsaw: The Drastic Change*
1874–1882

THE JEWISH QUARTER of Warsaw was created in 1809. The dishonesty, perfidy, and corruption of the Jews were cited as grounds for the segregation. In fact, Polish and Russian merchants had pressed the Russian authorities to eliminate the unwanted competition from the inner city. Jewish merchants were offered the opportunity to invest their capital in developing the outskirts of the city; the center remained off limits to them. Only 140 Jewish families obtained permission to live outside the quarter in the years 1809–1862. The prerequisites for permission included huge assets—60,000 Polish zloty (roughly the equivalent of $6,900 at the time)—as well as fluency in Polish, German, or French, public school attendance for the children, and Western attire. Whenever economic or political expedience required greater flexibility, the discriminatory rules were bent. This policy increased the mistrust between Poles and Jews. The Catholic Church warned against corruption of morals should Christian and Jew live together, and the Polish municipality insisted that only Jews distinguished in arts and sciences be permitted to live in Warsaw. Despite strenuous opposition, the Tsar's order of 1862 finally abolished residence restrictions, and the Jewish quarter formally ceased to exist.

The Luksenburgs carefully chose the neighborhood to which they moved. It had recently been opened to Jews and was halfway toward acceptance by Poles. Inhabited also by Polish professionals, it was a short but safe distance from the section occupied by the poor and Orthodox Jews. The Jewish neighborhood—with its exotic atmosphere, gesticulating men with earlocks and yarmulkas, their kaftans flying like huge black birds, women in wigs, beggars, and street vendors—resembled medieval theater rather than a Western capital. It was a source of embarrassment and resentment to assimilated Jews, who felt shame for their people's backwardness and longed not to be associated with it. They reformed their religion; they no longer spoke Yiddish "in front of the children"; they softened their Semitic features by wearing Western clothes. And yet, just a few streets away was that other world, the main obstacle to acceptance: noisy people in bizarre costumes; laborers who refused to work on Saturdays; tsadiks who performed miracles; rabbis who made laws. Ordered by tsarist decree to dispose of their beards and garb, they found ways to keep both; expelled from one part of the city, they emerged in another; urged to learn Polish, they elevated Yiddish to a literary tongue.

Warsaw represented a step toward assimilation for the Luksenburgs. But as in Zamość, each move in that direction required a decision and each decision presented a new problem. The Luksenburgs could not follow an established pattern—none existed; nor could they comfortably consider themselves either Jews or Poles. They chose to loosen the traditional ties and to assume an altered but not totally new identity. To gain access to the Polish world without renouncing Jewish tradition was more difficult than a clear-cut conversion to Christianity; nor was it welcomed by most Poles. To a Pole, a Jewish Jew was easily identifiable and therefore less of a threat than an assimilated one. Moreover, after Russia, Prussia, and Austria partitioned Poland, a Jew was no longer simply a Polish Jew but also a Russian, a Prussian, or an Austrian subject. That made the road to emancipation yet more slippery.

Złota Street Number 16 was in the middle of a short block that connected two streets, Bracka and the main artery, Marszałkowska. Złota Street cut through Marszałkowska and became more squalid as it continued west, but the short section where the Luksenburgs lived was a good neighborhood. Decades earlier Bracka Street had been the daily route of the Russian Grand Duke Konstantin, commander-in-chief of the Polish army. From his residence in the Belvedere Palace he had proceeded on horseback to Saski Square for the notoriously humiliating inspections of his Polish subordinates. One unquestioned benefit of the Duke's excursions on Bracka Street was that the street's surface had been paved with solid stone. Marszałkowska Street was bustling with life. Women dressed in the latest Paris fashions, stores offering choice imported wares, cafés, restaurants, and bookstores gave the metropolis a touch of European chic. It was multinational, multilingual, lively, and colorful. Smart horse-drawn carriages transported elegant ladies to their charitable functions and gentlemen to intimate dinners; glittering Russian uniforms mingled with priests' cassocks and girl-students' pinafores; dandies and nuns, Hasidim in broad-brimmed beaver hats and messengers in bright red caps, governesses in black capes and street musicians, all under the watchful eye of mustached Russian policemen, brought an aura of glamour to the street.

The picture changed drastically just outside the center of the city. Dilapidated coaches drawn by bony mares hobbled over the cobblestones; vendors harnessed to carts offered sand, water, fruit, and vegetables; ragmen, junkmen, waterbearers, and porters monotonously chanted the praises of their commodities and services. An organ grinder and his monkey, acrobats, clowns, and beggars joined in the chorus. Still farther from the city's center were the factories that lured peasants, Jews, and young people from the provinces.

Like the city, Złota Street also had an elegant facade and a less elegant backyard. The more expensive flats, like the Luksenburgs' home, faced the street and were occupied by a different class of people than were the tenements overlooking the yard. With little or no daylight, overpriced and overcrowded, the tenement buildings were occupied by tailors, needlewomen, milliners, and cobblers. Like all tenement dwellers, these people had a history of penury, disease, and despair. Often a family of six, a workshop, and apprentices lived in one room equipped with a makeshift oven, straw mattresses, a few chairs, and a table. Tuberculosis, scurvy, and rickets were common. The lively, clean street and the dark, filthy courtyard, the front apartments and the backyard tenements were Rosa's first introduction to differences in social standing.

The move to Warsaw disrupted her life. The three-room flat, housing her parents and four siblings, deprived her of space and restricted her movements. The comfort of familiar surroundings and familiar people, of consistency and predictability was gone. She was taken out for walks by her older sister, Anna, whose limp she disliked, or by her mother. Every time she went out she had to dress up. Anna took her to nearby Saski Garden, full of children, old trees, and flowerbeds. The children in Saski Garden were unlike her playmates in Zamość. Fancily dressed, they were accompanied by adults and spoke in a serious, deliberate manner. The loss of her former companions, who talked loudly and laughed loudly and were happy to play with her, was bewildering. Out of spite and anger she spoke loudly herself, only to be admonished to lower her voice, to behave. Why her behavior, acceptable before, was now criticized was difficult for her to understand. But just as she began adjusting to her new life, she suffered another yet more shattering blow.

The exact circumstances that prompted Rosa's parents to have a physician examine her legs remain unknown. She herself maintained that her gait was normal until, at the age of five, she was put into a cast and kept in bed for a year. She got up with one leg shorter. The long confinement indicates that she was treated for a tubercular hip, but in all probability she suffered from a congenital hip dislocation, common among female infants at the time. As an adult, she blamed her parents for her condition, which she believed could have been avoided if detected earlier and treated properly. It is doubtful that her parents were negligent, as she claimed; since the older daughter limped, they were surely alert to potential problems.[1] The effects of a hip dislocation may have been unnoticeable for a long time, and that probably misled both parents and doctors.

After the cast was removed it appeared that Rosa limped, but it was not clear whether her condition was curable. She was taken from one doctor to another and subjected to different treatments, often painful and finally useless. Baths, compresses, and stretching were prescribed, and she suffered the pain with patience. For a long time it did not occur to her that treatments might not help. She could not imagine herself dragging her leg like her older sister or being unable to walk like other children. Yet she limped heavily. She found the physical suffering easier to bear than the conspicuousness of the handicap. Urchins pointed at her and sang in unison, "Cripple, cccrriipplee." Children in the park observed her curiously, followed her, or ran away. The pitying glances and the whispers of adults were no less maddening. She dreaded the street, the strangers, the compassion. All her energy was concentrated on minimizing the limp; it was a triumph to pass in the street unnoticed.

Perhaps her parents believed the damage was not permanent; perhaps Rosa waited for her shorter leg to grow. It was unjust. She had three extremely handsome brothers, and her own body was deformed. Any rewards of family indulgence were suspect in the face of the calamity. In time she learned to accept her disfigured body and created an image of a happy, healthy child. In the years to come she so perfected the image that even her closest friends believed it was real.

On 5 March 1880 Rosa turned ten. In the fall of that year, after being tutored at home, she entered the first class of the state school, the Russian Second Gymnasium for Girls. No doubt she wanted badly to attend school, to escape the boredom, the isolation, the cramped apartment. But at the same time she was filled with apprehension. Like other applicants of Jewish origin, she had to score higher on the entrance examination than a non-Jew; there was a quota set for Jews. She was accepted, but it was not the kind of acceptance she wanted.

Being admitted under a quota system was her first confrontation with her inferior status. A sensitive child, she felt degraded. It was at this point that she started her protracted fight to remove the stigma, and the choices she made in later life, personal and public, were a direct or indirect reaction to the child's humiliation.

The experience deepened her confusion. With no religious up-bringing, she was, however, exposed to some traditions, like the celebration of Rosh Hashana or Passover. Her mother's attachment to Judaism, her father's typically Jewish occupation of small merchant, and her physical handicap added still more to her turmoil. Her school was Russian, her language Polish. Poland, her mother country, did not exist as an independent state. Being Polish, like being Jewish, provided no stronghold, no security.

Segregation at school was only one aspect of the quota system. Religion, a mandatory subject, further divided the students into Roman Catholic, Russian Orthodox, and Jew. Throughout their school years, students attended separate classes in religious instruction according to their creed. Unlike the Jews, the Russian and Polish students, more numerous and usually with strong religious ties, did not seek at school a way out of a predicament rooted in race and religion and therefore suffered none of the Jews' emotional stresses. Not that the Poles lacked their own trials; forbidden to speak in their native tongue, they were closely watched by teachers, predominantly Russians, and punished when they broke the rule. But if a Polish pupil had to be alert, a Jewish one, guilty by definition, had to be doubly so; he was more suspect, more severely punished, and an easy target of derision. A few months before Rosa entered the Gymnasium, a group of high school students were expelled for what was termed a political demonstration—they had offered a gift of flowers to the famous Polish actress Helena Modrzejewska (Modjeska). Among those involved was Ignacy Neufeld, a seventeen-year-old Jew. He threatened suicide if he was dismissed. The school director's reaction was typical: "A Jew! Shoot himself! I'll never believe *that!*" Neufeld was expelled and as he had promised, blew out his brains.[2]

Her experience at school confirmed Rosa's worst fears. She was different. She could not do what the other girls did. They could run into the school building and take two or three stairs at a time in order to beat the sound of the gong announcing the beginning of class. She could not. She had to get up earlier, leave the house earlier and climb the stairs one by one. Every day she made the long trek from Złota Street to Wilcza Street, where the school was located, totally concentrated on keeping her small body erect and her limp as imperceptible as she could manage. In the classroom she felt at ease, though walking to the blackboard was a trial. The sports and dancing caused her the greatest anxiety. Sports for girls were a novelty; besides dancing classes, schools introduced calisthenics, ice skating, and outdoor games. Rosa liked exercise, dance, and sports. She had no difficulties moving, but move with charm she could not. At a time when a graceful carriage was one of the chief feminine attributes, her physical awkwardness hurt all the more. Yet she stubbornly trained for the most difficult physical tests and passed them.

The milieu Rosa encountered at school was largely alien to her. Her classmates were the daughters of impoverished Polish gentry, the intelligentsia, middle-level officials, Russian functionaries stationed in Warsaw, and Jews of modest means. There was little socializing between the offspring of the rulers and those of the vanquished; and the latter, the Polish and Jewish students, formed no cohesive group. Rosa was by no means exceptional in her desire to identify with the

Poles; that was, after all, what assimilation was about—to overcome barriers and blend into the Polish culture, with the school providing the first bridge. But not all Poles were disposed to allow the Jews to cross that bridge.

In academic life Rosa established herself quickly; a hard worker, diligent, gifted, and eager, she was a model student. But social acceptance did not follow. She could claim an intellect but not a noble ancestry; she could impress her classmates with her individuality, but the masses of dark brown hair, the big deep-brown, intense eyes and protruding nose, were all too conspicuous. The impecunious status of the Polish girls mattered little. They were blond, blue-eyed, and creamy-complexioned, their fathers and grandfathers were martyrs to the national cause, their mothers and grandmothers took them, all clad in white, to Sunday mass and to church fairs. They attended soirées, danced mazurkas and polonaises, and celebrated Christian religious holidays, rituals that Rosa adopted once she left home.

Outside the school she had little in common with her new friends. Their fierce national pride intimidated her. Did she share in their heritage of Polish kings who made the country into a bulwark of Christianity and Polish queens, models of Christian virtues? Rosa's later fanatic antinationalism may have grown out of ambivalence over this heritage.

The nervous restlessness that was to set the rhythm of Rosa's adult life originated with the obstacle course that school presented to her. Had she been placed in a special but not inferior category—had she been the proud daughter of a distinguished father—she might have yearned less for recognition outside her family. Had she not been crippled, she might have been more confident. And had she felt a strong sense of belonging to the Jewish tradition, she might have fought less desperately to be accepted as a Pole. The fulfillment of her natural desire—to be like everyone else—was outside her reach. This she had to accept; she did, and concentrated on drawing attention away from her Semitic features and shorter leg toward her mind. And this is how Rozalia Luksenburg became Rosa Luxemburg. It was an arduous undertaking and she never stopped paying. Strong will was not enough; neither were drive, ambition, and intellect. She cast herself in a role of strength—strong will, strong mind, strong character—a role she came to play so convincingly that it became second nature. Arrogance and aggressiveness covered her insecurity; a show of self-confidence hid her fears. In her school years she became known as "strong," an epithet she appreciated more than "cripple" or "dirty Jew kid."

Rosa was not quite twelve years old when she experienced the greatest brutality of her short life. She had just started her second year at the Gymnasium and had won and enjoyed the recognition of her teachers and classmates. She was discovering that the attributes of her mind could override any misgivings others might have about her. Slowly, she was overcoming her anxieties.

On Christmas Day of 1881 a panic, whose origin remains unknown, seized the crowd leaving the Church of the Holy Cross. The panic ended in a pogrom. In the tsarist empire, pogroms held the Jews in check by making the impermanence of their security manifest. Pogroms found a fertile soil in Poland, where age-old tensions were aggravated by the large concentration of Orthodox Jews and by the country's economic backwardness and lost independence. The foreign occupation enticed some Poles into a fanatic nationalism. Their nationhood threatened, their dignity injured, the victims needed victims.

The pogrom in Warsaw was less shocking to the poverty-stricken inhabitants of the Jewish quarter than to the Złota Street Jews. The precariousness of their newly acquired status was not only exposed, it was legitimized by the authorities. The tsarist police did not interfere with the assailants. Because of the acquiescence of the police, the pogrom raged for three days and nights in the Jewish quarter. The workers, peddlers, cobblers, and shopkeepers rallied in self-defense and prevented the disaster from spreading. Two thousand families suffered losses; many were wounded and killed. Although more affluent neighborhoods usually enjoyed the protection of the police, this time even Złota Street was not safe. A rowdy crowd stormed the area, looting, breaking windows, throwing stones. Some Jews ran to their Polish neighbors for safety, others barricaded doors and windows.

It is not difficult to imagine what was going on in Rosa's mind. The screaming and shouting, the jangle of glass broken under heavy boots, the coarse, roaring laughter, the curses in Polish and Yiddish, the sound of wailing women and crying children left her terrified. Her parents could not defend her. They could not stop the mob yelling "Beat the Jew!" from breaking into the house, beating her, murdering her. She could not run away. Dragging her shorter leg behind her, she would surely fall into the hands of the horde. Never before did her limp appear a danger, a threat to her life; never before was fear so real.

Rosa's parents may have hidden her, perhaps for hours, perhaps for days. They may have taken her to Polish neighbors or kept her in the apartment behind locked doors. But whatever they did to ensure her physical safety, they could do nothing about her mental anguish.

The pogrom left Rosa with a permanent scar. In later years when she herself could control crowds, could keep them spellbound, she avenged the horror-struck child. The crowds chanted, "Long live Rosa!" But she remained scared of the mob. "Do you know what thought obsesses and frightens me?" she wrote to her friend Luise Kautsky in 1917. "I imagine that again I must enter an overcrowded gigantic hall, the glaring lights, the ear-splitting noise, the mass of people pushing against me . . . and I feel an urge to suddenly run away! . . . I have a horror of crowds."[3]

She buried the childhood experience deeply. Meticulously scrupulous though she was, the one time she mentioned the pogrom—in passing, in an impersonal way, in an unsigned article—she mistook its date.[4]

3 | *Warsaw: The Adolescent Quest*
1882–1889

THE POGROM BROUGHT to the surface all Rosa's latent fears. Desperate for escape from the frightening reality, she found her refuge in poetry.

Adam Mickiewicz, a world-renowned Romantic who captivates the minds of young idealists to this day,* became the source of Rosa's inspiration. His appeal to unite "minds and hearts" in love and rebellion, his dreams of "good for all" entranced her because she was hurt, lonely, and threatened. All oppressed people, Mickiewicz taught—workers, Jews, peasants—wherever they live, will become equal once the old world order is destroyed.

Nothing could have been more alluring to the teenage Rosa than the sense of belonging to a community bound by a noble goal. "Shoulder to shoulder," the poet said, youth would raze the decaying universe and build a better world. The idea of relieving humanity's suffering eased her pain. In a world in which everyone loved everyone, she too would be loved, in spite of her origin, in spite of her deformity.

*For example, the closing of Mickiewicz's play *The Forefathers* in Warsaw in 1968 because of its allegedly anti-Russian overtones led to widespread student unrest.

In dimly lit rooms, behind closely guarded doors, girls and boys gathered in clandestine meetings and hungrily listened to the outlawed verses of Mickiewicz. The mystery of the poetry, the conspiracy, and the secrecy fueled the feverish excitement of the young audiences. Erotic and spiritual, the poems told them about ideal love, the meeting of two souls that become one.

The very facts of Mickiewicz's biography even now retain their magic for the Poles. They represent Polish experience in its purest form. Mickiewicz began as a conspirator and ended as a pilgrim. Born in 1798 in the Wilno region, he lived in exile in Russia and later in France and died mysteriously in 1855 in Turkey. He personified the drama of his country—torn between East and West, emotion and reason.

As a student at the University of Wilno, he was imprisoned for founding a secret Polish student society, and was deported to Russia in 1824. In Russia, 1824 was a year of hopes and dreams that were broken in the failed 1825 Decembrists' uprising against Tsar Nicholas I. Close to the Russian intellectuals, the Decembrists, and above all to Alexander Pushkin, Mickiewicz discovered a larger spiritual and intellectual world. The rebellious Pole became a rebellious European. Freedom now became not only Poland's freedom but freedom for all oppressed nations. The Russians, he saw, suffered no less than the Poles from autocracy, and their enemies were the same as his. Pushkin, an exile in his own country, and Mickiewicz translated each other's poetry into their native tongues and mourned together the slain or imprisoned Decembrists. In a poem called "To My Russian Friends," Mickiewicz lamented:

> Where are you now?
> Ryleev's noble head that I held in brotherly embrace
> hangs from the gallows by the Tsar's decree . . .
> Bestuzhev's hand, that he, the bard and knight
> stretched out to me, cut off by the Tsar from pen and sword
> tears at the stones in the quarry, chained to the arm of the
> Pole . . .
>
> Cursed be peoples that murder their prophets.[1]

The tragedy of the Decembrists did not discourage him. Indeed, his poetry preached battle the more forcefully. The insidious charm of Mickiewicz's ideas, his Samson-like readiness to destroy and perish under the rubble, and his Christ-like willingness to sacrifice played no small role in triggering the 1830 anti-Russian insurrection in Poland and every Polish insurrection since.

In the years of Mickiewicz's exile in France, where he settled in the 1830s, his beliefs led him to socialism—Messianic, mystical, but also rational. "Socialism," he wrote in 1849, "is an entirely new word. Who created it? No one knows. Words created by no one but repeated by everyone are most frightening. Fifty years ago the words *revolution* and *revolutionary* were also barbaric neologisms . . . The old world and all its representatives, though unable to grasp their meaning, read their death sentence in them . . . The old world . . . has no moral foundation."[2] The poet-warrior was the founder of *Peoples' Tribune*, an international journal that assembled revolutionaries, anarchists, and utopians. Mickiewicz became a socialist because he was a Christian, but one increasingly skeptical of the Holy See. "Rest assured," he challenged Pope Pius IX, "that God's spirit dwells nowadays under the work blouses of Paris laborers."[3]

Because of the prestige he lent to the ethos of the pilgrim who set out to seek freedom and justice for all, the poet may have ennobled Rosa's vague desire to leave her home and country. "The Polish pilgrims are the soul of the Polish nation," he wrote.[4] Throughout Poland's captivity, pilgrimage became an idea, a way of life, tragic and mystical and of deep moral significance. In his *Books of the Polish Nation and of the Polish Pilgrims,* Mickiewicz commanded the Poles to survive, much as the Old Testament had commanded the Jews living in the Diaspora. A Polish pilgrim, the poet wrote, is not a wanderer or an exile, for a wanderer strays without a goal and an exile is banished by decree. A pilgrim journeys in alien lands, but his homeland is within him, and the indissoluble bond, ethereal like a shaft of light and heavy like the slave's chains, elevates his spirit and guides his intellect.

Mickiewicz's pilgrimage brought him finally to Turkey. The last episode of the poet's life is not widely publicized by his embarrassed compatriots. Inspired by the Polish mystic Andrzej Towiański, Mickiewicz came to believe that in a popular war for the freedom of all peoples, the "Jews . . . who hold sacred the omnipotence of the people, equality and freedom" would defeat all oppression.[5] He resolved to organize a detachment of Jewish hussars (Russian Jews taken as prisoners of war by the Turks) who were to fight for the freedom of the people of Israel and Poland. Amidst the preparations Mickiewicz died.

What started for Rosa as a need to escape from reality gradually evolved into a decision to change reality long before she heard about Marx. Her belief in the moral obligation to fight for a more humane system, in the ethical dimension of social change—the essence of Luxemburg's philosophy—derived from the poet's vision. His faith in the healthy instincts of the common people underlay Luxemburg's famous theory of the spontaneity of revolution. Many years later, convinced of the power of the creative spirit and the intuitive wisdom of the masses, who, as the poet said, "know" because they "feel," she rejected Lenin's concept of a professionally organized revolution.

In the 1880s, when literature fought for "minds and hearts" and provided youth with poetic visions, reality confronted Polish society with new facts and new challenges. The unsuccessful 1863 insurrection bled the nation, leaving the Russian invaders unvanquished and more determined than ever to pacify the rebellious country. The hopelessness of armed resistance and the rapid industrialization in Europe opened doors to a new Western trend in Polish culture and economy known as positivism. Instead of looking back, mourning for lost glory, and dooming the country to extinction, the Polish positivists declared, the nation must become realistic, forget the past, and look to the future; productive work must replace the sabers, factories must replace the barricades. National independence was not indispensable to the nation's survival, the positivists maintained, but a sound economy was. Although positivism in one sense was just a different word for a liberal economy, late in coming to Poland by three decades, it was not welcomed by a large segment of the society.

If the shock of the crushed 1863 uprising against the Russians altered some attitudes, it did not change the national ethos. Rebelliousness, an inability to conform to reality, an aversion to pragmatism, and the worship of heroism made the Poles poor partners in capitalist ventures. While it was easy for a landowner to give his property to patriotic causes or gamble it away, it was difficult for him to turn into a merchant or a banker. Few Poles dreamt about making fortunes or building factories; many viewed with apprehension if not disgust the growing ranks of German, Russian, and Jewish industrialists. Material success remained very low on the scale of traditional values. One hundred years of foreign rule, political impotence, and isolation intensified rather than weakened the traits that had developed over the previous eight centuries of Poland's sovereignty. The descendants of "the royal tribe" nourished a contempt for the modern Huns in the West matched only by that for the Asians in the East.

Economic change required above all cooperation with the three invaders in the annexed territories: the Russians, the Prussians, and the Austrians. To many Poles in the 1880s, and in particular to the younger generation, for which the 1863 insurrection was yet another glorious page in the patriotic gospel, this amounted to explicit recognition of the status quo, an admission of defeat, and conformity for the sake of material gain. But some young Poles found a way to link tradition with modernity, though not exactly the one the positivists preached. The sons and daughters of the intelligentsia and the new bourgeoisie blazed with a different kind of rebellion—socialism.

In parallel with economic positivism, a literary trend also known as positivism developed. The successful businessman—rational, sensible, skeptical—replaced the doomed romantic rebel. But the new hero was largely confined to fiction. There was little in him that appealed to those who held an idealized vision of Poland's destiny; he could no more fire the imagination or inflame the spirit than he could inspire resistance. He was devoid of drama, for which his rational mind and his skill at making money were a poor substitute. Poland was not going to become a nation of entrepreneurs. The road to glory was not paved with bank notes.

Resistance to modernity could do no more than slow down its progress or ensure that it bypass the Poles to the benefit of non-Poles. Poland, at the crossroads of East and West, was much too important as a commercial route and a source of cheap labor to be left out in the Russian and Prussian designs of economic expansion. The 1862 waiver on restrictions for Polish Jews was a shrewd move on the part of the tsarist government; the Jewish worker was the cheapest, the Jewish entrepreneur the most eager. In the years 1874–1897 the Jewish population in Warsaw increased from about 90,000 to 220,000, while in Russia the big cities were largely off limits for Jews. By 1870 one-third of the factories in Warsaw were owned by Jews, and by 1895 there was hardly a street left with no Jewish property ("We own the streets," the Poles said half in jest, "and the Jews own the houses"). A chronicler wrote in 1885: "The role of the Jews in industry is not so extensive as it is in commerce; industry is dominated by Germans.

20

Recently the Poles too started to go into business but these are exceptions, whereas the Jews, ever since they were allowed to buy and own land . . . embarked on building factories and their enterprise is constantly growing."[6] The appeal for "positive action" and economic improvement was not lost on the Jews. It was their only chance for education and emancipation.

Positivism gave the young people an opportunity to turn their minds to facts and away from dangerous illusions. The generations that had been raised believing that the best they could do for Poland was to die for their country were being decimated, yet the first prayer children were taught was for Poland's freedom, the first facts they learned were about their martyred ancestors, the first poems they read exhorted them to follow their forebears' example. A pragmatic education was the way out of the vicious circle of doom and destruction.

The spiritual and political leadership of the Roman Catholic Church had been strengthened by Poland's military involvement in defense of the Christian faith against Turkey's Moslems in the seventeenth century. Education, from parochial schools to universities, was the exclusive domain of the Church until the Renaissance, which brought religious reforms and an increasing sophistication of the gentry. After a brief revival of classicism in the mid-eighteenth century, the French *philosophes* and later the German metaphysicians and idealists countered, though not very successfully, the influence of the Catholic Church, which could still claim to "rule the souls" of the vast majority of Poles.

It was therefore the Church's control of education that the positivists had to contend with. Their task was controversial and complex because of the undeniable, though intellectually limited, influence of the Church on education and because of its unifying role in the partitioned country, its enormous authority among the masses, and its alliance with the ruling classes, domestic and foreign. Even though both their point of departure and their goals differed, the Church and the positivists had a common cause: the defense of Polish culture and the Polish language. The loss of independence could easily have destroyed both because the invaders were well aware that the most expedient way to annihilate Poland was to annihilate her culture. Since the Poles knew this too, a guerilla war started the end of which is not yet in sight. Education became a patriotic duty, a defiance of the invaders' policy of Russification or Germanization, but it was an education steeped in the Christian faith and in literature. The priest and the writer had different, though overlapping, constituencies; the peasants and the workers were the former's domain, the gentry and the intelligentsia the latter's. The urban proletariat, illiterate though it may have been, grew less prone to accept suffering on earth for the promise of paradise in the afterlife.*

The writer became a sacred figure after the loss of national independence. In particular, the romantic prophet, the personification of the nation's dreams of freedom, was elevated to the rank of spiritual leader of the collective conscience of his people. He set humiliation and defeat against higher, universal values unfettered by any religious creed; he called for justice on earth and preached resistance and rebellion, not humility and obedience. But like the priest, he mistrusted the intellect. "Feelings and faith speak stronger to me," reads a poem by Adam Mickiewicz, "than the eye of the sage and his prism."

In response to a more stringent Russification program after 1867, more private boarding schools had sprung up with Polish teachers and administrators. But there was a hitch: only Russian state Gymnasia exempted male students from the draft and opened universities to them. The expensive private girls' schools, closed to Jews, were attended by daughters of the aristocracy, the wealthy landowners, and the well-to-do intelligentsia. Then in 1879 instruction in Polish was outlawed. Polish was taught as a foreign language, and the teaching of Polish literature and history went entirely underground. The repression defeated its purpose. The students, ten to eighteen years old and particularly receptive to patriotic fervor, matured early into conspirators and, with the cooperation and blessing of their teachers and parents, into defenders of the Polish creed.

The division of subjects into humanities and sciences ran along distinct, peculiarly Polish lines. The humanities, apart from neutral subjects, were taught underground and acquired a spiritual meaning alive to this day; the sciences, charged with no emotions unless applied to producing terrorist bombs, remained outside the battleground. Instruction in Polish literature continued to gravitate toward the Romantic tradition; the Romantics touched off "feelings and faith"

*A characteristic example of the workers' mentality is the following revolutionary song: "No one will die for the idea in vain / In the end Christ over Judas will reign." Leon Baumgarten, *Dzieje Wielkiego Proletariatu* (Warsaw: Książka i Wiedza, 1966), 579.

and quelled desperation, keeping alive the nation's past grandeur and mirages of its future glory. The positivist trend clashed with an abstract force, mesmerizing if deceptive.

An 1886 photograph of the sixteen-year-old Rosa shows a severe face, stern and stubborn. A look of determination all but conceals the sadness in the big eyes. The full lips are pressed together, and there is a barely visible trace of irony or perhaps smugness. It is an uncommon face: not a touch of shyness, only haughtiness, no softness, but suppressed impatience.

Rosa had matured early, had learned to control her limp, which became pronounced when she was tired, and had learned to control her face to conceal fatigue. Her mother took care of her clothes, which were tailored to hide her defect. Her large bosom towered over her small lower frame, but a pleat or a fold smoothed the disproportion. There was little, however, that Lina Luksenburg could do to smooth her daughter's inner discord. It is doubtful that she was aware of its extent; rather, she was convinced that family love and academic success made Rosa content or even happy. Rosa gave her mother no reason to doubt that. The affection she received at home she took as her due; obliging but not effusive, she repaid her parents' love and care with filial obedience and a fine academic record. Her family became accustomed to Rosa's keeping to herself, attributing her need for privacy to preoccupation with school work. In reality, Rosa was growing apart from them.

Elias Lukensburg did not fare well in Warsaw. From early in the morning until late at night he made his rounds in the city, striking a deal here, a bargain there. With new waves of his coreligionists crowding into the city and with growing competition from younger, more vigorous businessmen, Luksenburg, never aggressive, was now easily defeated. Overworked and overtired, he was not for Rosa a father who inspired awe or respect. He personified the world from which she tried to escape; in her eyes he lacked idealism, power, and dignity. Nor did Lina Luksenburg evoke in her daughter a desire to emulate her. Rosa was too young to recognize either the strength behind her mother's habitual sweetness or the determination needed to fulfill the role of good wife. In later years it occurred to her that strength may not be immediately perceptible and need not express itself as flagrant domination. Appearances notwithstanding, Lina Luksenburg achieved something Rosa never did: she appropriated two cultures, Jewish and Polish, and felt as comfortable with both as Rosa felt uncomfortable. It may have been precisely the ease with which her mother was bicultural that made Rosa envious and angry.

Rosa was not close to either of her parents. Their concerns— children, home, day-to-day existence—their petit bourgeois tastes and transparent Jewishness embarrassed her. Their strenuous efforts to find a husband for her sister Anna, now close to thirty, irritated her because she mistook their worry for bigotry. If as an adult Rosa Luxemburg looked down on her milieu it was because even as a teenager she had been at odds with it. She grew accustomed to the implications of anti-Semitism, but not to the notion that it concerned her; she believed herself to be Polish even if no one else did. Like the Poles, she frowned at the men with earlocks, long beards, and long kaftans, speaking Yiddish "with their hands," and like the Poles she wished them away. If others associated her with these Jews it was, to her mind, due to ignorance or malice, and though it oftentimes annoyed her, mostly she just ignored it.

The time when she so desperately longed for acceptance by her schoolmates was over. At sixteen she had found her soul mates in the social-minded students in the underground circles. No longer was she the petitioner. Friendship, which she understood from Mickiewicz to be the sameness of social conscience, changed Rosa's universe. It gave her a feeling of belonging to a group that she chose and that accepted her as an equal.

It was a tribute to Polish youth that the Russian system of public education—a religion of blind obedience, as Alexander Herzen, a nineteenth-century Russian thinker, called it—had not killed their soul. In Russia, wrote Herzen, "the naturally expansive feelings of youth were brutally driven inwards; instead, ambition and jealous, spiteful rivalry were encouraged. Who was not destroyed grew up sick, crazed . . . Before they reached the age of twenty, people became hypochondriacs, suspicious, worn out. Infected with the passion for self-observation, self-examination, self-accusation, they carefully studied their own psychological symptoms, and loved endless confessions and discussions about their own neuroses."[7] Herzen, who like Mickiewicz mourned the "decaying Europe," would have discovered in the Polish students' circles that not all ideals were dead.

In some of the underground classes for the study of Polish literature and history, students motivated by teachers or by the experience of injustice, as Rosa was, went beyond aesthetic sensibilities and artistic revelations. For them Mickiewicz's appeal to establish higher moral order had a direct bearing on reality, on the inequities in their own world. The poet was not the only source of political wisdom. Illegal literature, social and economic, smuggled into Poland—paradoxically from Russia and also from the West—was eagerly studied. Reality itself stirred up questions. In the streets striking workers were brutally beaten by the Russian police, and along with conspicuous new wealth grew the squalor of the new proletariat. And once the questioning started, everything was questioned: Mickiewicz and positivism, the Church and Darwin, materialism and antimaterialism. Fantasy and enthusiasm flared in heated discussions; "revolution" and "socialism" connoted a new, just world to come. Even if they were romantic, the students were not starry-eyed. Some came from workers' families, many were Jews, many were women. Their experience no less than their idealism made them identify with the underprivileged.

In her new situation, standing up for a cause instead of for herself, Rosa lowered her defenses. In this environment her "typical Jewish" qualities—ambition, drive, assertiveness, intellectual curiosity—were not automatically dismissed as alien.

At school, the girls now blooming into women invited the inevitable unflattering comparisons. Flustered, excited, they fantasized about romance and elopement, lovers and husbands. Rosa's awareness of becoming a woman—a replica of her older sister perhaps?—increased the strain, which impaired her behavior, her posture, and her looks. But in the underground circle her situation was dramatically different, and so was she.

School, however, lost nothing of its importance for Rosa. Learning had developed into a passion comparable only to her later intensity in love. Now that her anxieties had diminished, intellectual pursuits became an end rather than a means. With the ground firmer under her feet, she discovered the pleasure of learning for learning's sake, and the last two years of school became an experience very different from the initial ones. By then she knew that the Gymnasium was not the last but the first step in her education. The sad existence of her older sister, if still disturbing, was no longer an overwhelming burden; rather, she saw herself following in the steps of Józef, her youngest brother, a university student. If her academic interests had not yet crystallized, her desire for learning had.

It is difficult to say precisely when Rosa became seriously interested in politics. That her dream at the age of sixteen was for "a social system that allows one to love everybody with a clear conscience" is documented by an inscription in her handwriting on a picture of herself that she offered a friend. Still earlier, at fourteen, she had composed a poem, evidently affected both by Mickiewicz's ideas and by his means of expression. Written on the occasion of the German Emperor Wilhelm I's visit to Warsaw, the poem described its author as a politically unsophisticated "silly goose." The sarcastic disclaimer fleshes out her crucial message, "For the sake of Europe, / tell, nay order, thy foxy scoundrel, Bismarck / never to sully peace." The poem, clumsy though it is, displays a rather good sense of political realities— the precariousness of the alliance between Eastern and Western monarchs, the disparity of their interests, and the consequent threat to peace in Europe.* The satirical sting, her future awe-inspiring weapon, though slightly ponderous, creates a comically sinister aura. Whether or not Rosa early "transferred her adolescent rebellion from her family to the whole bourgeois society,"[8] she did challenge authority, displayed her superiority, and made a joke of the establishment.

On 14 June 1887, Rosa graduated from the Gymnasium. The school report attests that Rosalie Luxenburg,† seventeen years old, of Mosaic faith, completed the required seven-year course of instruction. The subjects listed on the report include religion, languages (Russian, Polish, German, and French), pedagogy, mathematics, algebra and geometry, world geography, world history, Russian history, biology, physics, cosmography, calligraphy, drawing, and needlework. In fourteen subjects Rosa was awarded an A, in five—Russian, German, French, geography, and Russian history—a B. Her overall performance was "very good."

After graduation Rosa joined an illegal socialist group committed to the program of the defunct organization called Proletariat. It

---

*Rosa continued to write poetry, but as an adult she knew it was mediocre. In a letter in which she described her drive to write, she consoled the recipient: "Don't worry, it's not poetry again or fiction." Róża Luksemburg, *Listy do Leona Jogichesa-Tyszki,* ed. Feliks Tych, 3 vols. (Warsaw: Książka i Wiedza, 1968-1971), I:421

†The spelling of both surname and first name was evidently changed from the Russian original in the German translation that Rosa later presented at Zurich University.

differed from the students' circles she had frequented because of its clearly set goal—the building of a worker's party. The extent of her involvement is not known. As an adult, however, she boasted to ten-year-old Zofia, daughter of Julian Marchlewski, her close political collaborator: "At your age I didn't play with dolls, I made the revolution."[9] Curiously, one of the members of her group recalled that Rosa was not at all interested in economics, but rather in writing fiction, as a short story she wrote led him to believe. Whatever her political engagement, it did not prevent her from applying for or being granted a passport. The passport was issued on 5 March 1888, Rosa's eighteenth birthday, and was presented by her to the Swiss authorities in February 1889.* Her parents probably delayed her departure to Switzerland because of her youth or their strained finances or both. Presumably, following graduation she worked as a governess near Warsaw, a typical job a Gymnasium graduate would take to earn some money for study abroad. It seems certain that Rosa's desire to study (there were no institutions of higher learning open to women in Poland) and to get away from home took precedence over her political activities. Besides, Switzerland, swarming with radical Polish students, held a promise of political freedom, whereas Warsaw held a promise of the gallows for her.

Who was the young woman who left Warsaw in February 1889? To what extent was she an exception in her society? Were her ambitions unusual?

The image of the woman-rebel was an integral part of Rosa's world. She was eleven when Sofja Perovskaja and Alexander Zheljabov, bound by politics and affection, were hanged next to each other for assassinating the Tsar in 1881; she was thirteen when Aleksandra Jentys was imprisoned together with her lover, Ludwik Waryński, the founder of the first Polish workers' party, Proletariat. With Jentys and Waryński, incarcerated in the notorious Tenth Pavilion in the Warsaw Citadel, the drama of love and revolution had been close at hand. For two years, from 1883 to 1885, before they were

---

*One story has it that Rosa was smuggled over the border in a cart (or carried on the back of a comrade) with the help of a Catholic priest who had been told that a Jewish girl was fleeing her parents to be baptized and to marry a Christian. No firsthand evidence exists to substantiate this story.

27

exiled to Russia, their mere presence excited young people. The twenty-two-year-old Aleksandra Jentys, a woman of great beauty and intellect, elegant and cultivated, was a teacher in the exclusive Institute for Girls of Noble Birth. Not unlike a character in an adventure story, Aleksandra lived a double life; by day a model of dignity for her adoring charges, by night a conspirator and the mistress of a married man.

Rosa was fifteen when two other women were imprisoned in the Warsaw Citadel—Maria Bohuszewicz and Rosalia Felsenhard. Bohuszewicz, a descendant of old Polish nobility, at the age of nineteen became the head of the Central Committee of Proletariat. Felsenhard, daughter of a Jewish physician, was her close friend and collaborator. During the 1881 pogrom Felsenhard's fearless posture saved the lives of her thirty small pupils when a rabid mob invaded her classroom. The year Rosa graduated from the Gymnasium, both women, still in their early twenties, died on their way to Siberian exile.

From a poem by Mickiewicz Rosa learned of another heroine, Emilia Plater, "a leader of great strength and fame," who died a soldier's death in the 1830 insurrection. The memory of Emilia Plater became a driving force during the 1863 uprising, sometimes called the Women's War. Russian chroniclers attributed "the frenzy of the resistance and the long desperate fight to the dazzling eyes and high spirits of the Polish women."[10] Still, Poland did not become a Sparta, nor did Polish women cultivate the military arts; it was the partitions of Poland and later the industrialization that brought a radical change in women's role and status. With men imprisoned, exiled to Siberia, or killed in the insurrections, many upper-class women took charge of running the landed estates and of the education and careers of their children. The belief that a woman is man's equal, borne out in conspiratorial work and on the battlefield, also gained ground at home.

The economic transformation brought yet another change: the impoverished nobility was forced into the labor market. With no skills other than the ability to converse in French and play the piano, a woman of the noble class could at best become a governess. Education came to be viewed as a means to independence and escape from an unwanted marriage.

It was in this atmosphere that Rosa decided to go to the university in Switzerland. She was not an impoverished aristocrat, but she did belong to a group oppressed for reasons other than gender. The lot of Jewish women in Poland also left a mark on Rosa's inner world and her aspirations. Seen by the society in which they had lived since the eleventh century solely in terms of their allegedly money-grubbing fathers and husbands, Jewish women were reduced to nonexistence in the country's culture in general and in literature in particular. No ballads praised their virtues, no poems their beauty. Their spiritual life was of no concern to writers and poets. Poland had no equivalent of a Rahel Varnhagen or a Sarah Bernhardt. An aesthetic sense, an idealism, and an ingrained understanding of nature were attributes associated exclusively with Polish women. Ironically yet logically, Jewish women, though oppressed as Jews, were free of rigors imposed by the feudal-patriarchal family. Thus they asserted themselves earlier than their Polish counterparts. As early as the seventeenth-century, they owned businesses and taverns, traded in liquor and fabrics, acted as matchmakers and go-betweens—occupations unthinkable for well-born Poles. In the 1830s a number of women registered in Warsaw as bankers and merchants and played a distinctive role in economic life. But their prestige did not increase—they were only Jews with money. On the contrary, if an outstanding Jewish woman emerged, she was regarded as antithetical to everything that was Polish. Despite her strong identification with Polish culture, Rosa Luxemburg would forever typify a Jew with no roots, no tradition, and no country.

At nineteen Rosa was fully developed intellectually and emotion-ally. The following thirty years of her life far from Poland were a continuation of attitudes already shaped. The unnatural living that began with her vague wish not to be a Jew inevitably led to secretiveness, to the chameleon-like behavior that was admired by some, condemned by others, and undetected by most.

If she did not know who she was, Rosa knew what she wanted: to escape the confines and canons of her milieu, to study, to work for a cause, to love, and to have a child and a home. She also knew what she did not want: to be a social outcast like her father, a housewife like her mother, or a spinster like her sister, to conform, to be dependent, to be afraid.

However different the famous revolutionary might seem from the child growing into womanhood in Warsaw, it was Zamość and Warsaw, not Zurich or Berlin as commonly believed, that shaped her. However strongly she wished to dissociate herself from the hurt child and the desperate adolescent, both, untamed and rebellious, dwelled within her, pressing upon her their fears and their dreams.

29

4 | *Wilno:Leo Jogiches,*
the Young Conspirator
1867–1890

LEO JOGICHES was the man whose life became inseparably linked with the life of Rosa Luxemburg.

Jogiches was born in Lithuania. Located on the eastern shores of the Baltic Sea, isolated from Europe by impenetrable forests, moors, and swamps, Lithuania was subjugated by a Gothic king in the fourth century and ravaged by the Scandinavians in the ninth. In the eleventh century, Lithuania emerged from obscurity. One of the largest states in medieval Europe, considerably weakened by wars against the Tatars in the East and the Teutonic Knights in the West, Lithuania joined forces with Poland. In 1386, Władysław Jagiełło, son of the Lithuanian Grand Duke, married Jadwiga, the daughter of Louis I, King of Poland and Hungary. The marriage resulted in the conversion of Lithuania to Christianity. In 1569, after establishing a union between the two countries, the king of Poland also held the title of Grand Duke of Lithuania.

The conversion to Christianity meant little to the vast Lithuanian populace, which worshiped pagan gods, personifying fire and flames, stars and waters, trees and flowers. The poetry of Adam Mickiewicz— a Pole born in Lithuania—is peopled by nymphs and elfs, sylphs and ghosts, and suffused with the sorcery and magic the common people never abandoned.

30

The baptism of Lithuania brought Polish Catholic priests and a swift rise in the power of the Church. A cathedral was erected in the city of Wilno in 1387 and the Lithuanian gentry who converted to the new faith were granted special privileges by the Polish king. The Catholic Church and the shared fear of Russia brought the Polish and Lithuanian upper classes together. After the partitions of Poland, when Lithuania was incorporated into Russia, resistance brought a new unity—Lithuanians along with Poles fought the Russians in the 1830 and 1863 insurrections. Under forced Russification, the indigenous culture suffered severely; Russian replaced Polish and Lithuanian as an official language.

Wilno, the capital of Lithuania and the center of the Catholic clergy, absorbed the Polish culture. The old Lithuanian aristocracy, now Christian, and the Church hierarchy built a successful coexistence. Polish artisans and merchants easily established themselves in the multiracial city, inhabited by Lithuanians, Ruthenians, Germans, Jews, Tatars, Armenians, and Italians. The establishment of the Polish University in Wilno in 1579 completed the process. It was the same university in which Mickiewicz founded the secret student society and which was closed in 1832 as a hotbed of dangerous nationalism and revolutionary ideas.

Wilno, set picturesquely on the banks of the Wilia River, was a treasure house of medieval architecture, with the castle of Prince Gedyminas, the wooden synagogue, and the shrine of the famous Black Madonna. The city became an intellectual center of two integrated cultures—Polish and Lithuanian. The entangled Polish-Lithuanian attitudes are mirrored in the opening words of the great Polish epic by Adam Mickiewicz: "Lithuania, my mother-country!" To this day, these words are a symbol of patriotism for the Poles.

The Jews experienced the familiar seesaw of laws alternately beneficial and discriminatory, depending on the times, the economy, politics, and whims; residence restrictions were finally abolished under Tsar Alexander II in 1861. At the beginning of the seventeenth century Wilno, called the "Jerusalem of Lithuania," became an eminent center of rabbinical studies—in 1847 a government-sponsored rabbinical seminary was opened—and in the nineteenth century the town emerged as a seat of Jewish learning unequaled anywhere until its annihilation by the Nazis. Regardless of such deceptive liberties, the policy of Russification centered primarily on Jews, an easier prey than the Catholic Poles. Consequently, the Russified Jews were seen by the Poles as double traitors—of Christ and of Poland. Although Wilno did not escape the pogroms in the 1880s, at the end of the nineteenth century the Jews constituted more than 40 percent of the population.

The name Jogiches first appears in writing on a document dated 10 October 1823. A certificate issued to a teacher was signed by, among others, Jakub Jogiches. Jakub was a learned man and one of the leaders of the Jewish Community Council in Wilno. His house was renowned for assembling intellectuals interested in Hebrew scholarship and in the emancipation. They discussed the printing of Hebrew books, of which Wilno was one of the world's leading centers, the divergent pressures—Russian, Polish, and Orthodox Jewish—and the establishment of modern schools for the Jews. Dr. Max Lilienthal from Germany was invited to advise the community on this issue. Jakub Jogiches exemplified the Jew who sought ways of integrating tradition with modern culture.

A successful businessman, Jogiches amassed considerable wealth consisting of a big water mill and four estates. He built a temple, known as the "Jogiches *shul*," and stipulated in his will that it not be closed or moved under any circumstances. Deeply religious, he never allowed himself to be photographed. He died during a cholera epidemic in 1848 at the age of eighty in his summer house.[1] His son Samuel inherited his entire fortune. Like his father, Samuel was a progressive Jew. He married a well-educated woman of great beauty, Sophia, and had four children by her: Osip, Pavel, Emilia, and Leo (Lev), the youngest, born 17 July 1867. After Samuel's premature death, Sophia Jogiches, still young and attractive, devoted herself to her children and to running the big household in a fashion appropriate to the family's station. She brought up the children in an enlightened Jewish tradition. The language spoken at home was Russian, they celebrated Jewish holidays, and the children attended Russian school.

Leo was a difficult child—moody, uncommunicative, close only to his mother. The older brothers, who took over the family business, seemed to Leo to be exploiters; apart from financial affairs the siblings had little in common then or later. Indeed, after his mother died in 1898, Leo wrote to Rosa: "Now, there's no one left at home," a telling confession considering that his sister and brothers were still living in Wilno.[2] Evidently home to Leo was his mother, with her weakness for her last-born and her passion for music. A contemporary of Leo remembers his "masterly" whistling of Bach and Beethoven, which he had heard his mother play.[3] It seems that she was the one woman whom he allowed to come near him, who loved him unreservedly; and he adored her. Perhaps she alone understood his fears and his dreams, his need to be admired and his inability to admit it. Perhaps she recognized her son's fear of rejection and failure and realized there was nothing she could do except love him. She did not object when he quit school and she allowed him to turn the family mansion into a conspirators' hideout. She played the piano for him and bailed him out of prison. His mother's death was a tragedy from which he never fully recovered.

Leo was "the grandson of old Jogiches," a man of property, a pious, scholarly Jew. The towering figure of Jakub Jogiches, nineteen years dead when Leo was born, shadowed the childhood of the fatherless boy. The Jogiches *shul* was a constant reminder of his grandfather's religious faith; the elegant house and the carefree life, of his financial success. The patriarch whom he had never seen, the long-gone provider, created a constant dilemma in Leo's life. Living on his grandfather's wealth, Leo used that wealth to fight people who, like him, lived on unearned income.

In 1883, at the age of sixteen, Jogiches left the fourth or fifth class of the Russian State Gymnasium. This was the first of his escapes from commitments that, if met, would give others the power to judge him. On finishing the Gymnasium, a student was awarded a diploma, a certificate of maturity. Students who, like Leo, failed to obtain it were regarded as little short of certified failures.

Time and circumstances were on Jogiches's side when he dropped out of school. The question "study or work?" had long been disturbing to some of the progressive Russian youth. "Was it necessary to devote ourselves to our studies, so as to obtain diplomas and then live the life of the privileged . . . or should we remember the duty to the people, recall that our learning had been acquired by the means provided by the people, who work as if condemned and are always hungry?" wrote a Russian medical student. "Should we not rather . . . give up our privileged position . . . and devote ourselves to learning a craft, so as to take part as simple artisans or laborers in the life of the people, and merge with it?"[4] While Jogiches did not exactly want to merge with the people, he did want to give up his privileged position in the Gymnasium. He apprenticed himself to a locksmith, earning his living by

33

manual labor; and although he never developed a taste for the work, he could now identify with the laborers. Indeed, he promptly established contacts with stocking makers, shoemakers, and printers. If these contacts were almost exclusively with Jewish workers, it was because workers were predominantly Jews, not because Jogiches felt any special interest in Jews.

Yiddish was the only language the workers knew. Most of the radical Jewish intelligentsia spoke Polish or Russian or both, so they had no common language with the workers whom they sought to save—a phenomenon unknown in most workers' movements. Nor were they eager to take a step backward by learning Yiddish "jargon," which they regarded as an obstacle to becoming truly European. Leo's and Rosa's contempt for Yiddish mirrors their fears of being associated with the stereotypical Jew. Free from such fears, a number of Polish and Russian socialists learned Yiddish in order to reach the workers. Jogiches too must have acquired some, for otherwise he would have been unable to communicate.

The Jewish Workers' Union in Lithuania, Poland, and Russia, known as the Bund, was founded in 1897, seven years after Jogiches left Wilno, but Leo had helped sow its seeds. He joined the workers' movement after the 1880s pogroms filled the Wilno factories with masses of fleeing Jews who became the main target of socialist agitators and who ultimately created their own organization. They came from *shtetls* and villages, from abysmal poverty and oppression. The cattle that shared their shacks were better fed, warmer, and safer than they. Racial, religious, ethnic, and national division fed on backwardness and poverty. The policies of the Catholic Church on the one hand and of the Russian empire on the other made abuse and pogroms a way of life. The city offered some kind of protection, which the backwoods did not. The concept of exploitation had yet to be explained to the newcomers. As police reports made clear, "revolution" was fashionable among students but not among workers.

During the mid-1880s two forces were shaping radical ideology: Narodnaja Volja (the People's Will), which advocated instant political action to achieve revolution and believed in the expedience of terror; and Marxism, which held terror to be harmful and futile and contended that only an educated proletariat could and would bring on the revolution. The evidence on Jogiches's allegiance is conflicting. The prominent Russian Marxist Georgij Plekhanov claimed that while in

Wilno Jogiches belonged to Narodnaja Volja, but once in Switzerland he became, for opportunistic reasons, a Social Democrat. Jogiches's later comrade Władysław Feinstein, who like Plekhanov did not know him in Wilno, did not deny Jogiches's ties to the terrorist organization but maintained that he worked closely with the future founder of the Bund—the Social Democrat Tsemakh Kopelson—and his group. With Kopelson as his second in command, Jogiches headed the Marxist Wilno Central Organization for one year and was "assigned to work among Jewish workers, and officers and soldiers."[5] There is thus no doubt about his close connection with the future Bundists and Marxists. And there is no doubt that he was irresistably drawn to terrorism.

Jogiches never formally joined the Wilno branch of Narodnaja Volja, allegedly because of its ineptness in conspiracy but more likely because he would not subject himself to the organization's rigid structure. Nevertheless, unlike the Marxists, he "deeply believed in terrorism and attributed great significance to it."[6] Terrorism implied secrecy, danger, daring. Its magic and mystery created the aura of power that Jogiches wanted more than anything else in life. A conspirator, like a god, controls destinies and lives—a proof of his extraordinary talent. No one knew exactly what Jogiches was doing or how, what he felt or thought. The visible result was perfect: a well-organized strike, a forged passport, a comrade smuggled across the border. His fanatic dedication and his organizational gift brought him fame before he reached the age of twenty. But he was also notorious among his comrades for the tyrannical manner that was to make his political and personal life so difficult.

With the workers, Levka, as he was called, was unguarded, open, sensitive. "I've met Jogiches," reminisced a female worker. "He was my teacher and the first to acquaint me with socialist ideas. He was clever, very able, a unique debater. One felt in his company as in the presence of a great personality. Totally devoted to his socialist work, he was idolized by his student workers."[7] That his comrades knew a different man, one they respected but did not like, apparently did not bother Jogiches. He was an undisputed authority on conspiracy and that was what mattered to him.

After the 1887 attempt on the life of Tsar Alexander III failed, Narodnaja Volja turned to Jogiches for help. Jogiches secured false passports and smuggled two men out of the country. "I spent the night before their escape with them and with Jogiches," wrote the future prominent French socialist Charles Rappaport. "The police ransacked the city while Jogiches was entertaining us with his stories and keeping our spirits high."[8] A transfiguration, no less: the enigmatic, taciturn Jogiches, hounded by the police, held forged passports in his pocket, harbored two outlaws, entertained, told stories, sparkled. He was in his element. The organization he shunned had turned to him for help, and he had carried out, brilliantly, a dangerous operation. His genius was evident and unquestioned.

Jogiches thrived in the atmosphere of danger. The superiority he had over people who would reason rather than gamble intoxicated him, as did the gambling itself. He used his grandfather's money to undermine the order in which his grandfather had believed; his grandfather had been successful, and so was he. He could now pass the Jogiches *shul* without a pang, for he himself was teaching workers to reject the religion the *shul* offered. He was no longer "the grandson of old Jogiches," but a man with power, feared and idolized.

With all the paraphernalia of conspiracy in his hands, Jogiches became an institution in Wilno. He jealously guarded his excellent connections with professional smugglers; his passport office, complete with forged forms, invisible ink, stamps, and photographs; and his collection of illegal literature. The prominence he achieved so early convinced him that force was an effective tool. Whether it was an actual bomb or an explosive idea, it worked. "You've too much faith in the magic power of force," Rosa Luxemburg wrote him years later, "in both politics and personal life."[9] Force was a shield against people who did not accept him on his own terms—just as Rosa's intellect had been her shield during her adolescence.

In 1888, at the age of twenty-one, Jogiches singlehandedly organized a printers' strike in the Wilno Syrkin printing shop. Forty workers went on strike, no small achievement for the young agitator. He spent some time in hiding, in the apartment of a young woman, Maria, to whom he was said to be attached. It was Maria who gave Russian-speaking Leo his first lessons in Polish. In September of the same year Jogiches was detained, spent seven days in jail, and was released on bail for lack of evidence. On 11 May 1889 he was again arrested and sentenced to four months in prison and two years of police custody. By then the police knew that they were dealing with a hardened subversive. Released in September, he was inducted into the army where, because of his record, he faced service in a penal batallion. He deserted, went underground, and in the summer of 1890 managed to flee the country with the help of his smuggler partners. He was never to return.

The seven years Jogiches spent in the Wilno revolutionary movement formed his political outlook and above all his character. While Rosa was fighting for acceptance in the Polish milieu, he made it known that he did not need acceptance but merely obedience. This attitude was self-deceiving and self-protective. His fear of rejection was so pervasive that he would not expose his feelings. But his defenses did not always work. "Jogiches was a romantic in the full sense of the word," wrote Luba Axelrod, who knew him well;[10] and Charles Rappaport noted that "he was really not so hard as he appeared."[11] Yet Jogiches did manage to convey the impression of a superior being. Secrecy, he found, was an effective means to impress people, a cover for any inadequacy, including his fears; it could isolate or unite at will. Secrecy, for Jogiches, became second nature.

Switzerland

5 | *Rosa Luxemburg and Leo Jogiches* 1889–1894

Not quite nineteen years old, Rosa arrived in Zurich at the beginning of 1889. She was captivated by the city. Unlike Warsaw, which heaved with unrest and was patrolled by Russian police, Zurich was a beautiful and tranquil town.

Second to the Russians, Poles constituted the largest émigré group from the tsarist empire. Since entry into Russian universities was difficult for men unless they were politically acquiescent and was nonexistent for women, Zurich was at the time a center for the progressive Polish intelligentsia. A Union of Polish Students created in Zurich in 1887 and a Polish National Museum in Rapperswil, on the Lake of Zurich, kept the Polish spirit—sometimes zealously nationalistic—alive.

For the Russians Switzerland had been a refuge since the 1850s. Herzen and Bakunin were the first of the spectacular succession of exiles committed to the overthrow of the tsarist regime; Georgij Plekhanov, Vera Zasulich, and Pavel Axelrod were active there during Luxemburg's Swiss years. They were followed by Lenin, who put the final if idiosyncratic touches to the work of his illustrious predecessors and from there set out to the Finland Station.

The German and Austrian socialists boasted no less prominent names. In Zurich, Wilhelm Liebknecht, August Bebel, Eduard Bernstein, and Karl Kautsky laid the foundations of the most powerful European socialist party, the German Social Democratic Party (SPD). The German socialist club Eintracht, complete with a well-equipped library, a reading room, and a lecture hall, was a second university for those who, like Rosa, were searching, testing, trying to give shape to their model of the world.

For the first time in her life Luxemburg found herself in a truly international community. Like Rosa, many of its members had escaped from the confines of their native lands, from racial, political, or religious intolerance. To them, Switzerland—civilized and tolerant— was little short of a promised land. They shared a thirst for knowledge and an urge to reform the world; they also shared hardships. Many supported themselves with odd jobs and menial tasks, but these did not prevent them from studying or from becoming involved in politics. In the quiet town of Zurich, the bearded Russians, Slavic women, and Jews of pronounced Semitic appearance made a strange crowd, but the local burghers merely raised their eyebrows occasionally. The Swiss authorities were concerned with the influx of foreigners; anarchists presented a problem, and so did the vast majority of young Russians who did not attend the university. When Rosa arrived in Zurich, an office was already functioning where foreigners had to register and to report every change of address and any travel from and to the city.

On 18 February 1889 Rosa Luksenburg registered in the Oberstrass municipality under the name Luxemburg.* She was a subtenant of Herr Lübeck at Nelkenstrasse No. 12. The Lübeck family was recommended to her by friends in Warsaw; Karl Lübeck was a socialist and his Polish-born wife, Olympia, the guardian angel of Polish students. Lübeck, formerly an editor of the *Demokratische Zeitung* in Berlin who had been driven out of Germany by the antisocialist law, lived the marginal existence of an expatriate. Half-blind and broken by hardships, he could barely eke out a living by writing. In his young tenant, Lübeck found an enthusiastic assistant. At the same time Rosa gained an insight into the German Social Democratic press and, by revising Lübeck's articles and writing herself, started to acquire the skills of a political journalist. Olympia, energetic, intelligent, cheerful, became Rosa's friend. With an embittered husband and eight children,

---

*After Rosa changed the spelling from Luksenburg to Luxemburg she always made sure that the new, more cosmopolitan spelling was used.

her life was not easy. In later years Luxemburg would sometimes invite Olympia for a brief respite in the charming secluded village of Clarens, on the Lake of Geneva. "My dear Oleńka left today," she wrote to Leo Jogiches, "went back to her hopeless life . . . after catching a breath here, poor thing."[1] Mrs. Lübeck never forgot Rosa's kindness. At her insistence, her son, Gustav, later married Rosa to secure German citizenship for her.

Rosa became friends with another older couple in Zurich, Mathilde and Robert Seidel. Seidel, active in the Swiss socialist movement, had risen from being a weaver to become a member of the Zurich City Council. When Rosa met him he was an editor of the socialist journal *Arbeiterstimme*. According to rumor, he fell in love with Rosa. The Seidels were among the few intimate friends in whom she confided about her personal affairs, to whom she sometimes confessed her loneliness and unhappiness. Only to them did she sign her letters "Ruscha" (not Rosa), a phonetic transcription of the Polish Róża.

Between February, when she came to Zurich, and October, when she matriculated at the university, Rosa spent part of her time helping Olympia Lübeck with her children and working for Karl Lübeck, possibly in exchange for room and board, and the rest of her time exploring the German, Russian, and Polish student circles. It is unlikely that a strictly political career was in her mind in the winter semester of 1889–90 when she enrolled in Principles of Zoology, and Zoology Laboratory and Microscope Techniques. She was still uncertain about her future but in the meantime decided to concentrate in the field of natural science. Darwinism provided public-spirited students with a scientific tool and at the same time supported their materialistic ideology.

In early autumn 1890, Rosa Luxemburg met Leo Jogiches shortly after he arrived in Switzerland. The famous revolutionary was someone an aspiring socialist would have been eager to meet. At first sight he emanated strength, authority, confidence. Under bushy eyebrows, his steel-blue eyes were attentive and cool. He had reddish-blond, curly hair and a sensuous mouth, and he spoke Russian in short, concise sentences. Anna Gordon, an attractive young woman from his hometown, Wilno, appeared to be Jogiches's constant companion.

Rosa knew little about Jogiches other than the rumors praising his phenomenal feats in Wilno, unmatched courage, and conspiratorial genius. Jogiches, though he clearly enjoyed being the center of attention, never talked about himself. He listened to others, rarely throwing in a word, but then showing an unparalleled knowledge of political reality. His face seldom expressed interest; mostly it expressed impatience. Theoretical arguments and scholarly discussions had little meaning for him, and he made no effort to pretend otherwise. For a year or so after their initial meeting Luxemburg saw him frequently in socialist circles, but he remained an enigma to her. If anything, it made this stranger, straight from the pages of Dostoevsky, still more irresistible to her.

Jogiches too kept observing Rosa Luxemburg. His curiosity was growing. In discussion, she could make her point with flair, conviction, and an aplomb that impressed him. Though he knew women from the Wilno movement, none could match this fiery Pole with her intelligent eyes and firm voice. He sensed a strength in her and a zeal that, harnessed, could do wonders for the cause. He saw a born orator, an agitator, persuasive, hypnotic. She had shortcomings, of course, due, he rightly guessed, to dealing with abstract theories and consorting with talkers, not doers. But to him this was more a challenge than a hindrance.

The switch in Luxemburg's course enrollment in the winter semester of 1890–91 indicates that she had reached a decision about her future. She dropped natural science and devoted herself to the study of economy, philosophy, and law. Jogiches was no doubt instrumental in this critical step. During the same semester Jogiches matriculated at the University of Zurich. He took two courses in natural science, botany and zoology, subjects he had studied on his own in Wilno so that he could impart to workers the essentials of evolution and revolution. Luxemburg's course load was much heavier: political economy, philosophy of socialism, modern philosophy, classical philosophy, and statistics.

Within a year of his arrival in Switzerland Jogiches decided that joining Plekhanov and the first Russian Marxist party Plekhanov created, Liberation of Labor, was his best chance to establish himself and gain influence in the Russian revolutionary movement. The decision shows his political astuteness. The terrorism advocated by Narodnaja Volja was of the past; the future belonged to the Marxist party. In the summer of 1891 Jogiches left for Geneva to meet with Plekhanov.

Georgij Plekhanov, an internationally known Marxist theorist and political activist, was well acquainted with Engels and other leading European socialists. Ten years older than Jogiches, he was ready to take the daring and brilliant newcomer under his wing. But the newcomer did not appreciate patronage. He wanted influence. The party was chronically short of funds; Plekhanov made ends meet by addressing envelopes; his comrade Axelrod made a living by producing kefir, a kind of buttermilk, which he and his wife delivered to customers. Jogiches, on the other hand, possessed the enormous sum of 15,000 rubles. According to Plekhanov, Jogiches used his money to strike a bargain. In exchange for money, he demanded that his voice be equal to those of all the other members jointly in matters of publication and finances—an attempt to gain complete control of the party. Other sources maintain that he merely wanted an equal voice with other party members.[2]

Whatever the case, Plekhanov was outraged. He wrote to Engels that he found it arrogant and disgusting of this "upstart," this "careerist," to make such demands on him and to use money as a means of pressure. He referred to Jogiches as "Nechaev in miniature" (the anarchist Sergej Nechaev was notorious for resorting to provocation and murder).[3] A lifelong hatred ensued on both sides.

Ironically, it was Plekhanov whom Luxemburg had looked to before Jogiches became her mentor. Plekhanov's erudition and intellect intimidated her and made her realize that her mind, the weapon she had relied on in Warsaw, was not as formidable as she liked to think. "I was in Mornex," she wrote to a friend, "but won't go there anymore because Plekhanov is too sophisticated or, to be exact, too well educated for me. What could he possibly gain from a conversation with me? He knows everything better than I do, and I cannot create 'ideas'—original, genuine ideas."[4] Her insecurity, dormant for years, reemerged. It took Jogiches one year to dispel it, freeing Luxemburg to openly challenge Plekhanov's authority.

In July 1891 Luxemburg wrote from Geneva: "I'm completely happy living all by myself here . . . and am really a mature person, which makes me very proud of myself."[5] Her happiness had one source—Jogiches. It seems certain that Rosa went to Geneva at his behest. Either he wanted her at his side while he negotiated with Plekhanov, or he planned a rendezvous with Rosa while Anna Gordon was in Zurich. To Rosa, Gordon's absence must have been a relief and a signal. In any case their mutual attraction reached a climax in the heat

45

of Jogiches's political battle, and by the summer of 1891 he and Luxemburg had become lovers. Her emphasis on "living all by myself," while in fact she was with Jogiches, became a refrain in her letters to Warsaw. It caused much anguish to her family, who bemoaned her loneliness in the alien land. Luxemburg was proud of herself for defying the conventions of her milieu and living, unwed, with the man she loved. The decision was not easy. She was still the daughter of Lina and Elias Luksenburg, and she knew that a *liaison amoureuse* would offend their sense of propriety. To add to her conflict, Jogiches insisted on absolute secrecy about their intimacy.

The short period of courtship in Geneva was bliss. With nostalgia and longing Luxemburg later remembered the time "when I wasn't your wife yet," that is, before she became his lover. What was for Jogiches a natural development when a man and a woman were attracted to each other was for Luxemburg an immensely serious and dramatic step. Nevertheless she took the step willingly, and it made her "mature" in her own eyes. Not so in Jogiches's: ten years later she was still trying to convince him that "I'm an adult, a mature person."[6]

Life changed totally for Luxemburg. The liaison with Jogiches assuaged her fears that the ideal man would not find her attractive. And it opened broad horizons in political work.

Jogiches, however, remained totally preoccupied with the revolutionary movement. Determined to declare publicly his independence of Plekhanov, he purchased his own printing press and launched a new publication venture—the *Social-Democratic Library*, which translated Marxist literature for distribution in Russia.

In the fall of 1891 Luxemburg and Jogiches rented rooms in neighboring houses in Zurich and both took the winter semester off. From 1892 to 1897 they regularly studied at the university. Together they attended a number of classes: in the spring semester of 1892 a course in finance; in the winter semester of 1892–93, Roman law, international law, and political economy; in 1894–95, history of diplomacy; and in 1896–97, principles of jurisprudence, public administration, and public law. Though each of them also took other classes, the direction of their studies was the same—law and economy. Luxemburg took a course in medieval history for pleasure, but Jogiches never once deviated from his strictly planned curriculum.

The university was not their only interest. During these years they worked out a common political platform from which they never departed. In 1892 Luxemburg involved the isolated Jogiches in Polish affairs, that is, in creating a Polish political party. Jogiches had been unwilling or unable to join any of the Russian revolutionary factions; consequently he found himself cut off from the Russian émigrés and had grown increasingly hostile toward them. "I never liked the way you kicked every Russian who tried to get near you," Rosa wrote to him years later. "One may boycott or 'punish' some people, a group, but not *a whole movement!*"[7]

Luxemburg based her idea of a new Polish Marxist party on the premise of the defunct Proletariat. Like its founder, Ludwik Waryński, she disagreed with Marx on the issue of Poland's sovereignty. An independent Poland, Marx believed, would "deal a mortal blow to the Holy Alliance, to the military despotism of Russia, Prussia and Austria, to the domination of the Mongols over a modern society."[8] Luxemburg defined Marx's view as "fallacy and anachronism."[9] She maintained that nationhood divides rather than unites workers, that the Russian and the Polish proletariat should join forces in order to overthrow their common oppressor, the tsarist empire, and that Polish workers would gain nothing in an independent bourgeois state. Luxemburg failed to recognize the psychological aspect of the appeal that independence had for the Poles living under three invaders.

In 1892 the Polish Socialist Party (PPS) was founded; it subordinated socialist goals to national independence. A year later, Luxemburg and Jogiches cofounded the antinationalist party Social Democracy of the Kingdom of Poland (SDKP)* and its organ *Sprawa Robotnicza* (*The Workers' Cause*). The issue of an independent Poland forever divided Polish socialists. The PPS existed until 1948, when it merged with the Polish Workers' Party, which fallaciously claimed heritage with the Social Democracy of the Kingdom of Poland and Lithuania.

In August 1893, twenty-three-year-old Rosa Luxemburg made her first public appearance. In an impassioned speech in Zurich to the Congress of the Second International[†] she appealed for recognition of

---

*The Social Democracy of the Kingdom of Poland merged with Lithuanian Social Democrats in 1900 and became the Social Democracy of the Kingdom of Poland and Lithuania (SDKPiL).

†First International, 1864–1876; Second (Socialist) International, 1889–1914; Third (Communist) International (Comintern), 1919–1943.

the SDKP. Joseph (John) Mill, Jogiches's comrade from Wilno, remembered her: "Small, with a disproportionately large head, she had a fleshy nose in a typically Jewish face . . . She walked with a pronounced limp, heavily, haltingly. At first glance she didn't make an agreeable impression, but after a short while one saw a woman bursting with life and spirit, endowed with a remarkable intellect."[10] The Belgian socialist Émile Vandervelde recalled: "Rosa, at twenty-three, was completely unknown outside some German and Polish socialist circles . . . Her adversaries had a hard time keeping up with her. I can still see her dashing out of the crowd of delegates and climbing a chair to make herself better heard. Small, frail, and looking neat in her summer dress, smartly cut to conceal her physical defect, she defended her cause with such magnetism in her eyes and in such fiery words that the majority of delegates, captivated and spellbound, voted in favor of accepting her mandate."[11] Nevertheless, Luxemburg did not obtain the mandate due to a later committee vote. The newly created SDKP was no match for the more influential PPS.

Then and there the acrimonious fight started between the PPS and SDKP. The ideological differences between the PPS and Luxemburg's small group appeared insurmountable. The Polish Socialist Party did not address itself exclusively to workers but to "all classes economically oppressed by the bourgeoisie and politically by the tsardom: small landowners, peasants, the yeomanry and the lower middle class."[12] The independence of Poland was its foremost goal. The program of Luxemburg's group, outlined editorially in *The Workers' Cause*, called for a common struggle by Polish and Russian workers and ignored the fight for Poland's sovereignty. Predictably, the PPS pointed to Luxemburg's Jewish origin as inevitably blinding her to the real needs and wishes of the Polish nation. The same was said in 1970, at a symposium in Warsaw commemorating the hundredth anniversary of her birth.

At the time the SDKP was created, it had about two hundred members. Beside Luxemburg and Jogiches, its cofounders were Julian Marchlewski, whom Luxemburg knew from Warsaw, and Adolf Warszawski-Warski. Marchlewski, born into a well-to-do Polish-German family, became a revolutionary out of sheer idealism. He arrived in Zurich in 1893 after one year of imprisonment in Warsaw, enrolled in the university, and, unlike Jogiches, four years later obtained a doctorate in law and political science. His wife, Bronisława Gutman, Rosa's schoolmate from Warsaw, was the first Polish woman to obtain

48

a diploma in bacteriology in Zurich. Warszawski was a Jew and was married to a Pole, Jadwiga Chrzanowska. He lacked the intellect of the other three but not their zeal. A hard worker, totally immersed in the movement, he lived with his growing family in great financial straits. Luxemburg was extremely fond of Warszawski and over the years tried to help his family, at one point offering to adopt one of his children.

The four collaborated on an informal basis, with no rigid party structure or hierarchy, though Luxemburg more than once had to curb Jogiches's dictatorial bent, which Marchlewski in particular dreaded. Jogiches, however, saw himself at the helm principally because his opinion of Marchlewski and Warszawski was not very high but also because the money was his—and so was Rosa.

The history of the small band around Luxemburg and Jogiches is one of long periods of stagnation and rare moments of glory. Because the party strove for a unity of Polish and Russian workers it never became popular in Poland, despite Mickiewicz's poetic vision in which Poles and Russians were brothers and despite its claim to be the successor of Proletariat. The renunciation of Poland's independence, whether for lofty or pragmatic reasons, hardly added to its appeal. With the leadership in Switzerland and the small following in Poland depleted by frequent arrests, the party was at times all generals and no soldiers. It was joined by such influential socialists as Cezaryna Wojnarowska, a former member of Proletariat, and Feliks Dzierżyński, who was instrumental in uniting the Lithuanian and Polish Social Democrats.

After the setback at the Zurich Congress in 1893, the SDKP was recognized at the next Congress of the International, in London in 1896. Upon its merger with the Lithuanian Social Democracy in 1900, the existence of the new Social Democracy of the Kingdom of Poland and Lithuania was no longer questioned.*

Much as Luxemburg wanted to draw Jogiches out of his isolation, it was not compassion that prompted her to involve him in the Polish movement. He was a priceless asset for the fledgling party. Even if she had known that Plekhanov had informed Engels that Jogiches had used her, his mistress, to gain control of the Polish movement, it would

---

*The Social Democracy of the Kingdom of Poland and Lithuania (SDKPiL) is hereafter often also referred to as the Polish Social Democracy or the Polish Social Democrats.

not have bothered her. She was impervious to party gossip. Likewise, Plekhanov's innuendos about Jogiches's "very wealthy mother" would not have touched her.[13] Jogiches's money helped, of course, for it financed publication of *The Workers' Cause*. But even without his money, with only Luxemburg's talents and his, they would have succeeded.

Luxemburg's oratory and writing were the chief assets of the party. Luxemburg was editor-in-chief of the party's organ, *The Workers' Cause*, and its main contributor. Two, three, or four articles written by her, unsigned or signed with different names, would sometimes appear in a single issue of the paper.

The years 1891–1893 were crucial for both Luxemburg and Jogiches. They brought the two close, but they also bred unrealistic dreams and illusions. Luxemburg had found her knight-errant and thought she held him firmly in her hand; Jogiches had found a disciple and thought he held her firmly in his hand. Neither realized just how fiercely independent the other was, how unlikely to "belong" to the other. In the frenzy of political work, they saw that which tied them, not that which divided them. Luxemburg's frequent trips to Paris to watch over the printing of *The Workers' Cause*, the brief separations, meetings and partings, enhanced the charm of their intimacy. Jogiches, in the newly founded SDKP, was organizing and commanding; he was needed and appreciated and, he thought, on his way to influencing history, his ultimate goal. Luxemburg saw their love growing into an indissoluble bond. She thought that her affection and the position she created for Jogiches in the party were enough to make him happy. Jogiches came to see them as a Trojan horse.

The two were drawn to each other for different reasons. Luxemburg was fascinated by the man; Jogiches was attracted by her mind. In time also their disparate attitudes toward exile divided them.

Unlike Luxemburg, Jogiches would not have left his country had he not been forced to. There was nothing that attracted him in western Europe—neither the possibility of study nor the status of émigré. He left behind his work, his mother, his home, and fame. In Wilno he was protected by his mother's love, by the web of secrecy, by the worshiping workers. Switzerland, peaceful, orderly, and trimmed—so different from Lithuania's untamed wilderness—grated on his nerves;

and so did the well-nourished burghers and his endlessly arguing fellow émigrés. There was no government to fight, no danger to court, no workers to organize. Instead, he lost his protective layers and was exposed to a motley group of émigrés who, he felt, could not measure up to him.

For Luxemburg, emigration amounted to liberation; for Jogiches it amounted to calamity. The air that let her breathe suffocated him; her reward was his punishment. At the same time, exile deepened their mutual dependence, which Luxemburg found natural and Jogiches burdensome. Exile breeds singular forms of dependence that bring some people close and make others drift apart. In their lives the two forms were intertwined.

Gradually Luxemburg came to know, but not to understand, the man. One of her first surviving letters to Jogiches, written in a Swiss mountain village and dated 21 March 1893, shows their closeness and her touching lack of inhibition. "A voice in the night woke me," she wrote. "Startled, I listened. It was my own words I heard, 'Dyodyo! Hey, Dyodyo!' I was pulling the bedclothes toward me, irritably, thinking my Dyodyo was there beside me (what an indecent dream)."[14]

But within a year things changed. "You reduced me to such a state that I am embarrassed to write about our personal matters," Luxemburg admitted unhappily. "It seems to me wrong to write about anything but the cause."[15] They lived together only outside Zurich, when they went on vacation to some remote village where their intimacy drew no attention. On these occasions Jogiches was more relaxed, warm, and patient. He shopped for groceries, scrambled eggs for dinner "with great finesse," brought Rosa her favorite cheese, took long walks with her.[16]

In Zurich the pattern was set in the fall of 1891 when Luxemburg sublet a room for herself on Universitätsstrasse No. 79 and Jogiches rented one at No. 77. They always maintained separate quarters, though at walking distance. But they were separated by more than just a few steps. Luxemburg became increasingly aware that "every word concerning the most stupid business is twice, no ten, a hundred times more interesting to you than my pouring out my whole heart."[17] She discovered that her lover was an "angry" man, with "no natural impulse to love." She promised, half in jest, to "wipe that anger" out of him, but she suffered from his inability to show his affection.[18]

Luxemburg yearned for a "peaceful and regular" life in which their love and their work would complement each other, and they would "shape a human being out of each other."[19] But Jogiches ruined all her efforts, she thought, with constant scenes over the way she looked, behaved, and worked. To him it was natural that he should assume the role of her teacher, and he expected her to conform to him unconditionally. But her attempts to change him were intolerable to him, her longings irritating.

Luxemburg had a fixed set of ideas about what makes a man a man and a woman a woman and what brings happiness or unhappiness, victory or defeat. Happiness was within one's grasp, she thought, provided certain conditions were met: humanity would achieve it if the downtrodden joined forces against their masters, and an individual would find happiness if he knew how to enjoy the beauty of spiritual and physical life. Her belief in *mens sana in corpore sano,* in keeping with the spirit of the time, was unshakeable. If something went wrong, it could be traced to improper living habits, lack of fresh air, or a poor diet. If Jogiches was depressed, it was because he smoked, did not take walks, drank beer instead of cocoa, spent nights brooding and days sleeping.

The Jogiches she first met was basking in the glory of his recent past, revered and admired. The past soon became remote and the present held no future; but Luxemburg, always an optimist, did not see it that way. At the time they became close, Jogiches was disheartened and bitter. Then his Russian publication venture and the Polish work revived him. So for the first two or three years of their association Luxemburg harbored many illusions. Jogiches exuded a burning passion that she had yet to learn was absorbed by a single thought—the revolution. His strength promised protection; she did not know he wanted to protect only the underdog. He seemed extravagantly giving; she was to find out that he gave cautiously and grudgingly. If he behaved "strangely," she ascribed it to his passing mood which her love or her well-written article would soon dispel. She did not know then that Jogiches was trapped in a vicious circle of conceit and self-doubt.

After Plekhanov's rebuff became public knowledge, Jogiches felt cornered. Defeat, exposed and visible, haunted him. Though he had no more use for Zurich University than he had had for the Wilno Gymnasium, he returned to the university. The 1891 summer in Geneva had brought him closer to Luxemburg, and after they came back to

Zurich, she persuaded him that attending school was the right thing to do. But to his mind, he had merely exchanged the "privileged position" at the Gymnasium for one at the university and the conspirator's independence for his grandfather's money. Ever since his teens he had tried to live up to the vision of a revolutionary, succinctly expressed in Bakunin and Nechaev's *The Catechism of a Revolutionary:* "The revolutionary is a lost man. He has no interests of his own, no cause of his own, no feelings, no habits, no belongings, not even a name. Everything in him is absorbed by a single, exclusive interest, a single thought, a single passion—the revolution."[20] In Wilno he had been close to that vision; in Switzerland he was losing ground. Because it was Luxemburg who drew him into the Polish movement, Luxemburg and exile became inextricably linked in his mind.

Jogiches's acceptance of Luxemburg's proposal that he join her in the Polish movement was a degrading concession. He was not made to accept, he was made to give orders. She insisted that he learn Polish. Politically astute, he knew it was necessary and mastered the language in a short time. Yet he never addressed her in her mother tongue. Though he found Luxemburg's mind unusual and intriguing, he may have found in her limp yet another humiliation; perhaps he was equally attracted to and resentful of Luxemburg's different appearance. And it is moot whether his insistence on keeping their intimacy secret was due to "the good of the cause," to his love of conspiracy, or to his reluctance to acknowledge publicly his liaison with a crippled woman.

Luxemburg had seen an aloof and supercilious Jogiches in company, but it had not occurred to her that he might behave the same way toward her in private. She could not know that he was at ease only in work, in the thick of activities, among workers, when his role was clearly defined and his superiority recognized. He felt threatened by unfamiliar situations or those he could not control; when he could not avoid them, he would become reserved and unapproachable. *Byt,* the dull, uncreative routine of ordinary life, was his nightmare. The small pleasures that Rosa enjoyed so much—a walk in the country, a dinner with friends, a novel, a concert—he saw as a waste of time, as a trap leading to a meaningless existence. Whatever was not relevant to "influencing history," whoever was not dedicated to the cause, was of no interest to him. Everything that distracted him or Rosa from this mission was to be eliminated from their lives. Social contacts were not only unproductive and wasteful but an unwanted, dreaded test he was determined to avoid.

In exile the revolutionary's greatest weapon was his pen. Jogiches's work in Wilno had not required a command of the written word: conspiracy is the art of silence. Marx, however, demanded that revolutionaries act "openly, in the face of the whole word, publish their views," as he wrote in *The Communist Manifesto*. Jogiches was not prepared for this, psychologically or in practice. He had neither Rosa's drive to write nor her talent. He had left school before he had mastered the art of writing, and the years of clandestine activities had further hindered its development. Aware that he could not impress by the written word as he could by action—that, on the contrary, he would invite criticism if his words were imprisoned in print—he took no chances. But he knew that battles are fought on the pages of newspapers, not only on the barricades, and that a good pen was the most needed and most effective weapon. To wield political influence he needed a pen. That pen was Rosa.

Many political exiles supported themselves by writing—Marx was a reporter for the New York *Herald Tribune*—but Jogiches's inheritance spared him the need to earn a living. For many radicals writing was the single way to communicate their ideas, defend them, gain influence, marshal support. Jogiches could do all this through Luxemburg. Thus, writing became a bond but also a chain.

6 | *The Uphill Struggle*
1895–1898

$\mathbf{F}$ROM THE TIME they became lovers Rosa Luxemburg considered her relationship with Leo Jogiches a marriage; in her letters to him she called him "my husband" and herself "your wife." Jogiches did not see their relationship in the same way.

Though many radicals lived in common-law marriages in defiance of the bourgeois institution, for Jogiches that was too much of a commitment. He insisted that Rosa pretend even to their close friends and to her family that they were merely comrades. Torn between her desire both to please him and to preserve her own dignity, Luxemburg alternately bowed to his demands and rebelled. "To go on pretending about our relationship [to the Warszawskis] is not just overdoing it; it is simply hypocritical," she wrote in the seventh year of the enforced secrecy.[1]

Jogiches resented her tearful complaints about how different he was "when I wasn't your wife yet." He had what he wanted: an adoring woman—part wife, part mother—and a disciple. With his role clearly defined as that of intellectual master, he felt comfortable. Acting from behind the scenes, through Luxemburg, he recreated the Wilno situation. Invisible yet omnipresent, he wielded power and challenged the established order and his political adversaries. His unwaveringly loyal yet enterprising apprentice was a godsend.

Jogiches's desire to reform Luxemburg equaled hers to reform him. He wanted to purge her of her sinful lust for life; she wanted to convince him that revolution and personal happiness were not mutually exclusive. She needed love, affection, and companionship as she needed air. Had Jogiches denied them to her consistently, she would not have stayed with him. He understood this, and rather than risk losing her he gave her what she needed—but meted it out guardedly, keeping her forever hungry. Her recurring plea—"as always I read greedily the few personal words at the end of your letter"—was sometimes effective, sometimes not.[2] She learned to live on memories of the rare moments when he had been "gentle, good, sweet," when the tone of his voice had been warm, his words caressing. Though at times he was all she wanted him to be, her ideal of "love and work together" was not his. Personal life and work were to be separated lest trivialities devour the cause.

Circumstances provided an outlet for their pent-up conflicting emotions. Luxemburg and Jogiches were often apart. From 1893, she went frequently to Paris to supervise the printing of The Workers' Cause and later to collect material for her dissertation; in 1898 she moved to Germany to further their cause while Jogiches stayed in Switzerland for two more years. Therefore, between 1893 and 1900 they often communicated in writing. Their letters served as a workshop in which they hammered out political strategies, negotiated alliances, gauged opposition forces, and jointly produced articles and speeches.

Letters kept the relationship from splitting asunder. Letters became their mutual addiction, a folie à deux. Throbbing with physical passion, abounding in reproaches and self-reproaches, Luxemburg's letters mirror their differing expectations and disclose their weapons: love, seduction, provocation, rewards, and punishments. Each used the letters as a substitute for a life lived together and as a means of controlling the other.

A "cold" letter or a "warm" letter became currency, a negotiable instrument. "Because of this letter you'll write me a tender one," Luxemburg wrote to Jogiches in 1895, "and when I send you a cold letter, I'll get a cold one in return."[3] Pet names and an intimate vocabulary that Luxemburg coined were important temperature gauges. The way she referred to herself or to him was patterned on a child's mode of expression. Violating grammar and syntax, the pet names are untranslatable. In Polish, it is not unusual to create exclusively personal words of endearment; those Luxemburg made up for Jogiches reveal an inexhaustible imagination; more, they show a sentimentality that would surprise even people who knew her well. The complete transformation of her personality in letters shows that Luxemburg needed an outlet for another self, one that was normally carefully disguised.

In writing, Rosa addressed Leo as Dyodyo or Chuchya, the former reserved for small boys, the latter for baby girls. If he misbehaved, she denied him the endearment and addressed him stiffly as "my dear." The punishment had the desired effect, and Jogiches clamored for her tenderness. "You are begging me to call you Dyodyo, but you have not deserved that for a long time," Luxemburg coolly informed him, "and I do not know whether you'll earn it soon."[4] The importance of the form of their written communications became still more transparent after they separated. To avoid any personal pronoun in her letters to him, Rosa invented a distorted lingo that only Leo could understand. To invest her letters with the substance of her emotions in love and in hate, she bent the language to her needs.

What Jogiches wrote could throw Luxemburg into despair: "I don't understand the tone of your last two letters in which you omitted even the heading. Do not torment me, I'm at the end of my rope."[5] Or it could open the gates of heaven: "You've no idea how happy your personal letter made me . . . I read it over and over again."[6] If Luxemburg craved to receive on paper what she could not get in person from Jogiches, to him her letters were information, an essential tie to the outside world and a window on the political arena. He found that she held a weapon she was not shy to use. Her mere threats to cut off the correspondence threw him into panic. Her insistence in March 1900 that "my decision to stop writing is *not* the act of vengeance you think it is" promptly brought Jogiches from Zurich to Berlin, where Luxemburg had been waiting in vain for two years. "Even to correspond in the manner we used to is no longer possible," she declared, assuring him that what he considered blackmail was a means to find out whether he genuinely cared about her. "I immediately decided to make the parting easier for you. I'd stop writing to you," she announced somewhat perversely after a month's silence. "I kept telling myself this was the solution. If he loves me and wants to live together he'll come, if not—he can take advantage of the break in our

57

correspondence."[7] That solution Jogiches could not accept. The endless sheets of paper covered by her neat, regular handwriting were at times the only reading he thought worth his effort. He demanded to be kept abreast of every development on the political scene, of her meetings, conversations, speeches, and articles. Nor was his demand merely an exercise in power. "Your recent letters have stimulated my thinking," Luxemburg wrote him, "and in your last letter you gave me an entire piece for my article, which stands out like a jewel . . . I translated [it] word for word from your letter."[8]

Luxemburg shared everything with Jogiches in her letters—political news and gossip, impressions of the politicians she met, views on Marxism and social change, comments on the books she read and concerts she attended, news of the latest fashions, details of her hats, shoes, jackets, and skirts, her health, and her diet. Fanatically attentive to detail, she described people, conversations, and events with humor and perception. No foible escaped her critical eye, not a word or a gesture. She painted in vivid colors a room dense with cigarette smoke, where she had chatted with workers well past midnight, or an elegant banquet closing a Congress. She discussed her ideas with him and asked for advice. "You've certainly got my point and recognize the potentially formidable topic. So think it over, and when you come up with more along these lines let me know immediately."[9]

Sometimes she described a book she was reading—"the autobiography of Benvenuto Cellini in Goethe's translation, an extremely original work, interesting as a mirror of fifteenth-century Italy and France"[10]—or enticed him—"I've two vases with violets on the table, and a pink lampshade . . . and a new pair of shoes, and a new veil, and new gloves, and a new hairbrush, and I'm pretty."[11] Her letters contained entire scenarios so that Jogiches could follow her, in spirit if not in body, on speaking tours, to meetings and social occasions, or into the privacy of her bedroom. She wanted him to know everything she knew, experience what she experienced, feel what she felt. Unabashedly she revealed her "indecent dreams," her sexual desires, her disappointments and hopes. Her unceasing demand for reciprocity—"I want you to write me about your inner life!"—remained mostly unanswered. "Our correspondence assumes a strange character. I'm writing to you about everything . . . and you respond with 'critical' comments. About yourself . . . not a single word. I do not like such correspondence, and since my questions are futile I'll write you as much about myself as you're writing about yourself."[12] But he knew the threat was empty.

Though they were equally dependent on each other's letters, Jogiches's coolness and composure gave him the upper hand. Only rarely did Luxemburg get a measure of satisfaction. "That you're furious because I wrote a short letter is a good sign."[13] Mostly she had to force a response out of him. "My dearest, write me something nice," she pleaded, "I'm exhausted, spiritually and physically. Your last letters were so dry."[14] She did not try to conceal her hunger. "Thanks for writing a few warm words at last. I needed them badly . . . it hurt when you wrote only of business. Not a single loving word."[15] Though Rosa knew that Leo impatiently skimmed the pages of her letters in search of political news, she made no effort to write less emotionally.

True to his nature, Jogiches preferred distance bridged by letters to a common daily life. Although he found writing a chore compared to practical work, he at least ran no risk of being censured; instead he could exert influence on Rosa.

His letters to Luxemburg have not survived; before every expected police search in Berlin, she destroyed his current correspondence. Much of their content, however, can be gleaned from her letters. She quotes him back frequently, verbatim or in paraphrase, sometimes with delight, more often with scorn. Her reaction reveals the temperature of his letters, mostly cool but sometimes angry or containing a rare emotional outburst. Repeatedly but unsuccessfully he tried to steer the correspondence away from the shaky ground of personal affairs to the safety of the public realm. Her resentment grew. "Your letters contain *nothing,* but *nothing* except for *The Workers' Cause,* criticism of what I've done and instructions about what I should do," she complained, not yet aware that his writing aptly reflected him as her letters reflected her.[16] Yet in spite of Jogiches's restrained and businesslike tone, the thousand or so letters he wrote to her were a measure of his affection.

Though less outspoken, Jogiches was as sensitive to the tenor of Luxemburg's letters as she was to his. He accepted her tributes as his due; but if he sensed an ebb in her emotion, imagined or true—"where have you discovered 'a personal, harsh tone' in my letter? . . . I was just writing in a great hurry"—he would become anxious.[17]

Luxemburg's thirst for independence, growing along with her reputation, made Jogiches increasingly fearful of losing control over her. That fear turned into ceaseless criticism, which, after she moved to Berlin, she was less and less willing to take. "You don't seem to see that all your letters are systematically and colossally distasteful," she wrote to him in Zurich. "They boil down to one long drawn-out stuffy *mentorship* like 'the letters of a schoolmaster to his favorite pupil.' Granted, you make critical comments; granted, they are generally useful, in some cases even indispensable; but for heaven's sake, by now the whole thing has become a *disease,* an addiction! I can't put a single idea or fact on paper without provoking a boring, distasteful harangue. No matter what I'm writing about, my articles, my visits, my newspaper subscriptions, dresses, family relations, anything I care about and share with you—nothing escapes your advice and instructions."[18] He knew that he incurred her wrath not merely because of his criticism, however annoying, but because his letters failed to abate her loneliness.

On her twenty-ninth birthday, in 1899, Jogiches wrote her a letter, a gift, as it were, absolving her from the sin of enjoying life. "You wrote," she quotes him, "that we are still young and able to arrange our life together." On that fragile foundation she erected an elaborate fiction—they would live openly as husband and wife in "our own small apartment, [with] our own nice furniture." They would entertain, go to the opera, take walks, spend the summer vacation in the country. "We will *both* work and our life will be *perfect!!* No couple on earth has the chance we have . . . we will be happy, we must."[19] One vague sentence of Leo's transported Rosa into a world of unattainable dreams.

A child by Jogiches was absolutely essential to fulfill the dream. "And perhaps even a baby, a very little baby?" she asked shyly. "Will this never be allowed? Never? Dyodyo, do you know what possessed me all of a sudden during a walk in the Tiergarten? . . . A little child got under my feet, three or four years old, blond, in a pretty little dress, and stared at me. A compulsion rose in me to kidnap the child, to dash home and keep it for my own. Oh, Dyodyo, won't I ever have my own baby?"[20] This was Luxemburg's first mention in writing of her desire to have a child. It was easier for her to write than to talk to him about matters that touched her deeply. "I constantly feel the need for a child," she confessed to Jogiches a few months later in 1899. "Sometimes it becomes unbearable. *You,*" she wrote, "you probably could never understand this."[21] It occurred to her that she might bring up a child alone. "If I have a child," she wrote him, "I will be able to support it by myself."[22]

Two letters Luxemburg wrote to Jogiches exemplify the ebb and flow of Rosa's emotions as the relationship developed in the 1890s. The first, angry and rebellious, was written by the twenty-four-year-old woman on 25 March 1894, not quite two years after they had become lovers. It reveals the roots of the disharmony that was to plague their life together. The second letter, intensely sad, was written on 16 July 1897, shortly after Luxemburg's twenty-seventh birthday. It is an admission of failure, though not devoid of the hope that was to linger for another ten years. These two letters disclose the vibrations that kept the pulse of the partnership beating.

In the 1894 letter Luxemburg rebelled against Jogiches's attitude both to her and to life. For her, she screamed at him, life is not about *The Workers' Cause,* it is not about the workers or the cause, it is about living. That she should and would work for the revolution she took for granted, but that life should be limited to "this issue, that pamphlet, this article or that" was tantamount to killing the soul. Destroying the spiritual bonds between people for the greater glory of an idea that seeks to create such bonds was to her a wanton aberration. "I have ideas and impressions all the time," she wrote, "the 'Cause' notwithstanding."[23] But she needed Leo, her other self, needed to share her thoughts with him, while he had nothing to share but deadlines, proofreading, editing. The thought that haunted Luxemburg all her life—whom does the revolution actually serve?—pervades that chaotic letter. She tried to come to grips with Jogiches's reality, a life sacrificed for humankind, but she could not. If the people that make the revolution are damned, won't the revolution be damned? If the revolutionaries are not human, if they don't understand the art of living, how can they create a better life for others?

Clearly this was not the couple's first argument on the subject. Clearly, Jogiches had previously reproached Luxemburg for lack of perseverance and diligence, for self-indulgence and weakness. "Don't tell me," she protested, "that I can't stand the never-ending work, that all I want is rest. No, no, I can stand twice as much, but what I can't stand is that wherever I turn, there's one thing—'The Cause.' " Jogiches had obviously been trying to pacify her, for she anticipated his response. "If you answer indignantly that you never fail to say tender words in your letters, let me tell you that *sweet talk* is not what I want." By then she knew that he shut her out of his inner life, and she was ready to trade body, brain, and pen for access to it. She would obey him, be his little pet or his invincible soldier, if he would open up to her. "Our only ties," she mourned "are the cause and the memory of old feelings." Plainly, she was at a loss. "I don't have a home anywhere. I do not exist as myself." Jogiches assigned her a role she found degrading. Commands, instructions, criticism—these were all she got from him. He presented her with decisions, patronizingly adding that her weak nerves should not be unduly strained. Her dream of equal partnership was imperiled, but she was not ready to give up. Shaken but determined, she put her cards on the table: if he thought that she would be content to "scribble articles" and acquiesce in what he termed his "modest opinions," he was dead wrong. It was her right to participate in political decisions and his obligation to respect that right. Their personal relationship aside, her position within the party was a serious matter to her. That Jogiches should make decisions behind her back was intolerable. That he should sweeten the pill by throwing in "sweetheart" when he reported this to her was disgusting.

As though to prove to Jogiches that she too could separate private and public matters, she wrote a second part to the letter, deliberately set off from the first. Its tone was dry and formal, and it contained a detailed accounting—printers, 118 francs; cocoa, 1.20; milk, 1.65; gloves, 2—to let him know that she was well aware she was spending his money. A meticulous report on a forthcoming issue of the journal discussed its layout, delivery, and distribution. Toward the end of the letter, typically, she extended an olive branch—she asked him about some economic and historical matters, an acknowledgment of his intellectual superiority and her dependence on it.[24]

The very different letter that Luxemburg wrote Jogiches three years later, late on a July night in 1897, describes a scene that had taken place in her room a few hours earlier. Leo had dropped by, preoccupied with something he did not care to discuss with her. Rosa's efforts to gain his attention were promptly dismissed as inappropriate sexual overtures. He gave her a disparaging look that silenced her and prepared to leave. Her heart sank, her eyes filled with tears. There was so much she wanted to tell him, while he was ready to leave, believing that all she wanted was to make love. As often before, she felt trapped, helpless, and angry. She could not speak, she could not move. She just stood there with a lump in her throat, ready to love, ready to kill. He looked at her, kissed her lightly on the cheek, and closed the door behind him. She lacked the courage to talk to him; absurd, even irrational as it might seem—"we live only ten steps apart and meet three times a day"—she found a letter the sole means to tell him the truth. She suspected that he wanted to be left alone and conceded that "all things considered," he would be happier without her. Her "female whims, impulsiveness, helplessness" got on his nerves, as did her scenes, her tears, her insecurity about his love. She contrasted her own spontaneity with his calculated way of "handling" her, her passion with his coldness; and she reproached him with interpreting her behavior "crudely," with turning their relationship into a "purely superficial" affair. Penitent, she took the entire responsibility on herself. It was her fault that the atmosphere was not warm and congenial; she had invaded his "pure, proud, lonely" life; she tormented him. Through her tears she could see him impatiently skimming the letter she had written. She could hear him asking, "What the hell does she want?" And she could hear him exclaim, "What a drama! What a bore! Same thing over and over again."[25]

This nocturnal confession retraced their struggle, now in its fifth year. The partners kept blackmailing each other into submission while at the same time delighting in the other's refusal to yield. Luxemburg wanted to merge with Jogiches completely, to become one with him, and that was what he most dreaded. To forestall her attempts, he was indifferent or abusive. To sublimate her insecurity, Luxemburg needed constantly to captivate and to capitulate; to sublimate his, Jogiches needed to display superiority. She depended on him for physical love and admitted this loudly and clearly; he was not influenced by sexual intimacy, and he told her so. In belittling her, he elevated himself. In public life she had a name, he had none. To compensate for this inequity, he would make sure he was the master in private.

Suspecting, as Luxemburg did, that Jogiches did not love her, that decency prevented him from leaving her, why then did she not end the affair? Jogiches would not let her go. He did, in an odd way, love her. More significantly, without her, with no anchor and no friends, he could not survive. She loved him passionately and was willing to live on crumbs.

By the mid-1890s, the seesaw that Luxemburg and Jogiches were to share for the next ten years had been constructed. The interdependence of intimacy and work started to weigh on her. In saying "I am convinced that you'll like me better once I've fulfilled my duties," she stated the plain truth.[26] When she made an error she berated herself and begged forgiveness—"if forgive you can"—and felt she did not "deserve" a caress. The strain showed. Rosa complained of migraines, a nervous stomach, exhaustion, and fierce menstrual pains. She was not as strong and healthy as he thought, she informed him. Nauseated, her head splitting in "rotten, noisy Paris," she carried on, she told him, only because of the prospect of resting in his arms. But Leo did not like to be cast in the role of slave-driver or to hear about her ailments, which she reiterated with some relish. "Don't be afraid," she comforted him after listing her complaints, "I'll do the work anyway."[27] If instead of the expected praise she received a reproach, instead of a tender word, a reprimand, she burst out, "The best machine cannot produce as quickly as I'm expected to. I cannot and that's that. I don't feel well, and even the healthiest person couldn't write that much. You're welcome to hire somebody else—there's no one who'd step into my shoes."[28] But then she told him that everything she did in the political arena she did because of him and for him. She oscillated between fighting with Jogiches for an equal voice in the party and relinquishing her adult responsibilities in exchange for the security of his embrace. "I no longer want, my dearest love, to be an 'adult,' a 'responsible person' . . . I just want to come back to you and find peace in your arms."[29] In such instances, Jogiches's roles as lover and mentor became inseparable. The lover rewarded her for the smooth execution of instructions and the mentor punished insubordination.

Gradually, Luxemburg learned to fend for herself, often at the expense of Jogiches's pride. "I'm returning the . . . proclamation [you sent me]. It is beautiful with regard to form and zeal. It has only one fault." She thrust the knife deeper. "Two most important issues are completely ignored—the benefits of an eight-hour day and of a common German/Polish platform."[30] The proclamation "can be easily fixed," she reassured him casually, eager to let him know that she had caught his mistake but careful to play it down. Of a short piece written by Jogiches in Russian, she remarked, "I've been translating till midnight . . . It would seem that translating is an easy and swift job, but alas . . . Now, finished it has turned into a strong and beautiful piece."[31] She informed him that she was working on his writing just as he was working on hers; if his article was good, it was because she made it so. There were no growing tolerance or mutual concessions;

instead, the constant ups and downs, the game playing, and even the quarrels intensified their bond.

In 1896, the Polish Social Democratic Party was destroyed by a wave of arrests in Poland, and *The Workers' Cause* was closed down. Jogiches lost the few soldiers who, under his command, had written, published, smuggled into Poland, and distributed the journal. The *Social-Democratic Library* closed down also, leaving him the desolate owner of a Russian printing press. Luxemburg was working hard to finish her dissertation. While she was excited and busy, Jogiches was growing more and more bitter. It may have struck him that she could go on by herself, that his creation might slip out of his grasp. She urged him to pull himself together and get his degree, with no effect. In the winter semester of 1893–94 she attended seven courses while he attended four; to her three in the winter semester of 1895–96 he attended one. No doubt the Polish journal occupied much of his time, but it occupied even more of hers.

The low point for Jogiches came in 1897. Luxemburg obtained her doctoral degree in law and political science *magna cum laude* on May 1.* A highly respectable publishing house, Duncker and Humblot in Leipzig, accepted her dissertation, "The Industrial Development of Poland," for publication; her article "Step by Step," a study of the Polish bourgeoisie, was published by the leading German SPD paper, *Die Neue Zeit,* to considerable critical acclaim. For Jogiches the future looked bleak. The discrepancy between his youthful aspirations and the disappointments of adulthood was never clearer.

Luxemburg tried to reassure him, but her attempts were sometimes wide of the mark. "I bought a mirror . . . in a nice wooden frame, high quality glass," she reported. "I did it *only* because you're always busy primping in front of the mirror."[32] Impeccably dressed, carrying an elegant cane or umbrella (one of his pseudonyms was Parasol), Jogiches hardly resembled an ascetic revolutionary; but this was the last thing he wanted to hear. Luxurious clothes were perhaps a substitute for the success that eluded him. The combination of ambition and fear, programmatic renunciation and self-indulgence, left him permanently dissatisfied with himself and with Luxemburg. His

---

*Until 1903, male students of law and political science were listed in the students' register as "jurists" and female students as "women students in political science." Verena Stadler-Labhart, *Rosa Luxemburg an der Universität Zurich* (Zurich: Hans Rohr Verlag, 1978), 47.

vanity suffered with each of her political setbacks; it suffered with her every achievement as well. Both showed him his own inadequacy. Their political platform was turning into Luxemburg's springboard. Moreover, she alone took public credit for their joint work; only the innermost circle was aware of Jogiches's share, and the credit that others gave him was limited to his organizational work. His close collaboration on her publications remained secret.

In April 1897 Rosa's mother developed stomach cancer. As often happens in calamity, Lina Luksenburg's illness threw family attitudes into sharp relief.

From the voluminous correspondence with her family, Luxemburg saved two sets of letters written in the years 1897–1900—letters preceding and following her mother's death and her father's letters preceding his death. She kept them locked in a box, and several years after their deaths, guilt-ridden, the thirty-five-year-old woman wrote to Leo Jogiches: "By a strange coincidence I took out the box with . . . the letters. I read them through and cried until my eyes were swollen, and went to bed wishing I'd never wake up. I cursed the damn 'politics' that stopped me from answering mother's and father's letters for weeks on end. I never had time for them."[33]

Anna, Rosa's older sister, wrote meticulous reports about their mother's condition—so meticulous, in fact, that her ambivalence, if not jealousy, comes through. Rosa, clearly was the apple of her mother's eye. "Rosa alone would do anything I asked of her for . . . she knows to value her parents and she'd do anything for us with pleasure," Anna quoted Mrs. Luksenburg.[34] But it was Anna who nursed their mother, not leaving her bedside for months, while Rosa left unanswered the single postcard her mother was strong enough to write; it was Anna who, after waiting for fifteen years to have her own room, let her mother sublet it for 10 rubles—the monthly allowance sent to Rosa— and it was Anna who gave up a library subscription to send Rosa a little more money on her mother's behalf.

In May 1897 Rosa's letter arrived announcing that she had obtained her doctoral degree. "Mother alternately laughed and wept," Anna reported to Rosa, "refusing to part with your letter for a single moment, eager for the whole world to know how proud and happy she was . . . Every morning mama and papa go through prolonged negotia-

66

tions about who's going to keep your letter—mamma at home, just in case someone drops by, or papa in his pocket to show it in the city."[35]

Her mind blurred by pain and morphine, Mrs. Luksenburg cried for Rosa to come to her. "I had no choice," Anna wrote Rosa. "In order to calm her down I promised her you'd come." Descriptions followed of the sick woman compulsively planning a trip to Zurich, of her hallucinations; she accused her family of plotting maliciously to thwart Rosa's efforts to see her. Then she calmed down, and—being "deeply religious," Anna stressed—spent most of the time praying. When she did not pray, her thoughts were on Rosa, on how to assuage her loneliness. If only she could send the love she had for her, she told Anna, she would feel better; failing that, the fine linen she had bought for Rosa and kept in her chest of drawers must do. Between fits of vomiting, Mrs. Luksenburg requested that Anna bake Rosa's favorite pastry and send it to her. "The inhuman suffering did not stop mother from figuring out, ahead of time, the date of the holiday and insisting that the parcel reach you in time." Anna, in her mother's stead, was to prepare the traditional High Holidays feast "for daddy to know it is a home and it is a holiday."[36]

Lina Luksenburg died on the night of 30 September 1897. "Mother was fully conscious till the very end," Anna related. "She knew she was dying; resigned and peaceful, she prayed constantly . . . and for the last two days she thought only of you, and whispered your name again and again. The last day she asked, 'why doesn't Rosa come to me?' and when I reminded her that you're away, she just kept repeating, 'Rosa, Rosa,' till her last breath."[37]

The strange way in which the news about her mother's death reached Rosa reflects the pattern of her relationship with her family. She and Leo were spending a working vacation in a mountain village, Weggis, in October. Her Zurich friend Olympia Lübeck suggested visiting her briefly, on some pretext. Rosa's family, anxious to protect her from the shock, had gone to great pains to find Mrs. Lübeck and entrust her with breaking the sad news. "Is there any close girlfriend with you?" her father worried.[38] "I thought Mrs. Lübeck would stay with you at least for a week," grieved Anna.[39] Indeed, Olympia Lübeck never went to Weggis. "You persuaded me not to let Mrs. Lübeck come to Weggis," Luxemburg reproached Jogiches eight years later, "lest she disturb my finishing the earth-shaking article . . . and she, she was coming with the news of my mother's death!"[40]

Rosa's agony did not end with her mother's death. Her mother, she felt, would have died more peacefully had she known that Rosa, unlike Anna, had met a man whom she loved and who loved her. In a mood óf utter despair she described in letters to her family her lonely life, making them feel wretched for abandoning her at a time when she needed them most. Anna was ready to pack and go to her sister. "I realize now how cruel it was to leave you alone," she wrote after the funeral. "No! Not for one more day will I leave you like that, lonely, abandoned . . . Dear God! How will I ever repair that wrong! I shudder at the thought of you, all alone in your little room, sitting alone, going to bed, getting up, with no one to cry your heart out to."[41] Instantly plans were made for Elias Luksenburg or Anna, or both, to join Rosa. Promptly, Rosa answered that she was leaving Switzerland. She compulsively kept writing, at the rate of two or three letters a day, intensifying their distress, guilt, and admiration. She did not want to live, Rosa wrote, there was no reason for her to go on with her mother gone. "It will kill me," wrote her father, his shaky handwriting reflecting his agitation, "should anything, God forbid, happen to you."[42] Anna's reaction was no less vehement. "How can you, how dare you to even entertain such thoughts! You must never forget mother's words—that you alone will make our family's name famous."[43]

Rosa's emancipation, confirmed by the solemn *doctor juris publici et rerum cameralium* (doctor of law and political science), and her mother's death, lamented by *Kaddish,* suggest more than the obvious differences in cultures. Two worlds clashed inside Rosa: that of her ancestors, from which she was running away, and the new world whose acceptance she eagerly sought. To succeed in the latter she had to detach herself from the former. But the tie was not easy to cut. The letters from home depicted the rites of mourning—her family sitting *shiva;* her brothers intoning the Jewish prayer for the dead day after day in the *shul;* and her family at the Jewish cemetery in Warsaw, at *shloyshym,* the official end of mourning, singing *Kaddish,* "naturally in your name too." Her mother's death and the Mosaic religious rituals that followed it thrust upon Rosa the world she wanted to forget.

Her mother's last words summoning Rosa to her bedside filled her with remorse. She lived a life of lies to please Jogiches yet somehow was never able to please him. But she was not discouraged. "Our entire regime is going to change," ran the refrain. "We'll go to bed and get up *regularly and early,* we'll dress nicely, the room will be elegant, and we'll have our own things."[44] The obstinate belief that discipline would create harmony, that the perfection of their relationship would emerge in a home filled with clothes and furniture, sustained her. If she could avoid discord, if order replaced chaos and beauty the mess, life would be ideal. Though she berated herself occasionally, she really believed that the key to their happiness was in Jogiches's hands. "It is all *your fault*—when I'm alone I live an orderly life, I keep the place neat and think about how to make it pretty. Why? Because I'm not constantly frantic, disheartened, driven crazy by you. *Be good!* And I'll do my best to make us a nice home. Only be good and love me."[45]

It was probably on the advice of Alexander Parvus-Helphand, a trusted and respected friend, that in 1896 Rosa and Leo first entertained the idea of Luxemburg's move to Germany. At the time Helphand held the position of coeditor of one of the best SPD dailies, *Sächsische Arbeiterzeitung.* That a Russian Jew had achieved such status in the German Social Democratic Party suggested an open-minded attitude toward foreigners. With a doctorate, more than fifty articles to her credit, and a name not unfamiliar among socialists, Luxemburg could look confidently to a new experience.

Yet the decision to move was not easy. "My success and the public recognition I'm getting are likely to *poison our relationship* because of your pride and suspicion," she wrote to Jogiches in July 1896, two years before she settled in Berlin. "The further I go, the worse it will get. That's why I'm having second thoughts about moving to Germany. If, after mature consideration, I should come to the conclusion that I either have to withdraw from the movement and live in peace with you in some godforsaken hole, or else move the world but live in torment with you, I would choose the former."[46] Since Luxemburg was committed to the movement and intent on finding happiness with Jogiches, she resolved to have both. Offensive as the thought was to her, the success of her union with Jogiches hinged more on her political performance than on her love. The dreary feeling was back— as in Warsaw, it was her mind that commanded affection and attention.

Perhaps Germany was her chance? Perhaps there was still time to start a new life? Luxemburg felt inextricably tied to Jogiches; she would go to Germany not just to save humanity, but to save her love.

For his part, Jogiches longed for greater influence, and his keen political sense told him that the German Social Democratic Party could provide the forum. He would work his way in through Rosa Luxemburg, whom he had trained over the past years. The articles they had conceived and polished together, the contacts she had established under his watchful eye, the name she had made with his help, all enhanced her chances. Her mind, he believed, was as exceptional as was her pen, and both would be put to good use in Germany. The prospect of staying alone in Zurich was not unwelcome. Broken by the recent death of his own mother in Wilno, he candidly confessed to Rosa that he could not stand the presence of a woman. He would be free to suit himself, with no mandatory attendance at the university, no fresh air, no rising early; free to dispatch instructions to Berlin, as he once had to Paris, he could pull the strings behind the scenes. He may have felt that their relationship would benefit from the parting because, as Luxemburg succinctly put it, "as long as we have political work at hand our personal affairs are all right."[47]

Like a commander planning an invasion into foreign territory, Jogiches devised the strategy for the German operation down to every detail. The people Luxemburg was going to contact, the topics to be discussed, the tactics to be used were carefully examined. The list included meetings with August Bebel, a towering figure in the SPD; with Karl Kautsky, the editor-in-chief of *Die Neue Zeit,* who published her articles; and with comrades familiar with the territory. Luxemburg was to send Jogiches detailed reports of each step and consult him before taking the next. He briefed her thoroughly, envisioning possible drawbacks and complications. Should unexpected developments emerge she was to wait for new instructions from him. As *The Workers' Cause* had been earlier, the German operation was financed by Jogiches, who prepared a detailed budget. It included 30 marks for rent, with the proviso that Rosa was to find a room appropriate to her station and not take "just anything." Their correspondence was to be divided into "personal" and "political"—most certainly Leo's idea. He did not want her to skip his instructions in order to "search greedily for the few personal words" or himself to fish for items of importance in pages filled with her emotional outpourings.

As a Russian subject, Luxemburg was liable to extradition on political grounds; it was therefore crucial that she obtain German citizenship. It is not certain who suggested that she marry Olympia

Lübeck's son, Gustav, but since Jogiches organized the entire venture, it was probably he. Rosa turned to Mrs. Lübeck—slightly embarrassed, one might guess, for Gustav was not a friend or comrade but a grudging stranger. The marriage, simple as it seemed at the time, was to take five years and a great many unpleasant legalities to dissolve so that freedom could be restored to the hapless bridegroom.

The wedding took place in Basel on 19 April 1898. The duly married couple—Rosalia née Luxemburg, twenty-eight years of age, and Gustav Lübeck, mechanic, twenty-five—gave as their residence Jogiches's address in Zurich. On the marriage certificate Luxemburg's date of birth, for unknown reasons, was given as 25 December 1870 (instead of 5 March 1870), in accordance with a statement signed by her father and two witnesses before a notary public in Warsaw.* The newlyweds parted after the ceremony and, except for the legal document, that was the end of the marriage. A few days later Luxemburg petitioned the registry office to change her husband's occupation from mechanic to merchant. It might have occurred to the ever-alert Jogiches that a marriage between a doctor of law and a worker would look suspicious to the German authorities. The petition was denied.

On 12 May 1898 Dr. Rosalia Lübeck left Zurich.

---

*In a letter to her Dutch friend Henriette Roland Holst, Luxemburg wrote on 30 January 1907: "I thank you . . . for your birthday wishes—they made me laugh. My 'official' date of birth is false. . . . Respectable person that I am I don't have an authentic birth certificate, but an 'adjusted' and 'corrected' one." Henriette Roland Holst-van der Schalk, *Rosa Luxemburg, Ihr Leben und Wirken* (Zurich: Jean Christophe-Verlag, 1937), 220.

Germany

7 | The German Conquests
1898–1900

THE BROKEN JUG, by the eighteenth-century French painter Jean-Baptiste Greuze, adorned a postcard Luxemburg sent Jogiches as she traveled to Germany. If the picture carried a message, it was lost on Jogiches; he was not given to symbolism. A letter from Berlin, dated 17 May 1898, one day after her arrival, was more explicit: "Despite everything you told me before I left, I cling, as I always have, to my right to personal happiness. Yes, I do have a damnable longing for happiness and am ready to haggle for my daily portion with the stubbornness of a mule." Sitting at night in a temporary lodging, amid her suitcases, in the huge, unknown city, she gave vent to thoughts which had tormented her for a long time. "I feel," she wrote, "like a forty-year-old woman going through the symptoms of menopause." She felt robbed of her womanhood and attributed it to Jogiches's refusal, not inability, to live a "normal" life and to satisfy her emotional needs. "It has become clear to me," she wrote, "that I left nothing good behind, that things would not have been any better had we stayed together, and I would have gone on living in an atmosphere of constant dissonance, trying to comprehend in vain and in pain."[1]

The first days in Berlin Luxemburg spent looking for a furnished room, possibly with board. After viewing seventy-five rooms in

75

different parts of the city, being fussy and choosy according to Jogiches's instructions, she reported to him that rooms within her 30-mark budget that were available in the "proletarian" section were beneath his standard and hers, while in better neighborhoods they were too expensive. Finally she found a room at Cuxhavenstrasse No. 2, "in the most aristocratic neighborhood, next to the Tiergarten." There was a problem, however: "I'm scared to tell you—it costs 33 marks! Do believe me, I wouldn't have taken it if there were the *slightest* possibility of finding something cheaper . . . I'm positive that this is the very room you'd have chosen yourself and am therefore less upset . . . but it is 3 marks beyond our budget . . . I shall count every pfennig, I already do . . . Do write back immediately that you don't disapprove of me because of the 3 marks."[2] Clearly, Luxemburg did not want to start the German venture by annoying Jogiches, nor did she want him to interpret the extra three marks as an act of insubordination.

Rosa Luxemburg descended upon the massive gray city like an exotic colorful bird. She was learned, witty, and elegant. If there were many accomplished women in the German metropolis, they were not members of the Social Democratic Party. She approached this bastion with modesty and perspicacity, well aware of the odds. She was a Jew, a Pole, a woman, and young—hardly a combination to inspire confidence. She worked out her own step-by-step strategy, following her common sense even if it occasionally meant crossing Jogiches. Fending off his frantic questions and undisguised doubts about her performance, she also carried out his orders, like the disciplined party member she wanted to appear to be. In two weeks she had learned about the policies of the German Social Democratic Party (SPD), studying its publications, listening to people, collecting information. She knew no one of importance in the party's leadership; but she did know that its venerated leader, Wilhelm Liebknecht, supported her adversary, the Polish Socialist Party (PPS). Diligently, she cooperated with the middle echelon of the SPD—functionaries whom she found mediocre and bigoted but whose support she needed. In Germany this was an election year; the SPD was struggling for votes, and she wanted to join the campaign and use her gifts. At the beginning of June she was sent to Upper Silesia, the part of Poland annexed by Prussia in the eighteenth century, to agitate among the Polish workers. Unlike Jogiches or her German comrades, she had never been an agitator. She charged head on, apprehensive but determined. The apprehension, it turned out, was mutual, as was the attraction. The workers had never before seen a *Fräulein Doktor*.

In Zurich Jogiches suffered birth pangs—would Luxemburg fail or succeed? She strained his patience with her lengthy letters in which she dissected their relationship, shed tears over the past, fantasized about the future, reminded him about drinking cocoa and taking walks, and inquired about his doctorate. It was of no comfort to him that her mind was in Zurich, not in Berlin. And it was certainly bad luck that just as she was ready to start her work, stomach cramps sent her to bed. Within a week, however, he received more welcome news. "If you think a lecture of mine will go unnoticed you're absolutely wrong," Luxemburg assured him.[3] After ten days she spoke German "like Bismarck" and could compose a lecture "no worse than Bebel"; after four weeks, she wrote, "I'm convinced that in six months I'll be one of the best speakers in the Party."[4] Jogiches sensed a slightly patronizing tone: there was no reason for him to get impatient, she suggested, since his counsel followed on the heels of action she had already taken. If he was proud of her progress, he was injured by every sign of her independence, which he interpreted as defiance. He did not expect her to make a decision and tell him, "I had no time left to consult with you."[5] Her letters were becoming more businesslike, reports of what she had done and what she planned to do, the few personal words thrown in hurriedly. With slight irony, she wrote, "As you see, I shifted to business—your style. Perhaps you are right, and in another six months I will at last turn into your ideal."[6]

Her Silesian tour in June 1898, barely three weeks after her arrival in Berlin, was a triumph. It gave Luxemburg the first taste of power; her contagious zeal kept the crowds spellbound. The news about the woman from Poland spread quickly. The lecture halls and makeshift quarters overflowed with Polish workers as interested in Dr. Rosa Luxemburg (she retained her own name) as in her speeches. Unattractive at first glance, she only had to open her mouth to mesmerize the audience. Age had not blurred her Semitic features; if anything they had become more pronounced. But she spoke Polish and she spoke with ardor and an inner strength that made the miners in German-annexed Poland proud of their outlawed language. They could not take

77

their eyes off the small figure with sparkling eyes and expressive face, who in a voice that rang like a bell talked about exploitation, their deprived wives and children, and their duty to fight for justice. They cheered and applauded her and showered her with flowers.

Luxemburg's success was beyond all expectations. Filled with confidence and pride, her heart went out to the workers and to her mother country. "What a delight—cornfields, meadows, woods . . . the Polish language and Polish peasants . . . a barefoot little cowherd and our magnificent pine trees," she wrote to Jogiches. "True, the peasants are starved and filthy, but what a beautiful race!"[7]

Jogiches was not moved. Day and night, sitting over the proofs of Luxemburg's dissertation, he pondered recent developments. The proofs gave him an excuse to interrupt his studies and a chance to improve Luxemburg's work, but his efforts did not please her. "You've left some spelling errors," she scolded him. "Your correction doesn't make sense . . . you missed the point."[8] The Silesian tour, Jogiches thought, successful in terms of her personal popularity, was far from making history. To distribute proclamations and voting papers "is in your eyes . . . degrading," she admitted, "for me it is an honor."[9] Luxemburg was not moving in the right direction, he feared. "You're probably very displeased," she acknowledged. "I, on the contrary, am very optimistic."[10] She pointed out to him that the difference in their assessments was caused simply by his ignorance of the situation. Although she apologized profusely when she made a decision on her own, she knew that he would not take her apologies seriously.

Cheering crowds, admiration, and reverence fulfilled Luxemburg's needs, at least temporarily. "You can't imagine how good my first public appearances were for me," she said to Jogiches.[11] Also her anxiety over being an intruder abated; and she no longer depended exclusively on Jogiches for acceptance or for confirmation of her womanhood.

Jogiches's sexual reluctance and his unceasing criticism of her looks and taste had almost succeeded in convincing her that she was not very desirable and that desirability did not matter. She learned to live with Jogiches's verdict but never quite accepted it and was childishly happy that men were attracted to her. The new glory enhanced her looks—her deep, dark eyes shone, she moved more lightly, more confidently. Stylishly and carefully dressed, a large-brimmed hat balancing the disproportions of her figure, Luxemburg looked attractive, and moreover she looked interesting. "Here . . . I made a great impression," she assured Jogiches. "In the black dress and in my new hat, I look 'charming,' the Warszawskis said."[12] Strikingly different in background and culture, in looks, behavior, and intellect from "that species," as she called German women, she intrigued the Germans.

Julius Bruhns and Bruno Schönlank courted her in a way she had not known before. Bruhns, the editor-in-chief of the Breslau-based paper *Volkswacht,* was a former deputy to the Reichstag* and a distinguished journalist. He had fallen in love with her five years before in Zurich and had remained under her spell ever since. Married to a woman whose needs and interests were incompatible with his own, he had, in his own words, "gone to the dogs." In Luxemburg he had seen the ideal wife and companion. Now he begged for her friendship, which she, flattered, promised. Schönlank, the editor-in-chief of the influential SPD daily *Leipziger Volkszeitung,* was an eminent socialist, a good journalist, former coeditor of *Vorwärts,* and deputy to the Reichstag. Instantly taken by Rosa, he announced his readiness to do anything he could for her. He invited her to contribute to *Leipziger Volkszeitung* and offered to write a review of her forthcoming book. "I can do with him what I want," Luxemburg wrote to Jogiches, assuring him that she kept Schönlank in his place. Contrary to Jogiches's suspicions, Schönlank could not "barge in on me any time," since she warned him, "no visits without a written note."[13] Her correspondence with Schönlank centered exclusively on philosophy and science, she informed Jogiches. Unable to contain the pleasure her success gave her, she sent Jogiches Bruhn's and Schönlank's letters. Jogiches returned them with the remark "too long to read."[14]

Although she kept insisting to Jogiches how much she hated Berlin and "the Huns," it took Luxemburg one month to come up with a new, distinctively German prescription for their happiness: efficiency. It would solve all their problems, and life would be sheer pleasure. They had been wasting time and energy being edgy and impatient with each other, she wrote to Jogiches. Efficient organization of work would free them from stress and tension; with more time just for themselves and a sense of accomplishing "maximal results with minimal effort," they would enjoy life, work, and each other. *"Frisch,*

*The German governing body.

79

froh, frei" (fresh, joyous, free), she happily quoted a favorite German slogan.[15]

Meanwhile Jogiches kept working on the galleys of her book, checking dates, figures, statistics, the entire apparatus on which her thesis was built. He rarely left his room and saw no one; and although he did not mind that, it irked him to be cast in the role of helpmate living between Luxemburg's galleys and her self-lauding reports. That she should pay attention to the dubious compliments of some German party hacks and, still worse, attempt to persuade him of the benefits of German efficiency, was an outright insult.

Hungry for recognition, Jogiches expected Luxemburg to praise his hard work lavishly. But she just wrote that her life was hectic, that she was "irreplaceable" in one district or another, that she was building important contacts. At the end of a letter that she said she barely could find time to write, he would find a jaunty "And my poor darling? still sweating over my proofs?"[16] He was furious that she made light of his work and offended by the condescending tone. He responded with one abusive epistle after another, and Luxemburg promptly reacted. She repented her criticism—"I was enormously impressed by your last corrections and I humbly ask your forgiveness"—but used the opportunity to discuss life with him once again.[17] Love, home, family, friends—all that makes life life—was sin to Leo, she told him. And life was what Rosa missed constantly and painfully. In Germany, conventional, orderly, hardworking, she became still more voracious for "life" than before and still less able to see the contradiction inherent in her passion for a man who was unable to satisfy her.

Soon after moving to Germany, Rosa told Jogiches that in Berlin she became "as though an entirely different person from the one in Zurich."[18] In fact, she was confronted with conflicts that Switzerland had alleviated. Her Jewishness, which was meaningless in Zurich, was not meaningless in Berlin. She could not but be aware that her looks were carefully scrutinized and that her face introduced her before she introduced herself. She found herself in a situation not uncommon for Polish Jews: she represented a nation the Germans considered inferior and a race that offended their sensibilities. The initial identification with the Poles during the Silesian tour prevented her from being identified with the Jews, and she was careful to leave it at that. But there was an issue she could not ignore. "One could do the Polish workers no bigger favor than to Germanize them," Ignaz Auer, the

Lina Luksenburg

Elias Luksenburg

Zamość, Poland; the house where Rosa Luxemburg
spent the first three years of her life

Rosa, age twelve

Rosa, a Gymnasium student in Warsaw

Leo Jogiches, in Wilno before 1890

Rosa Luxemburg from Poland

Leo Jogiches from Lithuania

Facsimile of Elias Luksenburg's last letter to Rosa: "An eagle soars so high he loses all sight of the earth below…I won't burden you anymore with my letters."

Facsimile of Rosa's letter to Leo, 6 March 1899: "Our own small apartment, our own nice furniture, our own library…And perhaps even a little, a very little baby? Will this never be allowed? Never?"

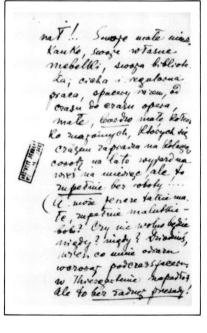

Luise Kautsky

Berlin, Cranachstrasse No. 28, where Rosa
Luxemburg lived from 1901 to 1911

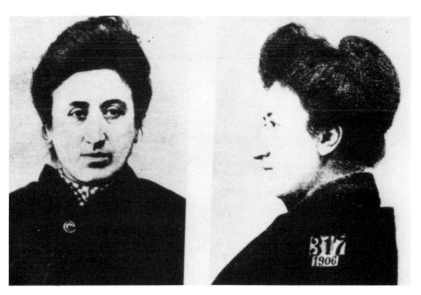

Police identification, Warsaw 1906

Leo Jogiches in Berlin—a commander
without troops

Congress of the Second International, Amsterdam, 1904. Rosa Luxemburg (center, with hat) surrounded by (clockwise) Victor Adler (Austria), Georgij Plekhanov (Russia), Sen Katayama (Japan), and Edouard Vaillant (France). Karl Kautsky (Germany) stands on Victor Adler's left.

SPD executive who sent her to Silesia, told her. "But this should not be mentioned to them," he said.[19] Luxemburg did not share Auer's view and wondered why he drew a line between "them," the Poles, and her? Because she was a Jew? Yet when Karl Gerisch, a party leader of long standing, asked her why she did not stay in Berlin, Auer explained to the "obese, bearded Jew," as she described Gerisch to Jogiches, that Luxemburg was a Pole and should work among Poles. Her ambiguous position as a Polish Jew was used for political expediency.

The suddenness of her success was deceptive; it camouflaged the anguish and vulnerability of any ordinary Jewish Polish expatriate. The years Luxemburg had spent with Jogiches had muted her anxieties. The transition from the Luksenburg family to Jogiches placed no demands on her perception of herself. Her family and Jogiches were Jewish, assimilated, middle class. Little during the Swiss years intensified her awareness of her origin until her mother's death in 1897. Six months later she became a German citizen by marriage. Even though hers was a marriage of convenience it added to her confusion. She came to Germany carrying the bundle of her Jewish family's letters, party instructions to introduce herself as a Pole, and the marriage certificate that changed her citizenship from Russian to German. If she had had a strong sense of belonging—to Jews, to Poles, or to Jogiches—all this might have mattered little. But with the link to her family further weakened by her mother's death, her Polishness never socially affirmed, and Jogiches's evasive attitude toward her, she did not, as she had said, exist as herself. Persistently, she had attributed this to external circumstances—lack of home, family, permanent job, regular income, regular life. The genuine reason, however, why her self could not emerge was hidden among the loosely plastered tiles of her existence, each painted in a different national color.

Anti-Semitism, on the rise in Germany since the 1880s, was absent in Luxemburg's letters to Jogiches. Yet some questions must have crossed her mind. If she referred to Karl Gerisch as "an obese, bearded Jew," how did people refer to her? If the German comrades spoke with unabashed contempt of the Poles in front of her, how did they regard her? The SPD leadership harbored no anti-Jewish feelings, and one could be "a Jewish socialist" though not "a socialist Jew."[20]

Luxemburg's ambitions went far beyond the Polish workers living in Silesia. In her mind's eye she saw herself addressing meetings of German workers in Leipzig, Dresden, and ultimately Berlin. The road from there was direct to the Second International. Suspended between the Germany she was expected to reject and the Poland that often rejected her, and burdened with the heritage she did not want, she saw the realization of her dreams in the socialist brotherhood.

The "deadening apathy" that seized her in Berlin did not affect her political activities. But her insistence on how brave and courageous she felt and her frequent indispositions—migraine headaches, stomach cramps, nausea, nervous exhaustion—indicate extreme tension. Her trepidation was not without reason: victory meant a new life, with her Jewish past successfully erased; defeat meant weakness, a triumph of the past over the future. "I feel detached and a stranger to everything and everyone," she wrote to Jogiches. "I'm just a corpse."[21] The recurring protestations—"I feel no fear, no pain, no loneliness"—and her inability to breathe without Jogiches near her—"I'm without air"—betrayed an anxiety she did not know how to fight on her own.[22]

For the first time she encountered the true power of modern, organized anti-Semitism, different from that she had known in Poland.* Luxemburg needed the protection of the man who, like her, was an outsider and who, unlike her, was not affected by his Jewishness—to whom it was a fact, not a calamity. Eventually she learned to deal alone with the conflict, but she went through a trying period, as her uneven, contradictory, and at times desperate letters to Jogiches indicate.

The self-imposed image, not unlike that which she had assumed in the Warsaw Gymnasium to deter embarrassing remarks or questions, produced the expected effect. Her German friends, drawing on Rosa's fantasized picture of her youth, unwittingly created an imaginary biography of her which is still widely accepted. In it, her father, Edward Luxemburg, was descended from a sophisticated family and was an ardent champion of Polish education and Jewish emancipation. He was the first to give Rosa foreign publications, which were eagerly studied and discussed at the family table; he drew her attention to social causes; his ideals fired her imagination and nourished the future revolutionary. There is no evidence to validate any of these claims. Like his father, Elias was an undistinguished merchant. He had no intellectual aspirations, no profession other than buying and selling, and no interest in things more esoteric. An unlikely candidate for Rosa's mentor and inspiration, he devoted all his energy to supporting his

---

*By 1893, anti-Semitic organizations sent sixteen deputies to the Reichstag.[23]

family. That he did not enjoy even a passing period of prosperity is attested to by the fact that the seven-member family never once moved to a larger apartment, that sometimes there was no money to pay the rent, and that he was destitute in his old age. He was typical of the first generation of assimilated Jewish fathers, mostly hardworking shopkeepers or merchants, of modest intelligence and few idealistic concerns.

Rosa described her mother as a saintly woman whose "shadow-like" existence left Rosa with "scant memories."[24] Lina Luksenburg, as Rosa was aware, had been a woman of great sagacity and strength. Cut off from her natural stronghold—the generations of Talmudic scholars—living in a new environment, she remained true to herself. She had to live with the sneers of the Jewish *arrivistes* and with dubious acceptance into Polish society, and she did so not as a victim or an interloper but as a victor. Lina sought acceptance for herself and her children in a world she perhaps did not admire but saw as more progressive than the world in which she had been raised. On her deathbed she implored her children to respect their father—a message that negates Rosa's invented portrayal of the venerated pater familias.

Although Rosa saw little of her father while at home, somehow she remembered him as a champion of noble causes. But of the mother, who was constantly with her in Warsaw, she retained "scant memories." That she continued to wrestle with the memory of her mother is shown by an experience she described to Jogiches some years later: "Did you hear me scream last night? . . . I wake up at two-thirty in the morning . . . don't know where I am, and in greatest fear I call my Mother . . . And it takes a long time till I realize I'm calling seven years too late."[25]

Germany brought back other shadows from Rosa Luxemburg's past. The style in which the SPD executives lived in no way resembled the humble existence of the socialist exiles in Switzerland. The salaries the party paid provided for pleasant apartments, entertainment, travel abroad, education for their children, a middle-class life. Luxemburg, having yearned for years for a "normal" life, was enchanted by the *Gemütlichkeit*. Though she tried to beautify each of her sublet rooms with knickknacks, fringed lampshades, and polished floors, they were still not a home. "The thought of sublet rooms makes me cringe," she wrote Jogiches.[26] The vision of a family home came back to her, now in an idealized version not much different from the cozy homes of her

German friends. The abnormality of her life, the constantly changing, unfamiliar rooms, the occasional visits she and Jogiches paid each other were in glaring contrast to the orderly German households of conventional families with maids and regular meals. Life with Jogiches, which she once had remembered as "joyless and drab," turned under her pen into an idyllic picture of "love and work together" in two comfortably furnished rooms, if only he would leave Zurich and join her in Berlin. Exhausted by her unsettled life, she craved stability. Letters arriving from her family in Warsaw evoked sentimental feelings. She remembered warmth, care, drawers full of linen, the festive dinners and everyday meals. The desire to have a home made her perhaps look differently at the role her mother had played.

The perplexing emotions, the conflicts, and unfulfilled yearnings inspired Rosa Luxemburg with courage. Over the summer of 1898 she prepared to do battle with Eduard Bernstein. It became a turning point in her career.

Eduard Bernstein, a prominent socialist theorist, is remembered as the first revisionist of some of Marx's theses. Bernstein questioned Marx's theories of the intensification of class struggle and the growing pauperization of the workers, which were to lead to the collapse of capitalism and world revolution. Bernstein argued that neither was inevitable in a capitalist economy and that some of Marx's theories, based on a reality fifty years old, were no longer applicable. His series of polemical articles, published in *Die Neue Zeit* in 1897–98, raised a virtual tempest in the socialist camp. The press, not guns, was still an accepted means to thrash out ideological differences, and since Bernstein appeared sacrilegious to his comrades, they took to their pens. So did Luxemburg. She sensed that a scientifically exact, rigorous rebuttal might elevate her to the position of a recognized Marxist. "I want this article so much I'd give half my life for it," she wrote to Jogiches on 2 July 1898. "There are two difficult problems: 1. to write about crises; and 2. to prove beyond doubt that capitalism must break its neck . . . Help, for heaven's sake, help!" The third difficulty was the timing. "*Speed is essential* because . . . if somebody gets ahead of us the entire work is wasted."27 Jogiches was no less excited. He too wanted the article to be perfect, and declarations of love flew to Berlin. "Dyodyo, you silly, I'm up to my ears in Bernstein and you ask if I love you," the

84

elated Rosa responded. "Yes, yes, yes, I do love you, yes, 'with a little passion' too."[28]

Luxemburg's article, "Social Reform or Revolution," published in seven installments on 21–28 September 1898 in *Leipziger Volkszeitung,* was hailed as a work of impeccable scholarship and the most comprehensive refutation of Bernstein's theory. As a result, the press commission of the SPD, composed of seventeen members, unanimously elected Luxemburg as editor-in-chief of *Sächsische Arbeiterzeitung,* an honor no woman has ever been paid, before or since. The distaste she may have felt at some party members' derisive protest, "What! petticoat politics!" was easily compensated for by the compliments of figures like Karl Kautsky, Clara Zetkin, Franz Mehring, and Jean Jaurès. Four months after her arrival in Germany, Rosa Luxemburg became an international celebrity. It is one of history's pranks that at a time when the entire socialist camp was up in arms against Bernstein, Luxemburg wrote jauntily to Jogiches: "What do you think about the new Russian 'party'? Naturally, just what I do—rascals, and yet they managed."[29] She was referring to the First Congress of the Russian Social Democratic Workers' Party, which became the Communist Party of Russia in 1918 and is still in power.

Rosa's life moved at a fast pace in 1898: marriage to Lübeck in April, arrival in Germany in May, the Silesian tour in June, the publication of her dissertation in July, appointment as permanent contributor to *Sächsische Arbeiterzeitung* in July, the publication of the anti-Bernstein series in September, editorship of *Sächsische Arbeiterzeitung* in September, and participation in the annual SPD Congress in Stuttgart in October. Luxemburg was now generally considered one of the top experts of the younger generation on scientific socialism. "Genius," she was called, and "the divine," she reported to Jogiches. Her writing was compared to "Marx at his best," she told him with a note of self-deprecating irony.[30] Though the applause pleased her, she was not impressed by the applauders. "Poor is the party," she wrote about the SPD, "in which a botcher, an ignoramus like me plays an important role."[31] But the "poor" party became her mainstay for the next twenty years, and Luxemburg made it her business to understand it and to imbue it with her rebellious spirit.

What she learned about the party was not heartening—the coteries, self-serving and self-congratulatory, barred innovation and progress. The party needed, she thought, a steady influx of young talent and intellect to counter routine, complacency, and growing conservatism. Her criticism, open and provocative, was not, as some party members maintained, "typical arrogance"; it originated in her broad, liberal education, her sense of history and taste for literature, and her impatience with those who lacked these perspectives. "Someone like me who does not belong to the family," she wrote to Jogiches in May 1899, "who has no backstairs influence only his two elbows, who is a potential threat to adversaries . . . and to supporters as well . . . whom they keep on the back burner lest he outdistance them . . . has no chance, and there's nothing one can do about it because all deals are struck backstage . . . I'm observing it very calmly. I knew all that in advance, just as I know that within a year or two none of this will matter—the intrigues, the fears, the venom. I shall occupy a position at the top of the party . . . My criticism is by no means limited to individuals," she emphasized. "I want to push forward the entire movement . . . to instill new life into the press, the meetings, the publications . . . to do away with the ossified forms of oral and written agitation to which almost no one responds anymore."[32]

There was also the unbridgeable difference in temperament between the passionate, imaginative, skeptical Luxemburg and the Germans—tenacious, rigid, passive. Never satisfied, forever questioning—be it Marx or Lenin, Plekhanov or Jaurès, the rule of the German emperor or the rule of the SPD—she was bent, the German government maintained, on overthrowing the kaiser and determined, the SPD maintained, on splitting the party.

Jogiches, however, reproached her for being an idealist in the ranks of an inert party she should use to gain influence. "Concerning your opinion that it is ridiculous to be an idealist in the German movement, I don't agree with you," she wrote. "First, there are idealists in this movement too, above all the huge masses of ordinary workers-agitators, and even among the leadership—for instance, Bebel. Second, I couldn't care less because my *suprema ratio*, reached in the course of my own Polish-German revolutionary practice, is to always remain my own self regardless of others, regardless of circumstances. I am and want to remain an idealist both in the German and in the Polish movement. This doesn't mean that . . . I don't want the most influential position in the party and that I'm not ready to fight for it."[33]

And fight she did from the start. Luxemburg's difficulties within the SPD began a few months after she joined the party on 25 May 1898, ten days following her arrival in Berlin. The troubles she encountered then and later have been variously attributed to her Jewish origin, her Polish provenance, her gender, and her aggressiveness. In fact, in a party that set great store by appearances and congeniality, or at least the appearance of congeniality, she simply was not a good team player. The elders in the SPD, Wilhelm Liebknecht, August Bebel, and Karl Kautsky, recognized that she was a unique asset to the party—hence her swift rise to the top echelons—but she made them and many others feel ill at ease.

A case in point was Luxemburg's criticism of the party press. "I am dissatisfied with the fashion in which most of the articles in the party press are written," she wrote to her old Zurich friends the Seidels. "The style is conventional, wooden, stereotypical . . . just a colorless, dull sound like that of a running engine. To my mind the reason behind it is that when people write they mostly forget to reach deep into their own selves, to relive the importance and truth of the subject. I think that with every new article one should experience the subject matter through and through, get emotionally involved, every single time, every single day. Only then will the old, familiar truths, expressed in words new and bright, go from the writer's heart to the reader's heart . . . The goal I set for myself is never to forget to reach deep into my own self, to be enthusiastic, inspired every time I put pen to paper."[34]

Rosa Luxemburg believed that the style of the press reflected the party's spirit, or rather the lack of it. Conversely, the style of her writing—vigorous, steel-sharp, witty, and often sarcastic—reflected her personality. It inspired the same mixture of admiration and nervousness as did her person.

There is no reason to assume that Luxemburg kept her criticism of the party to herself. Even if she did, it surfaced in September 1898 when she was offered the editorship of *Sächsische Arbeiterzeitung*. The offer came as a surprise and a challenge. Jogiches cabled from Zurich, *"rundweg ablehnen"* (refuse unconditionally), to no avail. She was not one to hide in a dark corner, she told him. Jogiches objected because he thought the job was way over her head, now dizzy from her recent success, and because he was in principle against her accepting a permanent job. He wanted her free, at his disposal, developing the talent he had been watching over and financing for seven years.

After she accepted the post, in October 1898 Jogiches rushed to Dresden, mistrustful of her ability to manage without his guidance and vexed by her disobedience—a proof of her growing independence. He could appear in no official capacity on the paper's premises and, because of the secrecy of their relationship, in no personal capacity either. From his hotel headquarters he supervised her work, not knowing whether the directions he gave her at night would be followed in the morning. For Luxemburg the pressure he exerted on her was unbearable. She remembered as dreadful the time spent in Dresden, in a third-rate hotel (due to the secrecy), and promised herself "to write everything by myself" in the future and to meet with him "only when I'm free, with no work at hand."[35]

On 2 November 1898 Luxemburg tendered her resignation over a conflict in editorial policy. It is difficult to say how deeply, if at all, Jogiches was implicated in her decision. But his initial reaction to the offer, his dislike of being contradicted, and the embarrassing circumstances under which he lived in Dresden probably played a role. He wanted her back in Berlin, uncommitted, and back to Berlin she went. He himself returned to Zurich.

But the party did not take her defiance lightly. August Bebel, with undisguised anger, accused her of "unbelievable tactlessness," adding that he was particularly disillusioned because she had behaved more like a woman than like a party member. "I considered . . . the elevation of the level and the improvement of the sorely neglected paper my foremost task," Luxemburg wrote to Bebel on 7 November, emphasizing that, denied "complete freedom" to publish her own articles and the right to publish outside articles of her choice, she could not fulfill her responsibilities as she saw fit.[36]

So she let the leadership know early who she was and where she stood. Their respect grew but so did their discomfort. The offers of editorship that followed were a measure of appreciation for Luxemburg's gifts: in October 1899 that of *Vorwärts*, which she turned down, and two years later of *Leipziger Volkszeitung*, which she held for a few months.

In Berlin Luxemburg found major SPD journals vying for her contributions. Though the fees were modest and irregular, for the first time in her life she was earning money. The improvement of her finances is attested to by the rent she paid. In 1898 she had tremulously begged Jogiches's forgiveness for the 33-mark extravagance, and a year later she paid 80 marks monthly for a room. Jogiches was still contributing 100 marks a month, but even this combined with her earnings was not enough.* She developed more expensive tastes, and her needs grew along with her success.

———

Jogiches's financial backing greatly helped Luxemburg's career. Free from everyday worries and badly paid jobs, she could devote all her time to studying and to political work. Jogiches's income allowed them both to live comfortably. In financial affairs Jogiches was a worthy heir of his grandfather. Money bestowed obligations; it was not meant for pleasure. Luxemburg's attitude, frivolous and irresponsible, was perhaps a reaction to the stereotype of the money-conscious Jew that haunted her youth. All her life she remained oblivious to the value of money, overspending, promising to improve, and never repentant. Jogiches did not begrudge her the money—he was anything but stingy—but demanded scrupulousness as a matter of principle. Unaffected by Jewish stereotypes, he knew that money bought him freedom in exile, allowed him to be his own master and to finance causes of his own choice. Until the outbreak of World War I, the administrator of the Jogiches estate sent Leo the accounts of the profits the family business produced. Neatly filed, they were found among his papers after his death. Among Luxemburg's papers were found scraps covered with quotations from Mickiewicz, Voltaire, Shakespeare.

If Jogiches ever tried to control Luxemburg with money, he did not succeed. She took freely, spent freely, and asked for more. Occasionally she threatened never to accept another penny from him, but the next emergency was never far away. "I'm very sorry but again I must ask you for 10 rubles." At times he became nasty and reproached her. "It always humiliates and irritates me when you request a detailed account of my pitiable expenses," she wrote, angry that he wanted to teach her to conduct her finances in an orderly fashion.[37] "Even if I had the terrible vice of being 'disorderly,' this would be no disaster," she declared. "Other women earn no money, have no particular intellectual or moral virtues, are 'disorderly,' yet their husbands are very pleased and don't pick on them."[38] The painstakingly meticulous accounts she sent him from Paris, itemized down to the last centime—1 or perhaps

---

*The rate of exchange at the time was 100 marks = $25.

1½ francs for flowers and pastry, 2.25 for a hat, 2 francs a week for sugar and bread for breakfast—turned the formality into a joke. The account would end, "What happened to the rest of the money? I've no idea."[39] Jogiches, always a mentor, insisted on teaching Luxemburg scrupulosity. But she refused to listen. She itemized the prices of tram tickets and milk just to demonstrate the futility of his attempts to reform her. When things were smooth between them, she apologized for both the accounting and the spending: "Our relationship is so wonderful now" that it would be silly to spoil it with petty explanations.[40]

Even if Jogiches thought frugality a virtue and advised her to "force" her brothers to support her sick father, he sent funds to extend a vacation she took with her father and requested that she go to the best tailor and live in an elegant neighborhood. In her eyes, by supporting her he was fulfilling the conventional role of husband. When she had a handsome income in Germany she still turned to him for a loan—"this time, I *really* mean a loan, so help me God"—or a gift—"if you want me to get a new spring jacket . . . and if you can spare 20 marks, send it"—or a convenience—"I could really use 15–20 marks."[41] Whether accompanied by a dramatic "this is the last time I'm taking money from you" or by warm thanks, it never became more than just money to her. Once only did she become genuinely upset, when she learned accidentally from Jogiches's brother that Leo kept the amount of his assets secret.

Money was never a barometer of their relationship. Even though by 1899 she was earning her living, Luxemburg did not feel less dependent on Jogiches. Money was not what defined her dependence or independence. But Jogiches may have seen her financial independence as a threat, and this may to some extent have influenced his discouraging her from taking a permanent job. Though she told him that "people's *primary concern* is to support themselves and their children or their parents, and *only then* should they think of becoming great scholars," she enjoyed the freedom Jogiches guaranteed her.[42] She did not object to accounting for the money she earned. "Since you're asking, here's what I made: *Sächsische Arbeiterzeitung*—80 marks, *Leipziger Volkszeitung*—60 marks plus 3 for a notice = 143 marks."[43] She did object when he pressed her to be more practical. "I'll do it my own way, following my instinct and my nature . . .I won't start out by haggling and making demands . . . —to appear petty and calculating would be very inappropriate."[44]

Jogiches liked his role of provider. When Luxemburg tried to assume the role for herself, she did not show much tact. "Why so sad, my golden boy?" she wrote. "Don't worry, you have a brave little wife. Your wife will work hard, make a great deal of money . . . with no great effort, almost playing . . . and every month she'll send some to her Daddy and some to her own Dyodyo."[45] That she could make money "almost playing" while he never earned a penny could not but have humiliated him.

Money, like their letters, was a tie when the relationship seemed to founder. When he refused to join her in Germany, Luxemburg told him to expect no more letters from her; "as for my financial needs," she stipulated, "in an emergency I'll get in touch with you."[46] Since emergencies were a natural part of her budget she was merely letting him know that one door was still open.

After Luxemburg moved to Germany Jogiches's newly regained freedom suited him well. As time went by, he felt increasingly hesitant about giving it up. The chasm between Luxemburg, swiftly moving ahead, and him, stagnating, was widening. His doctoral degree was not going to bridge it. But the university justified his staying on in Zurich. Luxemburg drafted letters to his dissertation adviser, watched the deadlines, and found a dissertation topic for him: "The State of the Economy in Russia." Although he finished only a seminar paper, which he presented in July 1900, Luxemburg kept referring to "your doctoral thesis" in her letters. To brush off her incessant questions, Jogiches told her that the thesis was in the works.

Luxemburg's desire that Jogiches complete his studies with an official stamp of recognition matched his longing to be left alone. He did not need the verdict of any institution on his intellectual capacity; he knew his own worth. Her wish for the degree, which she saw as a natural result of ten years of studies, he considered a pressure to conform, or still worse an aspiration on her part to have him meet the standards of her new German friends. Unwilling to move, he kept setting new dates for the mythical degree to materialize. "To leave Zurich after ten years without a doctorate would be very unpleasant indeed," she agreed when in the spring of 1900 he begged for just two more months.[47] Under the false impression that he was working on his degree, she wrote, "It makes me happy that you applied yourself with such passion to your . . . doctorate."[48]

A more personal problem was not as easy for Luxemburg to resolve. Jogiches still insisted on keeping their relationship secret. His demand to keep it hidden from Luxemburg's family bordered on obsession. Was it really his penchant for conspiracy? Or was it a fear of commitment? Whatever it was, she went along with it. "I'll do what you want and won't enlighten my family about us," she agreed in mid-1898 before her sister came to visit her in Berlin.[49] In order not to raise Anna's curiosity, he was to use plain envelopes, Luxemburg advised him. The somersaults she performed to avoid a meeting between Jogiches and her brother Józef, who with his family was staying with her just when Jogiches planned to visit her, she described as belonging in a cheap romance. Sometime later in 1898 Jogiches finally relented and gave Luxemburg his permission to reveal to her family his existence, though not his name. To them, Rosa's fiancé passed as Leo Grozowski, one of Jogiches's pseudonyms. Luxemburg, who in the past had never mentioned her father in her correspondence with Jogiches, now presented Elias as a dominant figure in her life. For his sake she wanted their union to be legalized. "Relying on your promises," she wrote to Jogiches in May 1900, "I told my father last summer [1899] that we would be living together by this month." Jogiches remained unmoved. "I can put off my father no longer," Luxemburg insisted. "I don't know what to tell him and have been lying to him like a crook. It is high time to end this procrastination."[50]

When Luxemburg realized that Jogiches was not going to join her, that he enjoyed his bachelor's life, that not even the evocation of her father's authority moved him, she presented Leo with an ultimatum. "The only hope for a mutual agreement and a more or less normal relationship is to live together in Germany," she wrote to him in March 1900. "I don't know and can't think why you keep putting it off, but I do know this postponement is abnormal, it humiliates me . . . If a person feels no need for a permanent union, I think it is simply a lack of courage to carry on a marital relationship at a distance and on fleeting visits."[51] And she hit where it hurt most—she threatened to stop writing. Thus, she was going to deprive him of his vicarious existence, leave him in a political void. Jogiches accused her of blackmail. But she was adamant—no more commuting, no more patching, no more beating around the bush. An exchange of dramatic letters followed, with Jogiches begging her to "renew our common spiritual life" and Luxemburg with a vengeance suggesting he take

92

advantage of "the break in our correspondence" and detach himself from her. He reproached her for never giving a thought to his "inner life," for egotism, for an inability to give. If that was true, she threw back, it was because "the only thing you let me do is keep my mouth shut." Their estrangement was his fault, not hers: "Even in Zurich we were spiritual strangers and the frightful loneliness of these last two years [1896–1898] is engraved on my mind."[52]

The reasons for the rift went beyond the "spiritual." Luxemburg's suspicion that he had "stopped loving" her, that he "might be involved with somebody else," was unjustified.[53] Jogiches simply wanted no constraint, no control, no closeness. After he agreed to join her in Berlin he still dwelled in his letters on their political partnership rather than on the feelings which keep lovers together. Fearful of losing each other, both of them were ready for some kind of compromise. Their mutual dependence, at once creative and destructive, personal and political, grew into a knot they could not disentangle.

Jogiches was coming to the forced reunion in Berlin empty-handed. In 1900, at thirty-three, he was too old to become the famous revolutionary's apprentice, too young to live in retirement. He had no name, no profession, no hope. He had yielded to Rosa's demand for want of another solution, feeling that he was giving up his last vestige of dignity. His life in Zurich, though far from gratifying, was his own, and he controlled it. At one point, before moving to Berlin, he stayed for several days in a hotel near Chur in the Swiss Alps, possibly alone, possibly not, but in any case without notifying her. Perhaps he needed to prove to himself that he was free; perhaps this act of defiance reminded him of happier days when he had enough pluck to challenge to a duel someone he found offensive. His act of submission, he felt, might make Luxemburg proceed on her course to improve him with ever greater authority. He was also aware that he himself was to blame. He had made promises he was not sure he was willing to keep.

Leo Jogiches was not made of stone, as Luxemburg maintained. He loved her, and her incessant demands that he love her differently deepened his sense of failure. He was no better, no more accomplished as a lover, she let him know, than he was as a husband. "Here in Berlin," she said, "I constantly see *the kind of women* men live with, how those men worship them and yield to their domination, and all the time, in the back of my mind, I'm aware of the way you treat me."[54] There was as little hope that he would yield to her domination as there was for his metamorphosis into one of the burghers whose attitude toward women she so admired. Her wish to live a comfortable, respectable life was to him proof of their estrangement. "Our free time we'll devote to studying art . . . a sheer delight, isn't it? The two of us, after a day's serious work, will read books on the history of art, visit galleries, go to operas!"[55] Each word hit him like a whip—the "free time" of which he would have plenty, the "day's serious work" of which he would have none, the art, the galleries, the operas—a German bourgeois dream. Everyday life embroidered was more of a curse to him than his solitary existence—tortured, but his own.

Jogiches's misgivings were justified. Luxemburg told him that the "mere child" she was when he met her was now a "mature person" and that his refusal to accept "that I've changed, that I'm not the same person I was eight years ago," created endless problems.[56] If he had come to her wielding power, he imagined, she would yield to him as she had before, occasionally rebellious but manageable. Her attempts to convince him of her independence were childish, he thought. "I don't like your telling me not to buy a jacket without you because I'll buy 'the devil knows what,' " she wrote him from Berlin two years earlier. "If I'm independent enough to perform single-handed on the political scene, that independence must extend to buying a jacket."[57] At the time it rather amused him that anything as insignificant as a jacket would stir her; now that he was to join her, it was her "single-handed" performance on the political scene that stuck in his mind. She intended, she said, to share *her* work with him once he came, and that defined his role.

On her own territory, Rosa held the trump card. What Leo could ignore at a distance as a passing whim or discard as a nuisance now threatened him. He let her indulge in observing religious holidays but thought it undignified and ridiculous. After she gave him for Christmas *Das Leben Jesu* (The Life of Jesus) by P. F. Strauss, he sent her a comedy by Molière. The mockery did not escape her. Nor did her fervor diminish. "I hope it is the last Christmas Eve we are spending separately," she wrote him in 1899. "But, by god, when I go back to those first years we spent together, what kind of holidays did we have then?! We never even knew how to celebrate holidays properly; but—without children there are no holidays, no family life."[58] Christmas, children, family life—it filled him with horror. If Rosa imagined him presiding over a festive Christmas dinner, surrounded by children intoning "O Tannenbaum," she was in for a bitter disappointment.

The two years Luxemburg spent alone in Berlin brought her fame and prestige. But the price she paid was high. She was afraid of succumbing to madness. She had her first bouts of depression. "I'm aware I did not achieve anything," she reproached herself. "And I'm aware I shall not do one tenth of what I should do. *Dissatisfaction with myself* is my permanent psychological state, remorse that I haven't done this or something else gnaws at me day in day out, hour after hour. The feeling of guilt doesn't leave me for a single moment."[59]

Yet publicly, her achievements were spectacular. Personally, she had none. Loneliness was destroying her. Jogiches was going under. Being together, she firmly believed, would bring them both fulfillment, and together they would start a new life.

8 | "Love and Work Together"

1900–1902

ROSA LUXEMBURG informed her family in Warsaw that, since Leo Jogiches was a Swiss citizen, the marriage ceremony would take place in Switzerland, and time was too short for them to attend. "You know how much I dislike making up such stories," she wrote to Jogiches, "but what else can I do?"[1] Credulous as always, the Luksenburgs believed her. They were not aware that Rosa, married to Gustav Lübeck, could not contract this marriage or that Leo was not a Swiss citizen. He became "uncle Leo" to her nieces and nephews, and brother-in-law to her siblings. The "marriage" was greeted in Warsaw with joy and relief. The family reunion in Germany that she promised for a later time to celebrate the event never took place. Her father, who more than anyone looked forward to it, died in September 1900, a few months after Rosa's announcement.

Between Rosa's ultimatum to Jogiches in March 1900 and his arrival in Berlin at the beginning of August, Luxemburg pressed hard to settle her divorce from Gustav Lübeck. With the counsel of Arthur Stadthagen, a lawyer and prominent socialist, she hoped to obtain the divorce within a few months, possibly before Jogiches arrived. Since Lübeck was living in Switzerland, she entrusted Jogiches with handling the details. Virtually every letter she wrote during that period mentions the "Lübeck case" along with instructions. Jogiches was to go "at once and with no excuses" to the Zurich district court, introduce himself as her brother or cousin, and speed up the proceedings; he was to talk to Lübeck "gently" and obtain a statement from him, "written at your place and in your presence," attesting to Lübeck's infidelity—the grounds for the divorce.[2] Should the court deem the statement insufficient and require a deposition by Lübeck's partner, a prostitute must be found. "Your fear that a hired registered prostitute might refuse to 'confess' in court is ridiculous," she wrote irritably. "Stadthagen is an old hand at this kind of lawsuit and I must listen to him, not to you. Please, please don't try to be smarter and shrewder than everyone else."[3] But Jogiches was in no hurry. After he failed once again to convince Luxemburg to postpone their reunion, he discovered new obstacles, this time due to Lübeck. Luxemburg wrote in exasperation: "Will there ever be an end to this . . . ?!!! My dearest, put aside everything else and first of all take care of [the divorce]. I don't have to tell you, do I, how important and urgent the matter is!"[4] Another three years passed before Luxemburg's marriage was dissolved.

It was easy to mislead her distant family about her marital status, but Luxemburg's German milieu presented a problem. The Social Democratic Party (SPD) was anything but bohemian, and conventional mores were strictly observed. A common-law marriage was not acceptable. Both as a public figure and as a member of the party's elite, Luxemburg had to guard her reputation. From Berlin, she wrote to Jogiches, "It is impossible to live openly together, and short of that our life will turn into a caricature that I fear more than loneliness."[5] They could live part of the year in Italy, she planned, or settle in Heidelberg, "where we'll be free from comrades and thus gossip."[6] After much arguing and devising, and abandoning various schemes, Luxemburg made the simplest arrangement. "My landlady has another (small) room to let, and you'll rent it with board just as I do. In this way we'll be together all the time. I'll introduce you as my cousin and this'll cause no gossip or speculation because I'm highly respected by my landlords and in the whole building."[7] Rosa merely asked that he bring his own pillow and let her know the exact time of his arrival so as to avoid an embarrassing scene in front of the maidservant that would "spoil the first moments by artificial restraint."[8]

So Jogiches became an uncle in Warsaw, a cousin in Berlin, and a "friend" to the outside world, and Luxemburg's dream of "living openly as husband and wife" was indefinitely postponed. The couple carried on the deception, always cautious, never open except in private—an arrangement that suited Jogiches, who was not at all eager to appear as prince consort among Luxemburg's friends.

Her friends were the most influential people in the SPD. In the two years before Jogiches joined her, Luxemburg had become a "family member" of the Kautskys, a confidante of Clara Zetkin, a favorite of August Bebel, and a protégé of Franz Mehring. They were taken by her sophistication and her devotion to socialism and were attracted by her personality. Aware of some politicking behind the friendliness, Luxemburg still enjoyed the company of people who, apart from the cause, shared her taste for literature and music; but above all she was proud of being accepted by the highly selective party elite.

Karl Johann Kautsky, his second wife, Luise, and their three little sons occupied a spacious apartment not far from Luxemburg's. Kautsky, born in Prague in 1854 and educated in Vienna, was the best-known Marxist theorist of his time in Germany. As editor-in-chief of *Die Neue Zeit* and author of numerous publications, he made a comfortable living. He lived in a style consonant with his belief that for the pioneers of a new social system, leisure was indispensable in order to conduct the long and exhausting struggle effectively. The Kautskys held regular Sunday afternoon gatherings and their house was always open to foreign visitors. Their public and private life was limited almost exclusively to contacts with socialists. Kautsky's first wife ran Engels's household, his second wife occasionally did translations for the socialist press, his mother, Minna Kautsky, wrote novels about workers, and Kautsky himself was entrusted by Marx's daughter, Laura Lafargue, with Marx's literary legacy. In connection with the latter, Luxemburg wrote to Jogiches in May 1900: "The day before yesterday the Kautskys invited me for dinner again, and he took the opportunity to ask whether I'd help him work on Marx's fourth volume [of *Das Kapital*] . . . Knowing full well that neither our contemporaries nor posterity would ever learn about my silent contribution to Marxism, I told him straight out, I'm nobody's fool! Of course, I put it in an elegant form . . . I advised him to buy a Remington typewriter and to teach his wife to type."[9]

Luise Kautsky, a well-educated, lively Viennese, played the traditional role of wife and mother. With both her husband and her

98

mother-in-law devoted to intellectual pursuits, she found that role particularly distressing. The breakdown in the Kautskys' marriage eight years later was caused by Luise's attempt to escape this confinement and live with a man more understanding of her needs. The accusation that Luxemburg was responsible for Luise's eccentric desire was unjust; but she undoubtedly clarified for Mrs. Kautsky the limitations of her life. Impressed by Rosa's mind and her independence, Luise sought her friendship from the beginning. Rosa was not very keen. "I don't like her . . . ," she wrote to Jogiches, "she loves me enormously, showers me with kisses, addresses me as *du*."[10] At first she thought Luise shallow and spiritless and jealous of Rosa's relationship with her husband—a relationship of equals. "I go to the Kautskys' rarely and stay briefly; more often he comes to my place," she reported, and added as an afterthought, perhaps to assure Jogiches that he alone mattered: "They bore me to tears."[11] Luise Kautsky had another story to tell: "After barely a few weeks, Rosa announced, 'all my needs are fulfilled at the Kautskys'.' " Mrs. Kautsky maintained that Rosa discussed politics with her husband, cuisine with the cook Zenzi, and "everything" with her. Although she admitted that Rosa was initially shocked to find "Karl Kautsky's wife wearing an apron!!" in no time Rosa put one on herself to learn the art of cooking under Zenzi's experienced eye. "Christmas without Rosa was unthinkable," Luise wrote, "and it was a pleasure to observe her wonderful way with the children." Mrs. Kautsky remembered herself and Rosa walking each other home, back and forth, unable to part at the end of the evening. Rosa would sing operatic arias, the "Marseillaise," or the "Internationale," her voice ringing in the nocturnal silence. In the spring of 1900, while Luxemburg was complaining to Jogiches about the burdens the relationship with the Kautskys put on her, she was invited to stay with the children, Luise said, "as a substitute mother."[12] She moved in when the Kautskys went to Paris to take over Marx's literary legacy.

After she came to know Luise Kautsky better, Luxemburg's early reservations disappeared and she grew deeply attached to her. Although Luxemburg was adamantly opposed to a separate women's movement—she considered it divisive to the cause—she felt strongly about her women friends' personal freedom. Sometimes in a jocular way, at other times in earnest, she protested against Karl Kautsky's arbitrariness and his condescending attitude toward his wife. She encouraged Mrs. Kautsky to write and helped her with criticism and editing.

Luise Kautsky attributed to Luxemburg a need to "surround herself with an impenetrable layer of secrecy." She ascribed it to Luxemburg's romanticism and to her fear of a barren petit bourgeois existence. Her friendship with Rosa was possible only, she emphasized, because she asked her no questions. Rosa never opened up to her, she said; an embrace or a sigh was as far as Rosa would go when in distress. She never dared to talk to her about Jogiches, with whom, Mrs. Kautsky wrote, Rosa had a "special relationship."[13]

Luise Kautsky was not Luxemburg's intellectual equal nor was she, like Clara Zetkin, a political ally. But for ten years Luxemburg had a home at the Kautskys', a family complete with three youngsters who adored her and a grandmother who doted on her. Luise, statuesque and matronly, developed a maternal attitude toward Rosa. She understood that under the exuberant surface there was a lonely woman, yearning for a family, tied to a man who, Luise noticed, would appear and disappear "meteor-like."

Rosa Luxemburg's relationship with Clara Zetkin began as a political alliance and turned into a lifelong friendship. Different in age, looks, and temperament, Clara and Rosa became the *Frauenzimmer*, as August Bebel somewhat patronizingly called them, of the German Social Democratic Party. For two decades they incited anger, respect, and mocking jibes.

Clara Eissner, born in 1857 of German Protestant stock, had met a Russian Jew, Osip Zetkin, in her home town, Leipzig, in the 1870s. The young revolutionary had fled Russia and could not stay in Prussia because of the antisocialist law. In 1880 he moved to Paris where Clara joined him two years later. Two sons were born to the couple, Maxim in 1883 and Konstantin (Costia) in 1885. In 1889 Osip Zetkin died, ravaged by tuberculosis and prolonged manic-depressive illness. Clara's sojourn in Paris had helped her to make contacts with foreign socialists and to acquire Russian and Polish Jews as friends, something most of her compatriots found an uncomfortable experience. During the years of her husband's illness Clara came into her own. In 1890 she was offered the editorship of the socialist women's magazine *Die Gleichheit (Equality)*, a post she held for twenty-seven years. She then moved to Stuttgart, where Karl Kautsky was a fellow editor and became her neighbor and mentor.

It is possible that Luxemburg and Zetkin met in Zurich in 1893, at the Congress of the International at which Rosa delivered her maiden speech, or at the Congress, held in London in 1896. After Luxemburg's anti-Bernstein series was published in 1898, the most lavish praise came from Clara Zetkin, whose position in the SPD leadership was firmly established. By the following April Clara was Rosa's house guest, and in May Rosa stayed at Clara's in Stuttgart, where she met Clara's sons, then fifteen and thirteen. Thereafter Clara stayed with Rosa during her visits to Berlin and Rosa was her guest while in Stuttgart. The house in the country that Clara acquired some time later became Rosa's favorite retreat.

Rosa's first impression of Clara Zetkin was positive; unlike the "party crowd," "she alone is honest and decent," she told Jogiches. "Nice and affectionate," she eased Luxemburg's entrance into the party's inner circle and kept her informed of current gossip. But Luxemburg's friendship with Clara did not preclude criticism. If, as Bebel put it, Clara and she were "the only men" left in the party, courageous and strong, Rosa thought that intellectually, Clara was "an empty hose," easily filled by her latest interlocutor.[14] Capable of assimilating but not of creating ideas, "she never has her own opinion,"[15] Luxemburg wrote to Jogiches; and, she reported, "her entire speech was a *literal* repetition of my last five articles, as though learned by rote."[16] Luxemburg's assessment proved right when, toward the end of her life, Clara Zetkin became Stalin's mouthpiece.

In 1899 Clara married Friedrich Zundel, a painter, eighteen years her junior. Defying convention, she challenged the SPD establishment, indifferent to gossip and ridicule. She preached renunciation of personal happiness for the cause but refused to renounce her own. She praised the virtues of proletarian existence yet held musical evenings in her pleasant country house that were a great attraction to Stuttgart's artistic circles. Her version of socialism was imbued with the Prussian spirit of discipline and obedience. There was no room for the abstract in her thinking; every issue was reduced to black or white, capitalist or socialist. A zealot with a despotic dispositon, Zetkin substituted principles where she lacked imagination.

Friedrich Zundel was Clara's first weakness, Rosa Luxemburg her second. Luxemburg fascinated her as an intellect and as a woman. Surrounded by doctors of law and economy, history and literature, and uneasy about her lack of higher education, Zetkin came to depend heavily on Rosa. Manuscripts she mailed to Rosa were returned with Rosa's annotations and criticism; speeches were rehearsed in Luxemburg's apartment. That Luxemburg did not share Zetkin's views on or commitment to women's causes did not affect their friendship. Occasionally, to please her friend, Luxemburg would write an article for *Die Gleichheit* or accompany her to a meeting of "these hens."

What drew Luxemburg, so particular about the company she kept, to Clara Zetkin? As a member of the SPD leadership, Clara Zetkin was a desirable ally, in particular because of her radicalism; yet for Luxemburg friendship was a spiritual, not a pragmatic, matter. If Luise Kautsky's lively spirit attracted her, Zetkin could easily have repelled her by what Rosa disliked in "the Huns." But the solid, great, full-bosomed German woman, thirteen years her senior, met a need unrelated to ideology or politics—she personified security.

On his earlier visits to Berlin, Jogiches met Luxemburg's friends only fleetingly to remain inconspicuous and to avoid gossip. After he joined her for good in August 1900, not much changed. When friends came to visit he kept to his room; on the rare occasions when he accompanied Rosa he seldom said a word. Clara's *Musikabende* or the Kautskys' Sunday afternoon gatherings held no interest for him. Each contact was but a new reminder of his awkward position as "Rosa Luxemburg's friend," as Bebel still referred to him years later. Luxemburg was surrounded by people who, like her, were extraordinarily active, writing books, editing newspapers, legislating, attending meetings and congresses. No other milieu could have exposed Jogiches's deficiencies so ruthlessly. In no other milieu would his inability to write, to appear in public, to associate with people, be so glaring. Without a newspaper, without the written word, he emphasized, there is no party, no movement, no revolution. That he should be among people who had all the means and abilities to make revolution yet be condemned to the role of a spectator was grotesque and demeaning. Like them he was a Marxist, like them he devoted his life to social change. That like Luxemburg, he disagreed on issues of tactics and strategy need not have hindered contact or the exchange of views. But that was not what he wanted. He wanted action.

When in September 1900 Luxemburg left Berlin, her first letter to Jogiches was in Russian. Not since 1893 had she written to him in his mother tongue. Now she was letting him know how deeply she felt for him. She was in Mainz to attend an annual Congress of the SPD; he stayed in Berlin, on Wielandstrasse No. 23 in the room next to hers, waiting for news from her. The pattern was set—she was in action, he sat in his room and read reports of her triumphs and her growing popularity. "Everybody at the Congress treats me with great consideration," ran the report from Mainz, "in particular the Berliners. I received a lot of invitations to speak . . . Auer is all sweetness, calls me Róża (in Polish), came over to me several times . . . Clara is good to me, as usual, but slightly *meshugge* over that feminist stuff, doesn't address general issues. Am therefore *completely alone* . . . Am sitting between Bruhns and Molkenbuhr, both are courting me assiduously. I had a very friendly talk with Eisner. Fischer is toadying to me more than is good for him. Gogowski sits across from me and 'admires' me . . . Even Adolf Braun, though I treat him with contempt, tries to curry my favor . . . My behavior is excellent, everything according to your instructions."[17] In three days there was more: "Singer is ecstatic about me . . . I was asked to speak in big cities all over Germany . . . Eisner told me at dinner that I had mastered the German language perfectly (Herzfeld agreed) and that as far as style goes I was the best speaker at the Congress!! . . . Bebel and others call me the 'conqueror.' "[18] From Mainz Luxemburg went directly to Paris to attend the Congress of the Second International. There she was appointed to the committee on militarism and colonial policy. Three months later, in December she was in Hamburg to deliver a series of lectures: "I had a chance to listen to the best local speakers . . . Not a single one can compete with me."[19]

The year 1900 was drawing to a close. For Luxemburg it ended the painful uncertainty in her personal life, while for Jogiches it opened a long period of waiting for a change. They started their new life together in two rooms, next to each other yet separate. The division was not merely symbolic. Their first Christmas in Berlin was not the joyous family affair Luxemburg so badly wanted. After ten years the question of starting a family was still unresolved. The physical distance was removed, but what it had concealed, the closeness revealed. It was easier to correspond about having children than to talk about it, to conceal the nature of their relationship when living apart than to pretend all the time. It was easier for Jogiches to read Luxemburg's letters in Zurich than to see her in action in Berlin. A letter Luxemburg wrote on 30 December 1900 to old Minna Kautsky showed an effort to appear content and cheerful. Jogiches was not mentioned but Beethoven and Chopin were. Rosa wrote that after the shattering blow of her father's recent death she was again able to enjoy work and company.

Elias Luksenburg had died on 30 September 1900 while Rosa was in Paris attending the Congress of the International, or, as she sarcastically wrote in retrospect, "taking care of mankind's urgent affairs and making the whole world happy."[20] Her father had been buried for a week when she returned to Berlin. Rosa was left with the memory of the two weeks she had grudgingly spent with him at a spa in August 1899. Suddenly, on that last vacation with her father, the past had caught up with her. More than ever before, the sick old man had personified weakness, intimidation, humbleness, the attributes of the morally, socially, and physically crippled Jews. He had no interests other than money, no dreams but to strike a small bargain. He moaned at night and spoke in a plaintive voice; his hands trembled and he walked with a shuffle. Confronted with the source of her tension, she could barely contain fear, revulsion, and anger. "He looks so dreadful that people stare at him," Luxemburg wrote to Jogiches; and going for a walk with him was a "virtual ordeal because father creeps at a snail's pace—it sickens me."[21] Even the living quarters in the spa, a tiny room in an attic divided by a screen, had reminded her of the cramped Warsaw apartment and its lack of privacy.

As Rosa Luxemburg was composing the letter to Minna Kautsky, suppressed memories came back. From the moment of her mother's death, her father's only dream had been to see Rosa. But she had had no time and had kept postponing his visit for two years. His letters, filled with love and admiration and with apologies for taking up her precious time, embarrassed her; his clumsy efforts to draw her back into the family's life irritated her. She did not like to be told that her letters were his sole pleasure, so she rarely wrote to him. "I'm terribly upset not to have heard from you for such a long time, to receive no answer to my letters. I've been bedridden for three weeks," Elias Luksenburg wrote. "I beg of you, have pity, answer by return mail."[22] The mosaic of postage stamps on the missives forwarded from Berlin to Zurich or wherever Rosa happened to be were no less telling than their contents. Rosa tried to make up for her neglect with small sums of money, a gift, a hastily scribbled note, a newspaper article bearing her name. "I'm pleased and honored," wrote Elias, "by the comments our friends made about your article."[23] Stubbornly, as though refusing to give in to her entirely, he spelled her name "Luxenburg," though of course she signed her articles Luxemburg.*

Another thing she had failed to do, she knew, was to alleviate her father's financial difficulties. Almost till the end of his days, dependent on what little money he could make, Elias Luksenburg, hunched and feeble, limped to the city. "Uncle Morris . . . granted me a subsidy," he informed Rosa when his gangrenous leg incapacitated him, "and I had no choice but to accept it humbly since I can no longer work." He indignantly brushed away Rosa's promise to meet with him in the spring: "You keep repeating that we have to wait until spring as though the spring were many years away. But spring is right now— and I, I don't have many of them to live."[25] It was his last.

Now, at the end of 1900, her father's unanswered letters were lying in her drawer. In the last of them, written eight months earlier, Elias Luksenburg had said that he had to drain the cup of bitterness to the last drop. "Your total indifference reminds me of something I once read," he told his beloved, youngest child. "An eagle soars so high he loses all sight of the earth below. You are so busy with social causes that family affairs are not worth even a thought of yours. There is nothing I can do but accept it . . . I won't burden you anymore with my letters."[26]

The following year, 1901, brought Rosa more triumphs. "Brilliant," she assessed her speech in Breslau in a cable to Jogiches. "You've no idea how they love me," she reported after a meeting with Polish workers.[27] Two postcards in Russian written in June were the last she sent him in his mother tongue. He now had little else to do but check out the timetables and the most convenient train connections that would take her to meetings and speaking tours, send her the daily papers to keep her abreast of the news, and wait for her to come back. She could barely catch her breath between one meeting and the next or keep up with the invitations to speak and the demand for articles. Her position as a leading political journalist was established and her territory was steadily expanding. In eastern European affairs she had no

---

*"Did you make a mistake, or is this how you now spell your name?" her sister Anna had asked some years earlier. "I saw the change in *N[eue] Zeit* and was surprised."[24]

equal in the SPD press; and she appeared to be equally at home with Prussian, French, British, and Belgian politics.

Only the closest of Luxemburg's friends were aware of her dual role, in both the Polish and German movements. Her official ties with Polish workers were limited to the part of Poland annexed by Prussia. Unofficially, however, she set the policy in the Social Democracy of the Kingdom of Poland and Lithuania, (SDKPiL), guided it and participated in its implementation; the party was her brainchild, but beyond that it was an outlet for her long-standing personal conflict with Poland.

Both the SPD and the SDKPiL press organs published her discussions of theoretical questions intended to instigate action, to bring change and ultimately a revolution. With the SPD as her stepping stone she moved from Russian and Polish affairs toward wider horizons. Her articles and pamphlets addressed issues such as universal suffrage in European countries, armaments, colonialism, customs policy, world politics, the freedom of artistic expression, the works of Marx, Engels, Lassalle, and Adam Mickiewicz. The ease with which she crossed borders—intellectual, national, historical—the effervescence of her arguments, supported by colorful metaphors and quotations from classic and contemporary writers, and her ability to simplify the complex assured her a wide readership.

Jogiches's despondency deepened. For days on end he would open no book, no newspaper. He would lie on his bed, wrapped in dark clouds, chain-smoking. On the other side of the wall Rosa's pen, like a rushing locomotive, covered sheet after sheet of paper. Her energy deepened his inertia, her strength his impotence, her accomplishments his failures. Her protestations just made things worse. He wanted no consolation, no assurances that he made her triumphs possible, that his intellect was superior to hers, that his ideas generated her actions. Each attempt of hers to lift him out of the morass ended in more misunderstandings, more recriminations, more bitterness.

Overwhelmed by Jogiches's intellect, Luxemburg made the common error of confusing intellectual prowess with the ability to survive from day to day. She acted like a mother who does everything to make her child happy, who loves him beyond reason, indulges him, suffers his whims, puts herself between him and the cruel world, and all the child gives back is unhappiness. She thundered and raged, pleaded and cried. She brought books he never opened, friends he refused to see, news he ignored. She dragged him out of bed, fed him nourishing food, took him for walks. She pointed out the budding flowers, the greening grass, the twittering birds. She planned outings to concerts, operas, theaters to uplift his spirits. All to no avail.

Death in the family put an end to the impasse. In December 1901 Osip Jogiches, Leo's middle brother, arrived in Berlin ravaged by tuberculosis. Doctors advised bluer skies and dry, warm air. Leo immediately offered to accompany Osip to Algiers. Of Leo's three siblings Osip was closest to him. After Leo's mother's death in 1898, Rosa had written Leo: "Shouldn't you bring your [brother] over? Granted, it'll make things harder for you, but the poor man certainly feels terrible and misses you badly."[28] A year later, in 1899, Osip Jogiches had come and Leo had asked Rosa to receive him warmly, a needless request, she thought. Osip had stayed in Berlin with Rosa for two days and with Leo in Zurich for two weeks. He had handed over to Leo their mother's little gold watch, which Leo gave to Rosa. Touched, Rosa said that it was "a precious souvenir, which gives me a pang every time I look at it."[29]

Jogiches's biographer[30] saw Leo's willingness to accompany his dying brother to Algiers as proof of fraternal love at the expense of the cause. In fact, Jogiches would have missed no opportunity to get out of Berlin. The vacation he had spent with Rosa on the island of Sylt, in August 1901, had failed to relieve the tension between them. In September Rosa was frantically looking for an apartment in which, she again believed, they would start a new life. In December 1901, Jogiches left with his brother, and the parting resulted in an abundant correspondence. What had remained unsaid between them during the year and a half of their common life was spelled out in the letters.

Osip Jogiches was dying a slow death. Day by day he seemed to be shrinking, his eyes sinking deeper into their sockets, his face paler, his breath shorter. The warm sun, the dry air, the medication, could not halt the disease. "Doesn't he look better from all that fresh air and good food?" asked Rosa. "I'm surprised the doctor didn't recommend a walk every day, however slow; surely it would improve his appetite."[31] Osip was too weak to walk. He rarely left his hotel room, most of the time resting after his exhausting coughing fits.

Helplessly, Leo watched the approaching end. Was he himself doomed as his brother was? He staggered from one failure to another—Zurich, Berlin, Algiers—each worse than the last. Nothing, not even death, was worse than the pervading boredom. His attempts to explain this to Rosa were futile. She could not understand, she wrote, his words written "in the obscure language of your psychology." According to her there were "real" disasters—his mother's death and his brother's illness—and imaginary ones, which she attributed to his "self-destructive streak," symptomatic of a "senseless, savage spiritual suicide." Both his own and his brother's behavior was suicidal, she declared. His brother had "thoughtlessly savaged his own body," and Leo was doing the same to his soul. They were both suffering from "the same savage madness."[32] Luxemburg's outburst, if ill-timed, was one more desperate attempt to shake Jogiches out of his depression. Now, when death brushed him, she thought she might be able to save him from himself.

Before the two brothers left Berlin, one of Luxemburg's dreams came true. In the fall of 1901 she rented a two-room apartment, on Cranachstrasse No. 58, where she was to live for the next ten years. The nightmare of sublet rooms was over. Now, she believed, they would settle down, have their own things, hire a maid, and run an orderly household, and Jogiches would finally acquiesce. Officially, since they were not married, he was subletting a room from her. When the landlord came to inspect the renovated apartment, as was the habit, "I did not show him your room lest questions about you come up," she reported to Jogiches in Algiers.[33] Each of the two rooms was a bedroom-study. Luxemburg's doubled as a living room. Heavy velvet curtains matched the deep-red wallpaper, the floor under the woolen rug was waxed and polished. A sofa with bookshelves over it, a dining table, upholstered chairs, and a small side table were arranged to entertain friends and guests; the bed, a big desk, and a washstand made up the private area. There were pictures on the walls, some painted by Luxemburg, and the customary knickknacks among which the porcelain figurine of Amor and Psyche was her favorite. Jogiches's room, also referred to as "the study," papered in dark green, was more austere, containing a desk, a glass-fronted bookcase, a wardrobe, an armchair, and a bed. There was a kitchen where the maid slept, a toilet but no bathroom. Water for the weekly bath was heated on the kitchen stove and the ablution took place in one's room over a big enamel basin. With time the apartment became richer in porcelain, linen, ornaments, and books.

In Jogiches's absence Luxemburg was preparing the nest, eager to have him come back to a home he would appreciate. She assembled the furniture, decorated the rooms, arranged books—scholarship, fiction, poetry in Polish, Russian, German, French, and English—and kept Jogiches posted about every detail. "The wardrobe and the black wash-stand top were delivered today," she informed him on 18 December 1901. "The wardrobe is wonderful, the spots almost invisible, heaven knows why you raised such hell over them. With the black top the wash-stand looks entirely different, the white set on the top is striking."[34] A hired hand came to beat the rugs, and the maid Anna polished, dusted, and cleaned so that "not a speck of dust is dancing, not even in the sunbeams."[35]

Luxemburg took her new duties seriously; she liked to be busy around the house, to add a touch here and there. She kept the maid on a tight rein—"I trained her into a model servant"—and was hurt when Anna gave notice three months later. "I don't know why," she complained, "she lived as in a paradise, put on weight and looks like a barrel."[36] She came to know the frustrations of finding and keeping a good maid. But for the time being she was pleased with Anna and since Christmas was approaching wanted to show her appreciation. "After making *several* inquiries," she reported to Jogiches, "I found out that a maid one is pleased with gets presents to the amount of her monthly wages. I bought Anna a marvellous silk blouse (after all she has enough dresses) with a white gusset and black velvet ribbons for 10 marks, an umbrella with a gilded handle for 5 marks and a pair of gloves for 1.90."[37] Anna became a fixture. "I have to finish now, Anna came to lay the table." "Anna's going now to mail letters so I'd better finish."[38] Anna waited for Luxemburg at the train station to help with the luggage, and Anna made her feel like the Hausfrau she at last was.

Now that she had a home she could entertain. Christmas she preferred to spend alone "amid these walls that I like so much and which like me," but then she was ready to demonstrate her talents as a hostess.[39] In panic, Jogiches advised from Algiers that she had better ask her former landlady, Mrs. Neufeld, how to go about it lest she make a fool of herself. Luxemburg did not take the advice kindly; her dinner was even more elegant than Mrs. Neufeld's, she reported to Jogiches, and she had managed it all by herself. The table, she wrote, looked wonderful, with small bunches of flowers at every plate (at 10 pfennig each) and a potted hyacinth in the center. There were rolls with caviar—"don't faint, 50 pfennig only"—salmon and eggs, beet soup with sausage rolls, fish in sour sauce, steak with vegetables, compote, and cheese with radishes for dessert, followed by black coffee and cognac. The problems of entertaining were entirely new: to select well-matching guests, to make no *faux pas,* to be a success. The Kautskys, the Eisners, and Arthur Stadthagen were invited for the first dinner, the Mehrings with Clara Zetkin to the next, Rosa informed Leo. "As you see," she joked, "not even Count Bülow suffers as many headaches and such serious ones as I do."[40] Her "six-course dinners," she said half in jest, became the talk of the party's gossip network. For Jogiches this was no laughing matter. He wrote to her that a guest who had turned down her dinner invitation claiming an earlier engagement simply wanted to snub her. "You're dead wrong," she protested, "he did have a speech in his electoral district, I read about it in *Vorwärts.*"[41] One doesn't serve cheese with radishes, Leo instructed from afar, and certainly not *after* dinner. "Yes," she insisted, "here, in Germany, radishes are served with cheese *after* dinner."[42] The Berlin-Algiers-Berlin exchange on social propriety was no less spirited than that on Prussia's military budget.

On 1 January 1902 Luxemburg introduced a new regime. She began rising at 7:00 A.M., and though it almost killed her she was determined to stick it out. "Take my advice and get up early too," she wrote to Jogiches, "take a walk in the sun and don't stay up at night because this is what ruins you and contributes to your usually sour disposition."[43] Like a child trying to get attention, Jogiches teased her, and she responded: "Why do you write so late at night? Don't you have time during the day? Do you have to stay up that late? Haven't I begged you to go to bed early?"[44] Her regime included changes in her diet, regular meals, daily walks, and cold-water rubs. She was preparing a new "daily plan" for Jogiches to be put into effect when he came back.

She now had more than she had ever dreamed at the Gymnasium in Warsaw—professional success, fame, recognition. She had Jogiches, a home, a comfortable income. But she no longer knew, she complained to Jogiches, how to be happy. "I'd like best just to stay in bed all day long. I'm for ever and ever tired though I live as regularly as a clockwork, go to bed at eleven, and take a nap after lunch."[45] Her health was fine but her mind was "dazed," she couldn't think straight and moved "as in a slumber."[46] A glass of Haute-Sauternes—which as a child her mother gave her when she was sad—was no help. Neither success nor the apartment satisfied her unfulfilled maternal instinct.

Indeed, her home turned her dream of a child into a painful need. "For hours on end I can sit in one or the other room, looking around and thinking how happy one could be in these nice rooms!"[47] But she was not. She suggested they adopt a child, the Warszawskis' expected baby, because "without children it is so empty and silly at home, and I'm feeling so lonely, and it seems to me a child would make me come back to life," she wrote to Jogiches. "Meanwhile I would like to get at least a dog or a cat."[48] A succession of dogs and cats appeared; Mimi, Luxemburg's last and most beloved cat, acquired the status of her "daughter."

Osip Jogiches died in early March 1902, and after three months' absence Leo returned to Berlin. Luxemburg hoped for the best. He was going to live according to the "daily plan"—rise early, take walks, replace tea with cocoa, and eliminate the nightly beer. He was to relish the home as she did. "The walls and the furniture simply *talk* to me. Always, they tell me something soothing and pleasant. I hope they'll have the same soothing effect on you."[49] Jogiches did emerge from his depression, but for reasons connected neither to a healthy life nor to the home.

In August 1902, the leadership of the Social Democracy of Poland and Lithuania decided to expand the party's activities, particularly in the sphere of publications. Leo Jogiches took charge, informally, of the party's work abroad, including the editorship of *Przegląd Socjaldemokratyczny* (*The Social-Democratic Review*) and of *Czerwony Sztandar* (*The Red Banner*). Work and new responsibilities helped him to overcome his crisis.

9 | *Prison:*
The Real Initiation
1902–1904

In 1902 Luxemburg and Jogiches settled into a life almost exclusively devoted to the movement. In their private life each made concessions without quite accepting them; and the small brushfires were more wearying than violent explosions. Jogiches, back in control, promptly assumed his former attitude of mentor. Traveling most of the time, Rosa, exhausted, assured him again and again that she read his letters carefully, followed his advice, remembered his instructions. And she repeated mechanically, "Go for a walk every day, live quietly and regularly, go early to bed and get up early."[1] Her need for his care and approval had not diminished, but she learned to live without them. Or so it seemed to her.

In 1902 and 1903 Luxemburg spent long stretches of time away from Berlin on speaking tours. To counter the influence of the Polish Socialist Party she cofounded an SPD-sponsored paper in Poznań (German-annexed Poland) in 1902. Published in Polish, it was called *Gazeta Ludowa (People's Gazette)* and was devoted, the subtitle said, "to the affairs of the working people." Its aim, the unification of Polish and German workers, never became popular among the Poles. The readership was modest and the paper folded in mid-1904. For its duration, however, Luxemburg, the editor-in-chief and main contributor, covered a wide range of topics, domestic and foreign. It was on the pages of this paper that she made one of her few public statements on the issue of women's emancipation. In an article called "Ladies and Women," she castigated an international women's congress in Berlin as "a congress of *ladies* . . . representatives of the fair sex from the bourgeoisie or at best the petite bourgeoisie" who, "bored with the role of doll or husband's cook, seek some action to fill their empty heads and empty existence."[2] Their working class counterparts, Luxemburg wrote, understood the close connection between the cause of women and universal social change; women must strive for equality and fraternity for humanity and abolition of oppression everywhere, not merely for rights and freedom for themselves.

Despite her other obligations she devoted much time and effort to the paper, almost single-handedly putting it together, shaping the editorial policy, and overseeing printing and distribution. But Jogiches was dissatisfied. "I'm simply too exhausted to make the 'Gazette' better," Luxemburg told him wearily. "I'm very sorry the paper doesn't please you but there's nothing I can do about it. Should you find somebody else, not even better but just willing to take over the sweet burden, I'd be *immensely* grateful to you."[3] Nor was Jogiches happy with her general performance: if she tried harder, she could do more and could do it better. His grumbling did not bother her as much as it used to; but his neglect of her personally did. The arrangement of their common life in which she acquiesced irked her, and her bitterness broke through. "Unfortunately I can't give you a report covering the entire gamut of affairs that, as you say, I was supposed to set in motion. I cannot because *as I've written you several times* I'm completely exhausted and can barely move. Though you say you're very upset, obviously you think my health should not influence my work. I'm doing as much as I can. As usual, not *all* of your projects can be carried out. ('Why??!!!') That this and that 'should' be done I know as well as you do but I have no intention of killing myself. It doesn't make much sense to write to you about details. Perhaps my weakness will pass in a day or two—then I'll be able to do more."[4]

On the back of a telegram announcing her arrival in Berlin there is, in Jogiches's handwriting, a day-to-day itinerary of a speaking tour Luxemburg was just completing. In two weeks in mid-1903, she addressed workers in twelve different places, and from each she reported to Jogiches. She traveled from one town to another, spent hours on trains and in railroad stations, slept every night in a different bed, to appear the next morning ready to storm yet "another fortress." Her speeches were generally about two hours long, were followed by a question-and-answer period and often by meetings with local activists that ran late into the night. On 28 May 1903 she addressed 1,500 people in Bydgoszcz, the next day 500 in Piła, a few days later, 2,000 in Lichtenstein. "The audience naturally included the entire Jewish bourgeoisie," she remarked. Invariably she drew large crowds—"the local comrades said they have never had such a full house"—and the meetings, in her words, were "excellent," "superb," a "tremendous success." Between one tour and the next she sometimes stopped at home to catch her breath and to change clothes—"tell Anna to have clean handkerchiefs ready for me."[5] Though an emotional and physical drain, it was a triumph to reach the masses of people and see them react to her and her words. And when she wrote to Jogiches, with five meetings behind and seven before her—"I've little energy left. Time passes terribly slowly, for every day must be conquered in yet another meeting"—there may have been more to her weariness than she admitted.[6]

The reactivated Polish Social Democratic Party (SDKPiL) brought the Polish cause back into the couple's life, but it also re-created the situation of ten years earlier. Once again Jogiches was in Luxemburg's debt for his new position since she had been instrumental in the SDKPiL. But, unlike ten years earlier, she now was an influential figure in the German party; he was relegated to a marginal movement. Moreover, Jogiches "stubbornly insisted on remaining in the shadows, behind the scenes, without appearing publicly as the organizer of the movement and the leader of the [Polish] party."[7]

This time, his remaining as invisible as possible was due to necessity, not choice. For all their internationalism, the Social Democrats in Poland might have viewed with apprehension a leader whose mother tongue was Russian rather than Polish. While Luxemburg's name was becoming a household word in Europe, Jogiches had to conceal his because it betrayed his Russian Jewish origin and made him a perfect butt for the pent-up nationalistic feelings of the Polish victims of Russian expansionism. Though dubbed a "Muscovite," an opprobrious word on the lips of a Pole, Jogiches, in his own words, had "earned Polish citizenship" by fighting for the welfare of the Polish workers.[8] Yet to many Poles this was a questionable argument since his party was against Poland's independence. Leo Jogiches thus assumed a Polish-sounding pseudonym, Jan Tyszka. As Tyszka, he "remained an almost mythical figure to such an extent that the younger generation of Social Democrats . . . thought that Jan Tyszka was a new pseudonym of Rosa Luxemburg."[9] His most bitter enemy could not have come up with a crueler joke.

While Jogiches was struggling in the peripheral workers' movement, Luxemburg was moving toward its very center. In 1903 she became a member of the International Socialist Bureau. "Her political vigour and intellectual achievements were accompanied by warmth, charm and sensibility . . . rare in the socialist world, and made her one of the most fascinating figures produced by the International."[10] The Congress of the Second International, convened in Amsterdam in August 1904, brought Luxemburg still more prestige. She held two mandates—one from the German and one from the Polish Social Democratic Party—and she sat on two committees—on trusts and unemployment and on international socialist tactics. A photograph taken at the Congress shows a dark-haired young woman in a light dress and a matching wide-brimmed, black-ribboned hat, surrounded by older, impressive-looking men—the most formidable figures in international socialism. Twenty-four countries sent 476 delegates, among them, to name the best known, August Bebel, Karl Kautsky, and Rosa Luxemburg (Germany), Jean Jaurès, Jules Guesde, and Edouard Vaillant (France), Georgij Plekhanov (Russia), Enrico Ferri (Italy), Sen Katayama (Japan), Victor Adler (Austro-Hungary), Émile Vandervelde (Belgium), Morris Hillquit (United States), Hjalmar Branting (Sweden), Pieter Troelstra (Holland), and Keir Hardie (England).

The six-year-long struggle against Bernstein's revisionism was finally laid to rest. The International's tactics, along the lines Luxemburg expounded in 1898 in "Social Reform or Revolution," were accepted at the Congress after four days of learned but acrimonious debate: the theory of class struggle was approved while revisionism was sweepingly condemned; instead of "reforming" bourgeois society, the member parties were to strive for a socialist revolutionary order.

Another issue that deeply concerned Luxemburg and her German comrades was the split within the French socialist camp into the radical Parti Socialiste de France, led by Jules Guesde, and the parliamentarily oriented Parti Socialiste Français, led by the flamboyant Jean Jaurès.

The Congress recommended that the parties unite and that they did so shows what international solidarity can achieve; the following year, the two parties merged into Section Française de l'Internationale Ouvrière (SFIO), so called in recognition of its origins.

At the Congress Jaurès, the most outspoken opponent of the German-sponsored resolution condemning revisionism, delivered an impassioned speech directed against Kautsky, Luxemburg, and the entire SPD. The Germans' lack of revolutionary tradition, Jaurès claimed, and their penchant for gratefully accepting what the monarchy granted them, such as universal suffrage, deceived the proletariat at home and abroad, though the SPD's political impotence did not prevent it from imposing its party line on other countries.

Luxemburg had for years carried on a polemic against Jaurès, whom she had known since the early 1890s in Paris. She was incensed by the conciliatory stand he took when the French government offered amnesty to Dreyfus, whom she herself unconditionally defended. The battle between pro- and anti-Dreyfusards was to her between the French socialists and the military-cum-clergy, not between the Jesuits and the Jews. She has thus been accused of being indifferent or blind to the real cause of Dreyfus's plight—rampant anti-Semitism, which indeed was not her primary concern. Jaurès, after two years of valiantly defending the victim of the gross miscarriage of justice, finally acquiesced in the amnesty. Luxemburg claimed that it left Dreyfus unrehabilitated and strengthened the military and the clergy in France; Jaurès believed it "saved the Republic."

Now at the Congress, Jaurès passionately defended his policy during the Dreyfus affair, castigating Luxemburg and the German Social Democratic Party for manipulating the proletariat with technical formulas. At the end of the oration there was no one to translate it from the French. Spontaneously Luxemburg got up and, with her customary flair and drama, rendered his speech into German, the ardor of the original intact. Her gesture is a perfect example of the spirit that permeated the International, a spirit that died together with European socialism in the First World War.

Once the Congress ended, Rosa Luxemburg returned to Germany—and went straight to jail. This was the touch of glory she needed to feel a full-fledged revolutionary—a three-month prison sentence for insulting Emperor Wilhelm II in a public speech. With her wry sense of humor she must have appreciated the ironic twist: the

Jewish schoolgirl who back in Warsaw had ridiculed the Prussian emperor in a little poem was now a German subject defying him publicly. It mattered little that, as Kautsky pointed out in another connection, she was "not considered a fully authentic German."[11] She was German and influential enough to force the regime whose overthrow she advocated to defend itself against her.

Luxemburg entered the women's prison in Berlin-Zwickau on 26 August 1904 and left it on 24 October. An amnesty declared to commemorate the coronation of Friedrich August von Saxe reduced her sentence to two months; despite her protests, the commutation was enforced. As a political prisoner she was allowed to write letters and to receive clothes, newspapers, books (though *The Communist Manifesto* was stopped by the censor), and guests. Her brother Józef visited her; Maksymilian sent money from Warsaw to have a restaurant deliver meals. The money was not necessary because her publisher took care of the expenses. She needed a skirt—"the black one with the royal train isn't exactly appropriate for a cell"—a blouse, "not in a striking color," and stockings, "the smallest women's size," but she did not need a hat—"I walk in the yard hatless."[12] She read *The Divine Comedy*, listened to the quacking ducks in a nearby pond, wrote letters, kept abreast of party affairs, worked on a study in political economy, and spent "a great deal" of time thinking.

The frantic pace of life she had imposed on herself was, to some extent at least, an attempt to avoid reflection. Each of the successive regimes she introduced to bring "order" into her life was designed to fill every hour of the day. In prison, thoughts crowded in on her, unbidden. Though her letters to Jogiches and to the Kautskys sparkle with excitement, despair occasionally seeps through. Prison turned her into the center of loving attention by her family and friends, but it also prevented real human contact. The seclusion released thoughts that the normal everyday bustle had kept at a distance.

What is life about? What is it for? Is it worth living? Nothing, she wrote to Jogiches many years earlier, was as agonizing and frightening as these thoughts. Marx had no answer for her, but Tolstoy's groping for an answer aroused her boundless admiration. "Life constantly plays hide-and-seek with me," she wrote now to Luise Kautsky. "It always seems to me that it is not inside me, it is not where I am but somewhere far away." As a small child she used to break the rules, she wrote, by sneaking out of bed and silently opening the window to look out at the still, dormant yard. "I firmly believed then that 'life,' the 'real' life, is somewhere far away, hidden behind tall roofs. Ever since I've been trying to find it, but it always keeps hiding behind one roof or another."[13]

The life she had made for herself was not the perfect work of art she once believed she could create. Time after time she set a goal for herself, striving after "real life." But each goal achieved failed to make life more "real," and she would pursue the next with undiminished determination. She and Jogiches had youth, love, spiritual affinity, and a common purpose, and yet she did not feel as though her life with him was "real." What meaning did her success have in the face of personal defeat? Yet the realization that "real life" was still hiding behind those Warsaw roofs while she was pursuing it in alien lands did not discourage her.

"I promise myself," she wrote Jogiches from her prison cell, "*to live* life to its fullest as soon as I'm free." His lonely existence was insane and abnormal, she told him; she had always hated his "asceticism" (she put the word in quotation marks) and her isolation made her hate it even more. By emphasizing her resolve *to live* without including Jogiches in that life, she may have been alerting him. "When I come out of prison," she warned him, "your Nazarene bloodlessness will clash violently with my Hellenic full-bloodedness." Her tone was light but her heart was not. From her prison cell she saw the past fourteen years with great clarity: Jogiches never learned to live and to love her. That was why, she felt, his life seemed empty to him. To her not even her cell was empty. "The moral of the story," she wrote to him, was that "whoever feels poverty-stricken should sit down and make an 'inventory'. . . just to discover how rich he is. You should make an inventory of your riches more often, and if you don't forget to include my modest person . . . you will feel like Croesus."[14]

Her attempts to reform him continued. "When I left, you promised you'd read one book a day. Do you? You *must*, I beg you! Now I again appreciate the value of making serious books a part of daily life. It saves the mind and the *nervous* system." His mental condition worried her; he might have fallen back into his bad habits in her absence. "I hope you still get up early and go to bed early . . . But then *why* did Luise [Kautsky] have to ring the doorbell for so long?"[15]

Jogiches sensed her mood and could read between the lines. He could easily turn her arguments against her, but he responded with unusual calm. He was busy refurbishing his wardrobe, he wrote her, to assuage her fears about his asceticism. "I'm very pleased," she replied, "that you're thinking about your clothes. But please, no heavy or hairy fabrics. That is so provincial. Get light, soft English cloth, dark gray, with a thin white stripe perhaps; the overcoat should be black and full, well cut, as I like it." Anna, their former maid, wanted to come back, Jogiches informed Luxemburg—letting her know he was a responsible house manager but leaving the decision about the maid to her. She wanted the decision to be made jointly: "If you want to take Anna back, I'd be very pleased."[16]

The letters from the Zwickau prison remained unpublished for many decades. Instead, generations of young radicals were brought up on a volume of Rosa Luxemburg's letters from another prison—*Letters from Prison,* published in 1920. The revolutionary who emerged from its pages was a spiritual giant and a lyrical dreamer. She possessed an almost supernatural inner strength, was immune to ordinary personal tribulations and anxieties, loved humanity, animals, birds, and flowers. Written in the years 1916–1918 to Sonja Liebknecht with the purpose of lifting the spirits of the young wife of the imprisoned Karl, the letters created and perpetuated a myth. The Zwickau letters, on the other hand, reveal the real person—plagued with doubts about herself, about her lover, about life.

It was not prison, however, but another distinction bestowed on Luxemburg that year that assured her place in history. With an article published in 1904, "Organizational Questions of Russian Social Democrats," she took issue with Lenin's political thought, initiating a polemic which culminated in 1918, after the first year of his rule. "After Lenin's *One Step Forward** was published," declared the editors of *Iskra* (*The Spark*), a Russian émigré paper, "we asked comrade Luxemburg to comment on the book. . . . Her article will, we hope, make clear to comrade Lenin that his stand on organization has nothing in common with revolutionary Marxism."[17] Whether or not the hope of the editors was fulfilled, Luxemburg proved as has no one before or since that equating Marxism with Leninism was a fallacy. Millions of words have been written on the subject, but no one has surpassed Luxemburg's sober, erudite, and comprehensive argument. Questioning Lenin's rhetoric, she wrote: "The glorification of the inherent genius of the

---

*The reference is to Lenin's *One Step Forward, Two Steps Back,* published in 1904.

proletariat in the matter of socialism and the distrust of the 'intelligen-tsia' as such within the Social Democratic movement are not in themselves manifestations of 'revolutionary Marxism.'" Her final stroke was reserved for Lenin's "ultracentralism," a euphemism for autocracy: "The 'discipline' Lenin has in mind is by no means implanted in the proletariat only by the factory, but equally by the *barracks*, by the modern bureaucracy, by the entire mechanism of the centralized bourgeois state apparatus . . . The ultracentralism advo-cated by Lenin is permeated in its very essence by the sterile spirit of a night watchman *[Nachtwächtergeist]* rather than by a positive and creative spirit. He concentrates mostly on *controlling* the party, not on *fertilizing* it, on *narrowing* it down, not *developing* it, on *regimenting* and not on *unifying* it."[18]

Since the program of the Polish Social Democrats (SDKPiL) stipulated a common fight of the Polish and Russian workers against the tsarist autocracy, it seemed logical that Polish and Russian socialists join forces. However, apart from Luxemburg's personal difficulties in dealing with "the Asians," as she called them, not entirely in jest, ideological differences divided the parties. In 1902 an article entitled "Some Remarks on the Program of Russian Social Democracy" was published in *The Social-Democratic Review*. Though strongly resem-bling Luxemburg's mode of expression, it was signed by Jan Tyszka, that is, Leo Jogiches. Commenting critically on the program of the Russians, the author pointed to their "slightly artificial and also fundamentally questionable" agrarian policy, their underestimation of the customs policy, and their shortcomings in labor protection.[19] These issues, however, were not of such magnitude as to prevent unification. The "centralistic tendencies" of the Russians constituted the main hindrance.

The Second Congress of the Russian Social Democratic Workers' Party (RSDRP) in 1903, at which the party split into Bolsheviks (led by Lenin) and Mensheviks (led by Julij Martov), failed to produce an agreement between the Poles and the Russians. The Polish delegates walked out twice—once in Brussels where the Congress started and again in London where it ended—in disagreement over the right of nations to self-determination. To accept Lenin's conditions meant in fact "annihilating our party and turning it into one of the territorial organizations of the Russian party," Julian Marchlewski wrote to the Foreign Committee of the SDKPiL.[20]

The differences between Luxemburg and Lenin persisted. Opposed to Lenin's idea of an "armed insurrection," Luxemburg wrote to Jogiches in 1905, "I deliberately wrote the paragraph [in an article] about what it means 'to prepare an armed insurrection' so that we won't look like Lenin's *Schildknappen* [vassals]; Lenin *juxtaposes* insurrection with participation in the Duma, but what he really means by it is armament."[21] In her view a people's revolt must be achieved by raising the consciousness of the workers, not by arming them. Lenin, undeterred, sent a personal emissary to Luxemburg to sound her out on her attitude toward the Bolsheviks. Their differing views did not diminish the respect they had for each other. Luxemburg met Lenin in 1901 in Berlin. One of the first on the European scene to recognize his political genius, Luxemburg regarded him as a worthy partner. Not so Jogiches. He and Lenin, both autocratic and ruthless, were too much alike to develop anything but mutual antipathy. Lenin is said to have avoided any personal contact with Jogiches. It fell to Luxemburg to prevent a public clash between the two men who, in her opinion, were the most outstanding revolutionaries of the time.

10 | Back in Warsaw
1905–1906

On 22 January 1905 Russian troops opened fire on a peaceful procession of workers in St. Petersburg. Led by a priest, Father Gapon, the workers had come to the Winter Palace to beg the tsar for better working conditions. Singing hymns, carrying icons and portraits of the emperor, the workers continued marching when ordered to halt. The Palace Square was soon strewn with hundreds of dead and mutilated bodies, and mounted Cossacks chased the dispersing crowd. The Bloody Sunday massacre, as it became known, unleashed a wave of strikes in Russia that quickly spread to Poland. The hour for Luxemburg's party had struck. The Polish Social Democracy (SDKPiL) swelled from a few hundred to two thousand members on the eve of 1905 and to thirty thousand by 1906. By comparison, the much more popular Polish Socialist Party (PPS) only slightly exceeded that number; the Bund, the Jewish workers' organization, counted approximately 35,000 members. The three feuding parties vied with each other for the souls and bodies of the workers. The written word was their most effective ammunition.

On 6 February 1905 Leo Jogiches left Berlin. Unbeknownst to both him and Luxemburg, this was the end of their life together. Jogiches went to Kraków, in Austrian-annexed Poland, where the editorial offices of two party publications had been moved. The SDKPiL founded a new publication in Kraków called *Z Pola Walki (From the Battlefield)*. After ten years of semiretirement Jogiches was again active, in charge of editing the newspapers, pamphlets, and leaflets and of smuggling and distributing them in Russian-annexed Poland.

That year, when it seemed that the people's wrath would topple the tsardom, was for Luxemburg a time of intense work and extreme tension. Close to ninety articles of hers were published in the Polish and German press; she participated in the annual Congress of the German Social Democratic Party (SPD) in Jena and became a member of the editorial board of *Vorwärts*. All the while she was going through an acute personal crisis, a protracted, painful dismemberment of the life she had been building for the past fifteen years. Outwardly nothing changed in her relationship with Jogiches; political events necessitated their parting and, as usual when they were not together, they corresponded.

Over the years Luxemburg repeatedly reproached Jogiches with indecisiveness: "I beg you to stop this never ending irresolution . . . and *to make a decision*," she wrote him in 1900 when he kept postponing his move from Zurich to Berlin.[1] When she was offered the editorship of *Leipziger Volkszeitung* in 1902 and was anxious for his reaction, she was even more outspoken: "I hope," she wrote him in Algiers, "you'll rid yourself of your inherent reluctance to take a bold step . . . and your natural inclination to rear up in fear at an important moment."[2] These were odd accusations, considering Jogiches's legendary fearlessness. Evidently it did not occur to Luxemburg that he developed protective coloring to defend his independence, that the indecisiveness that annoyed her was a response to her behavior.

In contrast, Jogiches made the decision to go to Kraków promptly and without wavering. And he went, it seems, with Luxemburg's wholehearted approval because it was crucial to her that he be in charge of the Polish party's affairs. The chilly tone of her letters, however, indicates a discord that occurred either before he left Berlin for Kraków or during the initial three months when she did not write to him lest her letters be lost. Once away from Berlin, Jogiches cut the suffocating web of dependence. Kraków became his exclusive territory and he jealously guarded it from Luxemburg's interference. As in Wilno, he was his own master, but now it was no longer a matter of a few forged passports or of organizing a few dozen workers; it was a matter of organizing a revolution in Russian-annexed Poland and ultimately of overthrowing the tsar.

Jogiches orchestrated the complicated enterprise and saw the publications through every stage, acting as editor-in-chief, technical editor, designer, and manager. At the same time he participated in the shaping of the party's policy, and during his frequent illegal trips to Warsaw saw to its implementation. Luxemburg was well aware of his activities; thus her casual question "What are you actually doing over there, in Kraków?" aptly reflects the friction in the spring of 1905.[3] Jogiches "was in charge of all publications and in touch with all the writers whom he advised and instructed . . . to whom he suggested political ideas and for whom he defined the guiding ideological principles." The actual "leader of the party," according to one of his chief collaborators, he "stubbornly kept turning down offers and demands to assume an official responsibility for leadership and to join the party authorities."[4]

With almost absolute power in his hands, yet anonymous, Jogiches was in his element. He "kept a tight rein on his collaborators, allowing for no fatigue or 'moods' . . . His untiring work from early morning till late at night was contagious and drew everybody into the brilliantly organized operation . . . He watched the writers, the type-setters, and technicians closely." Overnight, the "superfluous man" turned into an inspired leader and revered teacher. "He constantly repeated," reminisced Karl Radek, "that each written line must serve a concrete purpose, that revolutionary journalism is not literature but a battle with pen in hand. And he showed us that a revolutionary newspaper is not a compilation of news but a fighting force whose elements, created by different people, serve one concrete purpose." "There is not a single one of our generation of 1905–1906," wrote another of Jogiches's disciples, Józef Rotstein-Krasny, "who doesn't owe him a lot. As organizer, editor, tactician, and a learned Marxist he left an imprint on all the younger comrades who worked with him."[5]

The respect he inspired restored his self-confidence and hardened Jogiches's autocratic bent. He was determined to defend his newly gained independence, but it did not follow that he was ready to grant Luxemburg hers. Since he had written off her dreams and desires long ago it probably never occurred to him that she might still cling to them. They had both settled into middle age, and distance freed him, always a reluctant lover, from her demands. All that mattered was her pen.

Jogiches took for granted that like his other collaborators she would carry out his orders unquestioningly. But she did ask questions, constantly and insistently. Letter after letter is studded with angry requests: "Don't you really have a minute to write anything about the publication? . . . I demand and *absolutely* insist that you let me know immediately which of our people were arrested."[6] "How can you leave me without any news, this is simply carelessness . . . I beg you to answer and to send me at least some news from Poland."[7] "What the hell is going on? I'm waiting from one mail to the next and still no word from you!"[8] "There was no letter from you either yesterday or today. I don't understand what this means."[9]

In fact, she did not understand. For a long time she refused to believe that Jogiches was deliberately cutting her off. He did write to her, but at his own will, to coordinate political strategy or to demand an article. "Today I felt more keenly than ever the abnormality of my work in Polish affairs," Luxemburg wrote in October. "I get an order from you: write an editorial about [Poland's] autonomy . . . Fine. But, damn it, in order to write it, I must read the Polish and the Russian press, I must be *au courant* with society's mood, I must be *in touch* with party affairs."[10] For the previous two or three months, she said, she had seen no Polish paper, legal or illegal. She was left in the dark at a time when the revolution seemed close and her life's work was finally bearing fruit.

Were Jogiches's protracted silences due to lack of time or lack of goodwill? As Luxemburg impatiently pointed out, he could have had one of his people send the news or the papers. But he did not. She explained that she needed material to keep the German public informed; she pleaded and pressed in vain. If in the past Jogiches merely did not bother to consult her, now he adopted a firm policy. The more successful he was—and the growing membership of the SDKPiL was proof of his success—the more obstinately he entrenched himself in his fortress.

A glaring deviation from the principle of a common political platform with Luxemburg appeared in Jogiches's stand toward the Bund, the Jewish workers' party. Luxemburg's attitude, shared by the leadership of the Polish party, was uncomprisingly negative because of the Bund's Jewish national ideology. "I do not agree to *any* alliance with the Jews," she wrote to him in June. "For the same reasons that you turn down a 'maximum' alliance, I turn down a 'minimum' one. Of course, *vereint schlagen*, aber—*getrennt* marschieren [*fight together*, but march *separately*]. This rabble needs us, we don't need them."[11]

Jogiches defied her. It would be erroneous to attribute his defiance to anything but political strategy. The fact that in Wilno he had worked together with the future founders of the Bund and had inadvertently contributed to its foundation had no bearing on his policy. His disregard of the position adopted by other members of the party's leadership was symptomatic of his mood. He sought in the Bund an ally against the Polish Socialist Party and was ready to pay the price. In mid-July of 1905, at the initiative of the Bund and with his party's approval, Jogiches went to Warsaw to negotiate. He reached an agreement with the Bund on future cooperation and mutual support. Consequently, Jogiches was accused of making excessive concessions to the Bund, taking a dangerously reconciliatory stand, and of a "betrayal of the interests" of the party.[12] Feliks Dzierżyński wrote to the party's Foreign Commission: "[We] cannot reach any understanding with him. Even in the negotiations with the Bund he behaved so outrageously that it is simply hard to believe he'd carry things that far."[13] In response Jogiches resigned from his work on the party's publications. Luxemburg had to use all her diplomatic skills to patch things up between the party and Jogiches. No agreement with the Bund was signed, and Jogiches withdrew his resignation and resumed his work in Kraków.

A serious conflict in their personal life was triggered the same year, 1905, by the appearance of a young man to whom Luxemburg referred to as W. in her letters to Jogiches. When exactly W. appeared in her life is unknown, nor can the exact nature of their relationship be established. His identity is not certain. In all probability he was Władysław Feinstein, known as Witold and by five other pseudonyms each starting with the letter W. A Polish Jew from Warsaw, he was an active member of the SDKPiL, a disciple and close collaborator of Jogiches, and, eventually, under the name Zdzisław Leder, Jogiches's only biographer. Ten years Luxemburg's junior, W. was one of several men much younger than she who fell under her spell.

When in June 1905 Leo asked Rosa about her vacation plans, she answered that she was perfectly fine at home and was even putting on weight. She had received invitations she had turned down. Clara

Zetkin tired her with her ceaseless chatter, Henriette Roland Holst, a Dutch friend, bored her with her racial theories, the Kautskys' family reunion in St. Gallen was not much of a rest. Without suggesting that they spend the vacation together, she advised Jogiches to take two weeks off. It was not difficult for Jogiches to join Luxemburg or for her to join him. Clearly, neither was keen on meeting. Luxemburg finally decided to visit Clara Zetkin. Suddenly, on 7 August, she cabled Jogiches that she was coming to Kraków.

She stayed with Jogiches for about twelve days. In a birthday letter she sent Luise Kautsky from Kraków, she explained that she had been all ready to go to Clara's but had changed her mind at the last minute. If she sounded cheerful, it was because she had learned to sound in her letters exactly as she chose to. But the meeting with Jogiches was tragic. Luxemburg told him there was another man in her life.

Why did she go to Kraków? Why did she make the confession? Was it yet another, final attempt to shake Jogiches, to make him understand that he had failed her and that she was no longer willing to continue the pretense? The shock, she may have thought, was her last chance to save their union. Otherwise she had little reason to tell Jogiches about W.; it was an episode of no great meaning and she could have kept it to herself. But she did not, and telling Jogiches was a deliberate step.

It hit Jogiches hard. The one person he had trusted unreservedly had betrayed him; the one woman he was close to had deceived him. He felt cheated, wounded, lost. Her betrayal gave his fears shape and color: failure was now a fact, concrete and irreversible. And the realization of his total dependence on Luxemburg was certainly more crushing than her romantic involvement. He would never again take her for granted. But she wanted more.

On or about 4 September, two weeks after Luxemburg's confession, Jogiches went to Berlin. His visit was as sudden as hers had been to Kraków. Even considering the tense political situation, it is difficult to accept the standard view that he came to discuss party tactics with Luxemburg. Nothing, it seems, could have been further from his mind. He came not to plead, for he was unable to plead, but to obtain her assurance that she was his, that nothing in their life had changed. Luxemburg promised to break with W. and to tell him that the decision was final. When Jogiches was leaving Berlin, on 15 September, he was still in doubt. No sooner had he left than he cabled for reassurance. She cabled back

DEAR MISSED YESTERDAY'S TELEGRAPH MESSENGER.
MESSAGE JUST RECEIVED EARLY MORNING TODAY.
PEOPLE [VISITING] ALL DAY YESTERDAY. . . WAS
UNTHINKABLE TO WRITE. BE CALM DEAR ALL WILL BE
WELL. AM UNWAVERING. WRITING MORE TODAY
SPECIAL DELIVERY. THOUSAND GREETINGS. PLEASE
BE CALM.

The same day, 17 September, she wrote to him: "*Dear, my dear, why are you tormenting yourself, why? Now, all we must think of is our task, our work . . . I'm utterly unwavering in my decision, as I wired you today, so be calm and think only of the future* . . . W. arrived here aware that the decision has been made, and he didn't say a word to make me change my mind . . . That night on the platform a light shone in your window for a long, long time, till the train turned the bend. I intentionally kept standing in the light of the lamp so that you'd see me. I wanted so badly to be better, more cheerful in those last minutes, and I couldn't and you looked so ghastly . . . *Be strong, Dyodyo, be strong!*" In her third missive that day she said, "Remember, you cannot make any decisions about yourself without me. We'll think about it together as soon as you've finished with those conferences. Write to me, please, do. I'll write to you anyway. Your eyes! That look in your eyes."[14]

Luxemburg's tone had changed. But Jogiches could distinguish compassion from passion and guilt from love. If there was something more offensive than her disloyalty it was her pity. That his despair was so transparent added to his humiliation. His inner life, so jealously guarded, was suddenly laid bare. "How sad you sound in your letters!" she wrote. "Don't be so desperate and chase all your devils straight to hell. Stop philosophizing and start living with what's real. This damn philosophizing is good for nothing."[15] But he could no more stop "philosophizing" than accept defeat. And then, for all her sympathy Luxemburg was not ready to resume the relationship in its prior form: "You must let me do what I please and how I please . . . I simply live the life of a plant and must be left just as I am."[16] Yet he continued to analyze. "My treasure, where in my letter did you discover a 'personally harsh tone'?!" she protested. "I just couldn't believe my eyes. See, I wrote the letter in a terrible hurry to make the mail and toward the end

I was still more hurried. Perhaps that's why a certain *harshness* of style sneaked in (I didn't reread what I wrote). That you can *now* think I could be harsh with you is really incredible."[17]

There is a forced tone, a suppressed impatience in her utterances that could not have escaped Jogiches. Not even her plans for a future life together filled with "serious" books, work, and leisure sounded sincere to him anymore. "There was no letter from you yesterday, and today your Sunday letter came—so sad and so full of doubts, it amazed me. Why? What's the matter? It must be depression after unusually exhausting work," she declared, "that caused these hallucinations. And here I am, tidying your room."[18] If Jogiches had a premonition that the room would never be his again, if that was what his "hallucinations" amounted to, he was right.

His letters continued to be "short and sad." He kept harping on the past, mistrustful, suspicious. Still, his decision to keep Luxemburg out of his political domain remained unshaken. "Now something personal," she wrote, giving little thought to the reversal of their roles. "You're wrong, my treasure, thinking my mind is constantly on Polish affairs. Alas, the opposite is true . . . I think of nothing but German affairs, but I do want to be *au courant,* at least concerning the more substantial matters in *our* work. Please, please don't be so childish and don't cut me off from the Polish work so brutally by withholding all information from me. And please don't, my dearest, ever again use shock treatment with me. You must believe me when I tell you that a handful of news won't hurt me but on the contrary will fulfill a need."[19] Her pleas remained unanswered.

If Luxemburg made her confession so as to shake Jogiches out of his complacency she certainly succeeded. If his grief was a measure of his love—which to some extent it was—she had proof that he loved her, proof that he was human. But it had all come too late. She was burned out. "I feel a trembling, nervous restlessness," she admitted, "a need to drown myself in noise . . . I'm afraid of silence . . . and at night I suffer from nightmares and palpitations."[20] Work, she kept repeating, was the only remedy. It was difficult for her to write, and that, she said, was tearing her apart. "I can't be a genuine writer after all," she moaned, "if I have to pull myself by the hair to make myself write the least little thing."[21] In fact, she was quite able to write—in the three months following Jogiches's September visit she published over thirty articles. But she needed to lose herself completely in work, and the slightest setback threw her into a panic. The fear that she had destroyed Jogiches haunted her; could she have broken that man, so strong, invincible? It was like a bad dream. Somehow she would get him back, now on her own terms. The last act of her life's love was played out in Warsaw.

On 23 November 1905, Jogiches, alias Otto Engelmann, registered at the hotel Victoria in Warsaw. Other members of the leadership, including Dzierżyński, Warszawski, and Marchlewski, were already on the spot to attend a party conference and to found a party paper. Even in the thick of battle, Jogiches's mood did not improve. Not since the Wilno days had he been so conspiratorial (in Kraków he lived under his own name as he had in Berlin), with the Russian police on his heels and the entire apparatus of subversion in his hands. Yet he remained subdued and despondent. "Will this never end? Never?" Luxemburg anxiously wrote to Warsaw. "When will you stop thinking about what is aimless, senseless, and start living with what *is*?"[22]

Luxemburg decided to join her comrades in Warsaw, to make the revolution instead of writing about it. Upset by being deliberately cut off from Polish affairs, she may have wanted to prove to Jogiches the futility of his "childish" attempts and may have hoped to calm both him and her own conscience. She also felt a sense of discomfort at being the only member of the party's leadership to remain abroad in the volatile situation. German and Polish comrades objected to the trip as extremely dangerous, but she refused to listen. She was seen off on 28 December at the Friedrichstrasse station in Berlin by the Kautsky family. Old Minna Kautsky wrapped her woolen cape around Rosa, Karl Kautsky put a warm blanket over her legs, Luise presented her with her watch, incidentally bearing Luxemburg's initials (Luise's maiden name was Ronsperger)—so much for conspiracy. Luxemburg was traveling as Anna Matschke, but it would require a miracle for the Russian police not to recognize her face, well known from newspaper photographs, and her limp.

The Bloody Sunday massacre on 22 January 1905 and the strikes in Russia that followed set off in Russian-annexed Polland a reaction resembling a national insurrection more than an economic struggle. Not since the anti-Russian insurrection in 1863 had national sentiments risen so high and spread so wide. In the province of Warsaw, twice as many workers went on strike as in the province of St. Petersburg and three times as many as in the province of Moscow. Polish workers were temperamentally more prone to rebellion than were the Russians. Moreover, the Poles were fighting against Russification and for freedom as much as for higher wages. The striking workers were soon joined by Gymnasium and university students and the intelligentsia. The long-contained hatred of Russian domination united workers and intellectuals, students and peasants. It was a time of unique events and unique ethos. The mutinous sailors of the battleship *Potemkin* joined the revolutionaries in Russia, and in Warsaw a general strike broke out to protest the government-instigated pogroms of Jews in Białystok. Martial law was the weapon the Russians used against the Poles; it was introduced in August in Warsaw, extended to the entire Kingdom of Poland in November, lifted on the first of December, and reintroduced twenty days later. It was not an effective weapon. In October, on the heels of a general strike in Russia, Polish railroad workers went on strike along with workers in large and small industrial centers. Under the banner of a "common fight against the tsardom," a massive political strike, the largest in Poland, completely paralyzed the country. To get the situation under control and make a show of goodwill, the Russians promised the Poles a constitution and civil liberties. It was an empty promise. The sole concessions the Russians made were a political amnesty declared in October and the abolition of preventive censorship in December. A short-lived period of illusory freedom blunted the pent-up anger, and on 30 December, the day Luxemburg came to Warsaw, all hope for a general strike had died.

It is doubtful that Jogiches was enthusiastic about Luxemburg's coming to Warsaw. She was encroaching on his territory and taking away his glory; moreover, her presence would be a constant reminder of his humiliation. Yet her pen was badly needed, and as a politician he accepted her coming as a necessity. The sixty-five days of hectic activity in a city where they both were political criminals were the last they spent together. Day and night Luxemburg was turning out articles, pamphlets, and proclamations. The leadership met frequently, for strategy had to be adapted hour by hour to the unpredictable and uncoordinated developments. Not a day passed without a mishap. "Yesterday from early in the morning lots of bad luck—the printing shop was searched, then sealed, and there were frequent arrests, though nothing really serious went wrong, for today we've put together a new press and I must immediately sit down and write an article," Luxemburg reported to the Kautsky's in mid-January 1906.[23]

She was happy in the rebellious city. After years of talking and writing, theorizing and philosophizing, after the complacency of her Berlin comrades, the "senseless clichés" and the " 'radical' gibberish" of *Vorwärts,* the battlefront brought back the excitement of her youth. As had often happened in her life, reality did not disturb her dreams. Though the general strike she hoped for never took place, she wrote to the Kautskys, "It is not unfeasible that a mere 'chance,' a new Manifesto or something like that may suddenly bring on a spontaneous strike."[24] St. Petersburg, she reported to them, was in a state of chaos, and no instructions could be expected to come from there. Still she planned to go to St. Petersburg herself to "strengthen the ties" of the German party with the revolution, whatever she meant by that. Tremendous difficulties with printers, daily arrests, and factional strife were strenuous, yet she was excited. "In spite of martial law, we're publishing *[The Red] Banner* every single day and it is sold in the streets," she wrote to the Kautskys. "The minute martial law is lifted we'll resume the publication of the *[People's] Tribune.* Every day, gun in hand, we force the bourgeois printers to print the *Banner.*"[25] If she was not personally holding a gun to the printer's head, Jogiches perhaps was, or at least he directed the operation.

Meanwhile the harsh winter persisted, the families of the striking workers suffered from cold and hunger, and the workers were exhausted. The number of strikes fell drastically in 1906, and it became clear that not even the support of numerous European trade unions could counterbalance the Russian police. In the end, victory was on the side of the Russian force, as it had been so often before. Death sentences and prison, the liquidation of trade unions, and increased oppression reduced the workers to resignation and passivity for many years to come.

As became evident later, the shared work and danger failed to bring Luxemburg and Jogiches closer together. What happened between them during the Warsaw interlude remains a matter of conjecture, but it is clear that they both made efforts to save their relationship. What else could have prompted Jogiches's reckless move from his hotel to the pension of Countess Walewska where Luxemburg stayed? It could have been a conciliatory gesture or a deliberate courting of danger. Perhaps he thought police intervention a fitting end to the disintegrating affair. Perhaps he needed her closeness, perhaps she needed his. The decision cannot be justified on practical grounds; the two hotels were close to each other and the risk of walking the short distance was smaller than that of staying in the same place. Neither of them was in hiding; Luxemburg visited her family once a week, and both met with comrades, albeit with caution, in apartments in different parts of the city. Had they lived apart, there would have been a better chance for one of them to escape if the other were apprehended.

It is an iron rule of conspiracy to live or hide separately, to avoid conspicuousness, to reduce risks. No one was more aware of this than Jogiches. Both he and Luxemburg carried false passports, both came from Berlin where they had lived together, and both were notorious with the German and Russian police. They must have discussed the possibility of arrest. Luxemburg, a German citizen, was in much less danger than Jogiches, a Russian subject and a deserter; Luxemburg was a first-time lawbreaker, while this was Jogiches's fifth illegal trip to Warsaw within a year; in the event of an arrest, the German Social Democracy would protest on Rosa's behalf, but it would not lift a finger for Leo.

On Sunday afternoon, 4 March 1906, one day after Luxemburg's thirty-sixth birthday, the tsarist police entered her hotel room to find an abundance of illegal literature, proofs, and correspondence with the SPD leaders. The circumstances of the arrest are puzzling. According to the available sources Jogiches was not in the hotel when the detachment of police and gendarmes appeared. When he did arrive, he opened the door to his room, saw the search under way, and without being stopped by the police went to Luxemburg's adjoining room to warn her. They were both arrested in her room. If Jogiches was not in the hotel when the police came, however, it is unlikely that he would have entered it. On a Sunday afternoon, in the quiet neighborhood, the police could not have invaded the premises of the respectable pension without drawing the attention of neighbors and passersby. If the street had been conspicuously deserted or conspicuously busy, Jogiches would have smelled the hounds and spirited himself away. Even if he had noticed nothing unusual in the street, he would have become aware of the police upon entering the small hotel. It is unlikely that the police left the entrance unguarded, but even if it was guarded, Jogiches had time to run away or at least try. Instead, he supposedly went to his room unnoticed, saw the search in progress, missed yet another chance to flee, and went into Luxemburg's room, her recent personal letters in his pocket. Much more likely, Jogiches was simply in Luxemburg's room when the police arrived. He must have known all along that Rosa's presence in Warsaw was bound to end in disaster.

"On Sunday, the fourth, in the evening, destiny caught up with me—I was arrested. I already had a visa in my passport and was ready to leave. Well, there's nothing one can do about it . . . Long live the Rev . . . !" Luxemburg wrote to the Kautskys in an undated letter they received on 13 March 1906.[26] Her alias was not yet broken; she asked that their letters be addressed to Anna Matschke. Next she wrote to Karl Kautsky that the correspondent for *Leipziger Volkszeitung*, Herr Otto Engelmann (Jogiches) from Berlin—"you know him, of course, the same blond man who lived on Cranachstrasse for a long time"— was also imprisoned and asked Kautsky to confirm that Engelmann was on assignment in Warsaw, should the police inquire.[27]

Not surprisingly, the police knew their identities at the moment of the arrest. In the absence of police records, however, proof was needed. Luxemburg's case was relatively simple; within five days the police arranged a confrontation with her sister, Anna, who immediately identified Rosa. To break Jogiches's alias was more complicated; at the end of June, when Luxemburg was already free on bail, the Warsaw police asked the police in Wilno to identify a picture of Engelmann. Jogiches's older brother Pavel, more experienced than Luxemburg's sister, did not betray Leo's identity. Further inquiry, however, revealed that the correspondent of *Leipziger Volkzeitung* was none other than Leo Jogiches, sentenced in 1889 to four months of prison and one year of police surveillance, a fugitive and a deserter.

After she was identified, Luxemburg wrote a deposition in Polish: "My name is Rosa Luxemburg, not Anna Matschke as I previously stated."[28] She stuck to the rest of her story. She was a German Social Democrat, in Warsaw to see her family and collect material for German newspapers for which she worked; she had nothing to do with the Polish movement. Only after she was released did the police obtain an issue of *The Red Banner* containing an article signed by her.

The investigation tried to prove that the two defendants, along with trying to overthrow the tsarist government, had a personal relationship. Sensational articles about "bloody Rosa" and her lover appeared in the antisocialist German press. "This dangerous alien obtained German citizenship through marriage," wrote *Die Post*. "We, in Germany, can but rejoice that we succeeded in getting rid of her so easily."[29] Luxemburg maintained that she had been married to Gustav Lübeck in 1897 and divorced five years later; as for Otto Engelmann, he was a fellow journalist and their meeting in Warsaw was purely coincidental. There was no evidence to the contrary except for Luxemburg's clearly personal letters found on Jogiches; apparently these were not proof enough. In any case, in German law she was a German citizen, a fact impossible to refute either by the German police eagerly collaborating with the Russians or by the German press contending she had never lived with Lübeck and instead lived with Jogiches.

The leadership of the German Social Democratic Party spared no effort to get Luxemburg out of prison. August Bebel pledged money and every means at the party's disposal to prevent court-martial and deportation to Siberia. Luxemburg's family stood steadfastly behind her, trying to obtain funds, visiting her in prison, and ready to intercede with the Russian premier, Count Witte. Staunchly, she opposed this as she did an appeal to German Chancellor von Bülow: "In no case do I want to owe him anything," she wrote the Kautskys, "since I wouldn't feel free afterwards to criticize him and the government as is my duty."[30]

None of the escape schemes devised by the Polish party members worked out, partly because the prisoners were moved first from the Town Hall to Pawiak prison and then to the notorious Citadel fortress. It was in the Citadel that the youthful Rosa's heroes Aleksandra Jentys and Ludwik Waryński were incarcerated, and it was on its slopes that four socialists were hanged when she was sixteen. Pawiak reminded her of the prison in Zwickau, she wrote to the Kautskys: "Peace, order and solitude; I get more food than I need and can walk every day. Still, most important are the frequent contacts with the outside world: I'm in constant touch with friends, and—I can write."[31]

If Jogiches could ever reproach her with being frivolous, it certainly was not while she was in prison. She kept both business and personal affairs under perfect control. Jakub Hanecki, a Polish Social Democrat, visited her almost daily. They met without supervision to discuss party affairs, and he obtained her agreement for the Polish Social Democracy (SDKPiL) to join the Russian Social Democratic Workers' Party at the forthcoming congress. Karl and Luise Kautsky

135

had their hands full following her instructions. Karl was to represent the SDKPiL in the Bureau of the International; Luise was to pay her rent—"the hope of being back in my 'red' and 'green' rooms fills me with joy"—and a bill of 25 marks to Jogiches's tailor—"be sure to get a receipt from him."[32] With calm efficiency she attended to significant political matters and practical details, never once letting prison disrupt her life. The depression and apathy she had complained of a few months earlier disappeared; her letters to the Kautskys radiated humor and excitement, as though she had met with a great adventure. In the Citadel fortress, conditions deteriorated—she was forced to see her family from inside an iron cage—but her spirits did not. Her physical strength waned. When the doctors attested to her ailments—anemia, enlargement of the liver, and gastrointestinal catarrh—to obtain her release, they were hardly exaggerating.

In the end it was money that bought her release: 2,000 rubles to bribe the Russian officer who agreed to release her on bail and 3,000 for bail. The bribe money was raised by family and friends. The bail was deposited by her brother Maksymilian, though it was probably supplied by the German Social Democratic Party.

Luxemburg was released toward the end of June 1906 but was not free to leave Warsaw. Under the care of her family, she promptly regained her health. "We live in a spendid time," she wrote in July to her friends Emanuel and Mathilde Wurm. "Splendid I call a time that generates problems on a great scale, *significant* problems, a time that stimulates the mind, breeds 'critique, irony and essence,' releases passions, and above all is a fecund, pregnant time. It gives birth on the hour and becomes still more 'pregnant' with each delivery, and most important it does not deliver dead mice and squashed gnats as in Berlin, but veritable giants—gigantic crimes (*vide* the government), gigantic shame (*vide* the Duma), gigantic stupidity (*vide* Plekhanov and Co.), etc." Rosa ended the letter with her guiding principle: "The revolution is splendid, everything else is rubbish!"[33]

The rebellious spirit of the Poles entranced her. Compared to Warsaw, Berlin seemed more stifling than ever before; she would rather be in prison, she said, than argue with her colleagues at *Vorwärts*. She was proud of her city, "the only oasis in Russia," fighting, suffering, and alive.[34] In Warsaw, she wrote after she had left the city for Finland, danger was commonplace, "which of course makes me itch to go back at once." Warsaw was ten times "more interesting than the sleepy Petersburg where, walking the streets, one wouldn't even guess a revolution was going on."[35] The moral power born in insurrections throughout Poland's captivity and extolled in romantic poetry was reborn. The ritual of sacrifice was re-created. Like the insurgents of 1830 and 1863, the striking workers confronted a military force they could not conquer. The revolution was doomed, but the proletariat continued the tradition and shared in the dreams of the nation. "In the storm of the revolution," Luxemburg wrote in her work on mass strike, "a proletarian is transformed from a provident father, who begs for support, into a 'revolutionary romantic' for whom even the highest good, life itself—not to mention material well-being—is worth little compared to the ideals he is fighting for."[36]

She left Warsaw, never to come back, on 31 July 1906. Doctors recommended a cure abroad, and the authorities granted her permission to leave the country. Facing trial for a seditious speech Luxemburg had delivered in Jena a year before, she could not go back to Germany right away. In any case she was eager to meet with the leaders of the Russian Social Democratic Workers' Party; after a brief stopover in St. Petersburg where she visited an imprisoned old friend, Parvus-Helphand, she went to Kuokkala, a small summer resort in Finland, twenty miles outside of St. Petersburg. There she lived under the name of Felicja Budziłowicz.

For all her admiration for the Russian revolution, she found Russian attitudes as exasperating as she had earlier. "Chaos, disorganization, and above all a confusion of ideas and tactics," she wrote to the Kautskys.[37] Yet the visit was very instructive. "From my intercourse with the people in the movement I am learning what one could never learn from books; moreover, one can achieve something through direct contact."[38] Almost certainly she had Lenin in mind. Lenin and his close collaborators Zinovjev, Kamenev, and Bogdanov had their base in Kuokkala. Her attitude toward the Bolsheviks, reserved at best, had started to change in Warsaw; like the Poles, the Bolsheviks had at least attempted to overthrow the government.

In Kuokkala she came to know Lenin well. He struck her with his exceptional mind, a quality always seductive to her, and with his enormous will power and broad knowledge of the Russian reality. He was erudite, shrewd, and determined. The theorists she knew paled in comparison. Lenin's genuine belief in his own infallibility and his lack of interest in anything unrelated to the revolution impressed her. "It is a pleasure to talk to him," she wrote to a friend later. "He is sophisticated and knowledgeable, with the kind of ugly mug I like so much."[39]

Though she found the meetings with the Russians instructive, she really wanted to be back in Germany. With her new ammunition—the work on the mass strike—and her new glory gained in actually making a revolution, she felt better equipped than ever to breathe a truly revolutionary spirit into the German party. Most of her time in Finland was devoted to working on a pamphlet called "Massenstreik, Partei und Gewerkschaften" (The Mass Strike, the Political Party, and the Trade Unions). "If the Russian revolution teaches us anything, it is above all that a mass strike cannot be artificially 'produced,' 'decided' at random, or 'propagated,' but that it is a historical phenomenon that at the right time results from social conditions with historical inevitability."[40] Her credo—the superiority of spontaneity over "organized action"—and her belief that the healthy instinct of the proletariat was superior to party leadership were supported by forceful arguments. No plan prepared ahead can keep pace with the spontaneous movement of the masses; it was a mistake, she wrote, to attribute to a political party the power the workers alone possess. Political mass struggle cannot be directed from above by a central party organization. "The overestimation . . . of the role of organizations in the class struggle of the proletariat usually goes hand in hand with the disregard of the unorganized proletarian mass and of their political maturity."[41]

How did the experience of Russia, that "semibarbarous state," apply to Germany where the Social Democratic Party had three million members and the working class had thirty years' experience in political life? The differences were largely illusory, Luxemburg declared, for "a worker from Petersburg, Warsaw, Moscow or Odessa is much closer culturally and mentally to his West European counterpart" than people reared by trade unionism and bourgeois parliamentarism believed.[42] Furthermore, the abject poverty of the German miners and textile, railroad, and land workers, not dissimilar from that in Russia, reduced the differences. But whereas in Russia the smallest conflict between workers and employers caused a storm, in Germany, France, Italy, or Holland even the most explosive conflicts were not followed by mass action on the part of the workers. Luxemburg felt that it was the class instinct, highly developed in Russia and underdeveloped in Germany and other western European countries, that aroused the masses to action. "The most backward country . . . shows ways and methods of furthering the class struggle to the proletariat of Germany and of the most advanced capitalist countries."[43]

The 1905 revolution exposed the gap between Luxemburg and the German Social Democrats, the gap between a revolutionary and theorists. It appeared unbridgeable. Luxemburg's rhetorical question "When will you finally learn from the Russian revolution?" was little short of a slap in the face of the Germans. While she conceived of revolution as a historical necessity, her German comrades saw it as a philosophical, abstract issue.

The epilogue to the Warsaw debacle came in November 1906. The court-martial found Luxemburg and Jogiches guilty of membership in the Social Democracy of the Kingdom of Poland and Lithuania and of attempting to overthrow the Russian empire by means of an armed insurrection. Luxemburg did not appear in court but sent a medical certificate attesting to ill health; she was declared a law evader and her bail was confiscated. In January 1907 the district military court sentenced Jogiches to eight years of penal servitude. By then Rosa's life had already taken a different turn. When she had returned to Berlin on 13 September 1906, among the friends who greeted her was Konstantin Zetkin.

11 | *Costia Zetkin*
1907–1912

K<small>ONSTANTIN</small> Z<small>ETKIN</small>, known as Costia, the younger
of Clara Zetkin's sons, was born in Paris on 17 April 1885. He was
four years old when his father died. His mother moved with her
two children to Zurich, sent them to England briefly, and in 1890
settled in Stuttgart. Before he was five, Costia had lived in three
different countries, could speak French, German, Russian, and
English, and had been cared for by as many different maids. The
scant time Clara Zetkin had for her children did not prevent her
from making and enforcing strict rules. Cold baths, clean finger-
nails, and a tight schedule were to make her sons tough, fit, and
disciplined. Costia had little choice, so he tried to follow orders—his
mother's, his older brother's, his teachers', the maids'. Nevertheless,
given the chance he would run into the fields, stare into the sky, and
dream. He was ridiculed by his schoolmates for being the son of a
woman who defied the stereotype of the ideal German wife concerned
only with "children, church, kitchen" *(Kinder, Kirche, Küche)*. Moreover, he was forced to exhibit his mother's political allegiance.
Although she sent them to the best schools, Clara dressed her sons like
working-class children. Costia never forgot the embarrassment this
caused him. Yet not even the more independent son Maxim dared

contradict her; arbitrary and dogmatic in politics, she was no less so at home.

Costia was not a happy child. Shy and sensitive, he had the tougher Maxim constantly held up to him as a model. He admired Maxim, who could easily shake off the malicious jokes of fellow students and whose attitude toward their mother impressed him. Maxim was correct and respectful but self-sufficient, while Costia depended on his mother's approval. Unlike Maxim, he was no comfort to her, rather a source of concern. His grades in elementary school and later in the Gymnasium were passable, though not excellent like Maxim's. And excellence was what his mother revered, as she did order and efficiency. Costia was not very efficient; he fell behind in his homework; he liked to read and to hike and most of all to daydream. But whenever he was late for supper his mother's worried look and his neglected homework made him miserable. He tried hard to improve, never sure the better grade he triumphantly showed her made up for his transgressions.

Costia was thirteen years old when Clara asked him and Maxim, then fifteen, for their consent to her marriage to an aspiring painter, Friedrich Georg Zundel. While she claimed that her decision depended on their agreement, the presence of Zundel in their house for the past year left this in some doubt. Zundel was closer in age to the boys than to his forty-one-year-old wife—eight and ten years older than Maxim and Costia, respectively—and he developed good relations with them. Disinherited (presumably because of his radical politics) and penniless, with great artistic ambitions, he appreciated the home, the family, and above all the studio Clara had had built for him in her house. Thirty miles south of Stuttgart, in Sillenbuch, the house was beautifully located, surrounded by a big orchard, with picturesque woods nearby. It remained Costia's sanctuary in his teens and twenties.

When Maxim graduated from the Gymnasium, he went off to medical school and came home only on occasional visits. Costia, however, did not want to attend the university; he did not know what to study and was relieved that school was over. Clara repeatedly tried to persuade him to "do something," but he did not want to part from her or from the country.

In 1906 when Costia turned twenty-one Clara Zetkin finally confronted him with a decision. There was an empty apartment in Berlin that belonged to Rosa, who was in Warsaw and was not expected to return soon. The apartment provided a perfect opportunity for him—he could move to the city and enroll in the university. She had discussed her plan with August Bebel and Karl Kautsky who, aware of her predicament, gave their blessing. Thus Costia was installed in Luxemburg's flat, at Cranachstrasse no. 58.

Luxemburg had known Costia since he was a teenager, had seen him over the years at Clara's house, and was not unaware of the problem he caused Clara. When she returned to Berlin in September 1906, she applauded her friend's use of her apartment. Clara brought her up to date about her younger son. With no profession and no desire to work, he lived off her, she complained, unconcerned and carefree. Neither her strained finances nor her social conscience justified his idle life. Clara's entreaties for help in editing *Die Gleichheit* remained unanswered. The office bored her son and the office hours interfered with his mountaineering. Something had to be done about him.

Since Luxemburg was leaving Berlin shortly for the German Social Democratic Party (SPD) Congress in Mannheim and was planning a vacation in Italy later in the fall, she put Costia up in Jogiches's room. In December she returned to Berlin determined to help Clara. She would persuade Costia to enroll in the university or get a job and end his unwholesome existence. Where the mother had failed, a trusted old friend, and one with fame and authority, might have a better chance.

The conversion Luxemburg had planned took an unexpected turn: she and Costia became lovers. They were ideally suited, it appeared—they liked to look at the crescent moon and at the rising sun; they liked the outdoors and long walks, liked to listen to music and read novels. Costia showed interest in her work, and before long she started giving him her articles to read and discussed her opinions and speeches with him. His admiration and the intensity of his reverence were in sharp contrast to Jogiches's constant dissatisfaction. Nor was Costia just a passive listener; he responded intelligently and inquisitively but without Jogiches's arbitrariness. Helpful without being competitive, proud of her without bitterness or self-pity, he delighted her with his youthful enthusiasm. She in turn eased his self-doubt, assuring him that geniuses are often late bloomers, that to realize their genius they need support, freedom, and time. Without directly contradicting his mother, on whom, she knew, he was strongly dependent, she started to shift his dependence.

Costia was extremely appealing to women. Not very tall but lean and strong, he had the muscular body of a sportsman and a weather-beaten, tanned complexion. His face was finely chiseled and his gray eyes were pensive. There was something boyish yet serious in his expression.

Everything about Luxemburg was different from the women Costia knew. None had her spark and her exuberant vitality. In her he found his first genuine friend and a passionate lover; he discovered the delight of being guided by a sensitive intellect and adored by a charming woman. "Poor little Costia," a misfit and a loafer, saw himself suddenly elevated to her "Zeus." If at the outset he was intimidated by her mind, her fame, and position, he found in living close to her that these mattered little in view of their affinity. While his mother bemoaned his weakness, Rosa celebrated his strength and made him proud of his manhood.

Clara Zetkin could not remain unaware of her son's infatuation, as probably both Luxemburg and Costia realized. But all three would have agreed it was the best thing that had ever happened to him. Costia knew how deeply his mother admired Luxemburg and perhaps hoped he had impressed her for the first time in his life. Luxemburg's conscience was clear, for she believed that she was no less devoted to Costia than was his mother and that she was better equipped to help him develop. Clara could not but feel relief that her son was under the wing of an exceptional woman who posed no threat to her. Although she did not express her approval outright, she certainly did not discourage the affair; she did not object to Costia's staying in Luxemburg's apartment, to the expensive gifts and vacations abroad that Luxemburg financed, or to Luxemburg's visits to Costia in Sillenbuch when he began to divide his time between there and Berlin. To preserve appearances, Luxemburg mailed several of her daily letters to Costia together in one envelope and inquired about Costia only if Clara broached the subject.

Luxemburg's reputation protected her from speculation. August Bebel, worried about Costia's living arrangements, wrote to Karl Kautsky in mid-April 1907, after Jogiches returned to Berlin: "If comrade R. L.'s friend [Jogiches] stays in Berlin for good and lives in her apartment, then Costia can hardly remain there."[1] That no one questioned the propriety of Costia's presence on Cranachstrasse testifies to the lovers' extreme caution and to Rosa's reputation among the

143

party elite. Rosa and Costia met at the homes of friends but came and left separately; in public they addressed each other formally; Costia's visits to Berlin were carefully planned in letters in which precautions were devised down to the smallest detail. In her reminiscences about Luxemburg, Luise Kautsky devotes much space to Rosa's friendship with Hans Diefenbach, Costia's contemporary and good friend, but Costia's name is conspicuously missing. Whether Luise Kautsky was ignorant of the nature of the relationship or protected Luxemburg's secret is unknown. It was Hans Diefenbach, for years a shield for the clandestine liaison, who passed into history as "one of Rosa Luxemburg's most intimate friends."[2] Costia Zetkin remained invisible.

In the third year of the affair, Luxemburg asked that Costia be appointed to the faculty of the SPD Party School, where she had held a chair in political economy since October 1907. The request, made jointly by Clara Zetkin and Rosa, outraged Bebel and Kautsky. "The most senseless thing one could demand is to have Clara's son appointed as a teacher in the Party School," Bebel wrote to Kautsky. "Totally unknown, never having given the smallest proof of his skills . . . he is supposed to take on a first-rank position in the party with all the responsibilities it entails." Neither a "mother's adulation" nor the "blind indulgence of a friend" excused the request, Bebel commented. "[It shows] an absolute lack of tact and responsibility," he concluded.[3] It also showed that the secret was well guarded, for Luxemburg's support of Costia was interpreted solely as an act of friendship toward Clara.

Foremost on Luxemburg's mind was Costia's intellectual development. She wanted to shape his psyche and groom him to be her partner. It was not her purpose to turn him into a party activist, for "party struggle is not for somebody with your nature . . . it is a life that demands suppression of everything that is fine and noble in man."[4] He was to devote himself to the study of philosophy, economy, and history without neglecting his interest in the arts. With his brilliant mind he could achieve magnificent things, she assured him. "One day," she promised, "you will write a scholarly work."[5] To ease the process of study, she provided him with her own interpretation of the French Revolution and of the history of the proletariat. Page after page of her letters was filled with reflections on the European revolutionary movements and economic and social conflicts. Balancing instruction and pleasure, the reading list included Kant, Babeuf and Marx, Tolstoy, Dostoevsky, Stendhal, and Balzac.

Costia was not an enthusiastic student. Marx was driving him mad, he complained. He must be patient, she advised, read, reread, and reread again: "You must find your own way to Marx and you most certainly will."[6] If Babeuf was too difficult, a French dictionary might help. Serious literature was indeed painful and apt to tear one apart. But, she maintained, that was *good* literature—it touched something deep inside, and after reading a good novel one was never the same. She implored him to read the books on the reading list. Costia did read some and eventually was entranced by Tolstoy rather than by Marx. Luxemburg was thrilled: "Of all people with whom I've discussed *The Death of Ivan Iljich* (including myself), you have grasped its meaning most profoundly."[7] That Tolstoy touched a chord in Costia was proof of his spiritual depth, which she alone never doubted. No wonder Costia could find no place for himself among people whose lack of sensitivity she had long deplored.

When Costia made no progress in either choosing a field of study or taking a job, Luxemburg decided he should become a novelist. "I wish you would start to write great novels," she encouraged him, persisting, "I believe you *must* write. You will write wonderfully."[8] Writing articles for *Die Gleichheit* while he should be writing fiction was a waste of his time. Costia protested that he could not write. That did not matter, she comforted him; a man who does not fit the mold will sooner or later discover his true destiny. To make a convincing argument she exposed Jogiches's most painful failure. "Let me just tell you about a similar case. Notwithstanding his brilliance and intelligence, Leo is simply unable to write. The mere thought of putting his ideas on paper paralyzes him. This was his curse for many years . . . His life was a complete mess . . . and he was almost forty," she wrote to her young lover. "And then came the [1905] revolution and suddenly he became the leader not only of the Polish but also of the Russian movement . . . Still unable to write a single line, he is the spirit behind party literature."[9] Evidently it had not occurred to Luxemburg that she might have brought out a latent fear in both men. To the end of his days Zetkin refused to commit himself on paper.

Like a Renaissance man, he was many-sided, Luxemburg insisted; so after the writer's career plans were shelved, she urged Costia to become a painter or a sculptor. He should proceed like a professional, find a model among the village boys—she offered to cover the expenses—and thoroughly study the anatomy of the human body, Egyptian art, and drawing. She too employed a model, a young girl, Gretel, and found this helpful in improving her art. The Polish cornfields inspired her imagination; she hoped that nature, which he loved so much, would inspire his. If it did, it was not for long, however; in a few months Costia lost interest in painting.

Costia continued to live at his mother's house, paying brief visits to Berlin and maintaining a lively correspondence with Rosa. His letters made her feel safe, she wrote to him. She carried them always with her and "the only beautiful moment in the day is when I go to the post office to collect the mail."[10] His visits were a feast; though he could not always stay in her apartment, he came after nightfall and had tea ready for her when she returned home. Only when she sent the maid away were they "finally . . . alone."[11]

In a brief postscript to a letter of 20 March 1907, Luxemburg notified Costia that Jogiches had escaped from prison and would no doubt soon descend upon Berlin. A few days later, still in the dark as to Jogiches's fate, she wrote that she would have been less scared at night had "little Costik" been in his "little room," that is, in Jogiches's room. If it disturbed her that the affair had started while Jogiches was languishing in prison for their common cause, she never expressed it.

Jogiches had been sentenced in January 1907 to eight years of penal servitude for criminal conspiracy to overthrow the Russian government and was put in the notorious Mokotów prison in Warsaw. There he managed to convert to his cause a guard who, risking his life, organized Jogiches's escape. On 15 March Jogiches was out of prison. Instantly on the wanted list, he went into hiding for about five weeks, mostly in the underground editorial office of *The Red Banner*. Appalled by the sloppy editing of the publication, he corrected a recent issue and left written instructions on improving the paper's standards. Jogiches is said to have had a love affair during the time he spent in hiding. But his alleged lover, Irena Szer-Siemkowska, was incarcerated at that time and was released after Jogiches had returned to Berlin. This fact did not discourage speculation, however, or the conclusion that it was Luxemburg, not Jogiches, who had been betrayed, that she had been deeply wounded, and that in typical feminine fashion she had shown

146

him the door.* In fact Luxemburg and Costia Zekin had been lovers since the beginning of 1907, before Jogiches's escape from prison and his alleged affair.

Jogiches crossed the Polish border illegally in early April 1907. He arrived in Berlin in mid-month, to be told by Luxemburg that their common-law marriage was over. Jogiches's violent reaction shocked and frightened her. She certainly expected some resistance since she presented him with an accomplished fact; but violence she did not expect. Once more she showed how little she knew Jogiches. After a year in jail he came home to her, only to be dismissed. She flung her rejection in his face, deprived him of everything he had, of herself, and then was taken aback by his furious rage. She did not tell him that there was another man in her life, but he suspected that W. had reappeared on the scene. Jogiches might have learned that W. had been in Kuokkala in August 1906, at the same time Luxemburg was there, and had then come to Berlin as she had. Although W. had been arrested on his way back to Warsaw in October 1906, appearances supported Jogiches's suspicion. W., released from prison in 1908—Luxemburg raised bail for him—came back to Berlin. The only thing he wanted from Rosa was that she return his old letters.†

Jogiches refused to move out of the apartment. Luxemburg acquired a revolver, she confided to Luise Kautsky, for Jogiches had threatened to kill her. But the worst was still to come. In a few weeks, at the beginning of May, she and Jogiches were to attend the Fifth Congress of the Russian Social Democratic Workers' Party in London as delegates of the Polish Social Democracy (SDKPiL).‡ Luxemburg also represented the German Social Democratic Party (SPD). They traveled together, for Jogiches threatened a public scandal if Luxemburg refused to go with him. "Unfortunately the vessel didn't sink," she wrote to Costia with mock seriousness; this was to be the last light

---

*Hannah Arendt elaborates on the findings of J. P. Nettl, Luxemburg's biographer: "Their deadly-serious quarrel, caused by Jogiches's brief affair with another woman and endlessly complicated by Rosa's furious reaction, was typical of their time and milieu . . . This generation still believed firmly that love strikes only once . . . Mr. Nettl's evidence shows that she had friends and admirers . . . but it hardly indicates that there was another man in her life." Hannah Arendt, *Men in Dark Times* (New York: Harcourt, Brace & World, 1968), 45.

†Luxemburg's letters to W. could not be located.

‡The SDKPiL united with the Russian Social Democratic Workers' Party in April 1906.

note in her communications from London.[12] Jogiches would not leave her alone for a single moment, she complained to Costia; they stayed in the same hotel, went on the same bus to meetings, where they had to behave correctly if not cordially, and spent evenings with old comrades who still regarded them as close friends. Then, one day, Jogiches opened and read an unsigned letter from Costia. He would kill her and her lover, he announced. He watched her day and night, she reported to her "darling boy," and under no circumstances would he let her go back to Berlin without him. She wanted Costia to know that she feared for his safety and was even ready to appease Jogiches so as to keep Costia out of danger. Luxemburg reveled in the theatrics; though she had a premonition of catastrophe, she was determined to fight for their happiness, she wrote to Costia. In letter after letter she went back over the drama with relish—the interception of Costia's letter, Jogiches's manic behavior, a scene in a restaurant.

The latter took place in an elegant hotel to which her brother Natan, who lived in London, invited her and Jogiches for dinner. The luxurious setting and a band playing the *Carmen* aria provided the background. Rosa's brother, unaware of the situation, escorted the couple into the restaurant; Rosa forced a smile, while Jogiches whispered into her ear: "I'd rather kill you than let you go back."[13] She was frightened, she admitted to Costia, but nothing would stop her from returning to him or smuggling out letters to him—"To give my Love good-morrow."[14] Had Jogiches caught her writing to Costia, she claimed, she might have paid with her life.

Jogiches let her return to Berlin alone. Perhaps her public performance at the Congress convinced him that she was in no mood for private concessions. In her speeches, discussed beforehand with him, she offered her own interpretation of Marxism and its application. She challenged Lenin's concept of "armed insurrection" and contrasted the Bolsheviks' "mechanistic" view of revolution with the Polish party's successful reliance on the active will of the proletariat. Marxism, she said, is not a dogma but a scientific method of analyzing an ever-changing reality; to adhere slavishly to *The Communist Manifesto*, written more than half a century before, was "a glaring example of metaphysical thinking," a distortion of Marxism.[15]* Her uncompro-

*Joseph Stalin, aged twenty-eight, listened attentively to Luxemburg. In 1931 Stalin was to excommunicate Luxemburg for creating a "caricature" of Marx's concept of revolution.

mising stand, her audacity, her challenge of prominent Marxist theorists might have been fueled by the private battle she was simultaneously fighting. Luxemburg defied the Marxist establishment and she defied Jogiches, and that language he understood well.

She returned to Berlin triumphant. Costia awaited her at the train station, as she had wanted. With two victories, one public and one private, she felt exuberant, youthful, "like a twenty-year-old girl."[16]

The drama between Jogiches and Luxemburg made her still more desirable and mysterious in Costia's eyes. She missed no opportunity to describe to her lover, in impassioned and imaginative language, the danger to which she exposed herself because of him. Costia, the quixotic knight, could be dissuaded only with difficulty from rushing to her protection.

Within twelve days after the London Congress, Luxemburg entered prison in Berlin to serve a two-month sentence she had earned for "instigating the use of violence" in a speech delivered at the 1905 Jena SPD Congress. From her cell she wrote to Costia about the hopes she had for him and for them. But prison had lost its novelty; she had had more than her share of heroism a year earlier behind bars in Warsaw; now incarceration meant being deprived of freedom and of Costia.* Her work on a book on political economy did not prevent her from thinking about her lover "every free second." He was certainly starving himself to death with no one to take proper care of him; a wholesome diet and fresh air were imperative to his health, she reminded him, for he was still growing. Glad that Costia enjoyed a new toy, Clara's husband's recently acquired automobile, Rosa thought how pleasant it would be to take trips together. But work, she stressed, should be foremost in his mind. Several months earlier she had induced Costia to read political economy and to study Russian, "soon to become a world language"; she was anxious now about whether he continued his studies in her absence.[17]

Once out of prison she had to confront Jogiches, who flatly refused to move out of his room. In August 1907 she informed Costia that Jogiches was to leave Berlin in two days. Jogiches finally left in

---

*Attributing her presumably dejected mood to the blow Jogiches had dealt her pride by his alleged betrayal with another woman, J. P. Nettl contends that, "unlike the time so proudly and impatiently served [in jail] in 1904, she now was depressed and uncommunicative." J. P. Nettl, *Rosa Luxemburg,* 2 vols. (London: Oxford University Press, 1966), 1:377–78.

mid-September for Finland, the seat of the Russian Social Democratic Workers' Party (RSDRP) Central Committee, to which he had been elected at the London Congress. Meanwhile Luxemburg lived in constant fear; she destroyed Costia's letters and advised him to destroy hers. She picked up her mail at the post office lest it fall into Jogiches's hands. Yet her nervous exhaustion, she assured Costia, was due to the London trip, prison, and the Congress of the International in Stuttgart, all having taken place within the previous three months.

In January 1908 Jogiches came back to Berlin. He moved to a small hotel, Schlosspark, in Steglitz. But he did not move out of Luxemburg's life. In his heart of hearts he could not believe that another man had replaced him; unable to accept the finality of her decision, he was determined to win her back. His attempts, however, were catastrophic. He spied on her, rushed into the flat to catch her unawares, followed her in the streets with his hand on the gun in his pocket. Once when he stormed into the apartment, she stood paralyzed, unable to utter a sound, and finally ran away to the Kautskys; when she returned in the morning she found her mail opened and her keys gone. To make matters worse, she ran into Jogiches in the street: "He knew well, he yelled, with whom I've spent the night."[18] All this she faithfully reported to Costia.

Fear of a scandal and their compulsive need for privacy locked Luxemburg and Jogiches in a silent battle. Luise Kautsky explained away the storm as a temporary falling out, in spite of Rosa's telling demand: "Do not ask L. about the keys," referring to the keys to her flat, "and do not mention me to him or anything about me at all (the date of my arrival, etc.) or you might unwittingly get me into a mess."[19]

Jogiches carried on the war of attrition for almost two years, until 1909. Luxemburg could not make a clean break because they were both at the helm of the Polish Social Democracy. Willing or not, she had to maintain contact with him. Nor did her intellectual dependence on him diminish. Even if she gave Costia her articles to read or informed him about the progress of her work, Jogiches's authority in party politics remained unquestioned. Her correspondence with Jogiches, interrupted in December 1905 when she left for Warsaw, was resumed in February 1908. From the home they had once shared Rosa sent memos and reports to Leo at his hotel. Elaborately impersonal, bearing neither salutation nor signature, flat and impatient, these communications more than anything else gradually convinced him that he had lost her. But he hung on. The library they had assembled over the years was indispensable for his work, he claimed. In the fall of 1908 Luxemburg informed Costia: "L. arranged things in such a way that he leaves for the night but stays here during the day and works . . . He lived here when I was in N[uremberg], now he is in K[raków], but I was told today that he is coming back to Berlin for the winter, perhaps even within a month."[20]

The arrangement did not work; a year later, in September 1909, she wrote to Jogiches: "As countless times before, I must again ask [you] to discuss business with me in writing and to leave me in peace in my own home. I do not need the other room; I never set foot in it. Whoever stays with me is put up in my room in order to keep out of the other. But in my apartment I must feel at home, not as if I lived in a hotel where anyone can come and go whether I like it or not . . . I cannot go on like this . . . I want a home of my own. If I cannot have it, I prefer to give up the whole apartment together with the maid and to sublet a furnished room . . . I request a reply as to whether this is going to continue because I must know what to do with myself."[21] Jogiches relented.

Perhaps predictably, when the Trojan War raging on Costia's account subsided, so did his infatuation. Jogiches's sinister madness impressed Costia no less than Luxemburg's cool determination. And though it was exciting to be loved by a woman capable of arousing insane jealousy in a man of Jogiches's stature, inheriting Jogiches's responsibilities was a different matter.

"Why, oh why must I always pass through jarring and painful experiences in my life, while everything in me cries out for serenity and harmony? Why do I always plunge into the dangers and horrors of unknown situations?"[22] One may surmise what went through Costia Zetkin's mind upon reading these words. Perhaps the outburst perplexed him, perhaps it made him ponder the disconnectedness of Rosa's drives and fortunes and his own role in that confusion. As long as Luxemburg treated him like a child—"is the little boy studying his Marx?"—or like a companion with whom she could share her impressions of art, music, and literature, he knew where he stood.[23] Luxemburg may have been Costia's idol since his teens, and this may have extended into adulthood. Now it slowly dawned on Costia that Rosa's happiness or unhappiness depended on him, on his performance as a lover rather than as a child. In his eyes Luxemburg still belonged to Jogiches; otherwise why should she suffer his presence and his insults, advise him, Costia, to change his handwriting lest Jogiches recognize it, and behave like a wife betraying her husband? There was more behind it than the political bond that tied them, he rightly assumed.

Almost from the moment her liaison with Costia began Luxemburg had been ambivalent. The fifteen-year difference in their ages seemed an insurmountable obstacle, though Clara Zetkin and her husband, younger by eighteen years, had enjoyed a happy marriage for many years. Luxemburg lacked Clara's confidence, and besides she was in love with love. Day-to-day existence stripped the dream of the dream; the bright colors turned to gray, the storm to drizzle. Always to look her best in order to compete with women Costia's age was a trial; to fight her limp was an ordeal: "Why didn't you wait for me? Were you angry? Uncomfortable? . . . you disappeared in the crowd . . . you walked quickly away and I couldn't find you."[24]

Luxemburg's deep-seated fear of losing Costia might itself have been a reason for his retreat. His every sign of attention was rewarded with an outburst of anguish, his adulation with apprehension. She smelled his letters for "strange" perfume and searched his words for hidden meaning. He came to realize that the conflict between the harmony she sought and the terrors into which she plunged dominated her life and that he was being drawn into that conflict.

As her anxieties deepened, the burden weighed heavier on him until it became unbearable. If at first he was allowed to write when he wished, within a year his letters became for Luxemburg "my air, my oxygen, my *raison d'être*, my *only* joy."[25] The elaborate schemes she made for them to meet—for instance, taking a vacation with Luise Kautsky and her boys as a cover—once amusing, lost their attraction. Most oppressive was her growing possessiveness. For her, every minute spent with other people was a waste; wasn't it so for him? She was fed up with everything—the opera, the automobile trips, the people; wasn't he? If she could just have him next to her when she was working, even if he no longer loved her, she would be happy; could he understand? Would he love her for ever and ever though she was old and her hair was graying and she was growing heavier?

Costia was suffocating. The freedom she had offered him was a poisoned piece of candy. In 1909 he worked for his mother, proof-reading *Die Gleichheit*, perhaps to curtail his dependence on Rosa, only to be told by his mistress that her little butterfly mustn't waste time on such tedious work, that he must remain a "free spirit." But was he? Were they indeed two "happy children," as she maintained? He no longer saw it that way. The chains that she claimed a job would put him in seemed less of a menace than her insatiable hunger.

It was after a brief vacation he spent with Rosa in August 1909 that Zetkin awkwardly started to distance himself. She reacted immediately: "What is my Niuniu doing?" she asked him anxiously. "I'm afraid he is sad and I don't know why . . . Doesn't he love me anymore?"[26] It was bound to happen one day, she prompted; if he did not love her he should say so. He obliged. In a letter she received in mid-August 1909, while she was vacationing in Switzerland, he wrote that the relationship had grown into an impossible burden that he could no longer carry. He felt trapped, lost, and unhappy. He wanted to be free.

Luxemburg responded in style. It took a great effort to write at all, she said, but she owed it to him to clarify a few points. It was she who had been his prisoner, not the other way around; it was he who implored her to be faithful to him, who begged her to never abandon him, who forced his love on her. She would have parted with him long ago but for fear of betraying the trust he had placed in her. To read his "false" letters, to endure his ambiguous attitude, to look at his angry face was excruciating, but she suffered to keep her promise because their bond was sacred to her. Far from catching her by surprise, the news found her well prepared, for after all everything had happened just as she had foreseen. She had decided before receiving his letter to bring more strength, more clarity, more chastity into her life. Now he was free. She no longer stood in his way.

Her letter to him was not that of a lover. She wrote as a close friend on whose loyalty he could rely. He was merely a helpless youngster, she said, to whom, out of compassion, she had offered the wonderful gift of her friendship. That he had misunderstood it was due to his immaturity.

The effect of her answer was predictable. He had hurt his only true friend, Zetkin belatedly realized. No one in the world had been as caring and devoted, no one could replace Rosa. Now he would be alone again, misunderstood and unappreciated. Shamed and apologetic, he wrote back begging her forgiveness, her friendship, and the continuation of their correspondence. She consented. But why? Apparently because she needed him to confirm her womanhood and because she could not face defeat. One day, it must have been clear to her, they would part—but it would be she who took the step, not he.

Zetkin's betrayal touched every nerve in her. Under the seemingly calm surface a volcano erupted. In the period 1910–1913 Rosa would wage ferocious battles against Karl Kautsky, August Bebel, Lenin, Karl Radek, and a host of political parties. The indulgence she showed Costia in these years was diametrically opposed to the inflexibility and intolerance she showed others. To what degree personal frustration was worked off in political fights is impossible to say, but the timing cannot be dismissed as coincidence.

For three years, until 1912, Rosa and Costia's relations continued, but they were not the same. Rosa was wary and alert, Costia guilt-ridden and anxious. He owed her everything: the freedom, albeit with strings, to do what he pleased, the chance to become "a great artist," partnership in her political work, absolution for disappointing his mother. Afraid of losing her but uneasy about their intimacy, impatient for her letters as Jogiches had been, he would have been content with a relationship mostly at a distance. Not so Luxemburg. Her passion had not abated, but she had learned to control it and to wait. For many months he was forbidden to call her "dear"—"you gave up that right . . . you asked for friendship—you have it"—until the fall of 1910 when they reconciled.[27] There were no more letters without salutation or signature, like those she was then writing to Jogiches; Costia was again "my dearest Niunius," and she was his "Niunia" or "Jaguga." But the ardent, frankly passionate confessions subsided. Instead, she mentioned Hugo Faisst, a pianist and singer, who within three days had sent her three long letters, two postcards, and an "enormously long" wire, supplied her with concert tickets, and asked for a rendezvous; and she told Costia she would be happy to send him on a trip south if she had the money, letting him know that she was not afraid he might meet another woman.

She made an enormous, although short-lived, effort not to intrude on him. When he wrote, she answered; when he was silent, she invented excuses for him. Her letters abounded in long descriptions of flowers and trees and above all her cat, Mimi, the only safe receptacle for her overflowing emotions. "All I really want is to live in peace with Mimi, she loves me and we understand each other so well."[28] She described how Mimi flirted with Lenin—she rolled on her back and licked him, but when he tried to touch her she hit him with her paw and roared like a tiger. It was Mimi whom she missed when she went on speaking tours, Mimi who waited for her when she came home, Mimi who, as Costia had in the past, accompanied her on walks. It was Mimi who missed Costia and sent him a kiss, who sniffed at his letters and read them. It was "Mimi and I" and "greetings from us both." Reports on Mimi's health problems—sore eyes, constipation, colds, rashes—sounded like those of a worried mother writing to a distant father. She told Costia that he could find pure, genuine happiness just by caressing the soft body of his own cat. Their exchange about cats, sad and obsessive, became a link through which they communicated emotions they no longer felt free to express.

Luxemburg was never again to feel like a twenty-year-old girl. Time, she knew, was working against her. Zetkin was growing increasingly uncomfortable with his dependence on her, too weak to cut himself off but no longer eager to perform his role as lover. He came to visit accompanied by his mother as a shield. Sometimes, in response to her desperately sad letters, he came without Clara. But his visits made her still more nostalgic; the house was empty after his departure, she wrote to him, she was lonely and there was no one to comfort her.

She did not disguise her state from Jogiches. After two years her letters to him lost their impersonal edge. In tense, pointed words she admitted to suffering from "such acute physical and moral depression that I was unable *to write a single sentence.*" Of course she did not reveal the cause. Jogiches's worried inquiry was put off: "nothing has happened; it is a depression pure and simple and the more annoying for that."[29]

With Zetkin she was candid. "Ida* . . . knows that my mood depends on what I receive in the morning mail."[30] Costia seldom wrote. Her black moods frightened him; he felt both betrayed and guilty. He sent flowers from his mother's garden, he sent books. But her mood hardly improved. Her letters, sometimes signed Gina Stendhal, were lifeless, repetitive—she played with Mimi, finished an article, read Tolstoy, went to the opera, spent a boring afternoon with Hans Diefenbach. Sundays were quite superfluous; she did not know what to do with herself. The only consolation was Mimi, who liked

---

*Ida Radnin had temporarily replaced Luxemburg's housekeeper, Gertrud Zlottko.

best to spend Sundays "with Mama alone."[31] She kept waiting for Costia to express a genuine wish to see her. When he did invite her to his mother's house, "I thought . . . we were doing all right with letters," she hinted, not without malice, suspecting that he had invited her merely out of respect. "It now seems to me that you do want to see me. Well, I'll come of course."[32] Monotonously, she repeated, "feel free as a bird," but when the bird fluffed up his feathers panic set in: "I hear Fräulein Manya paid you a visit again, so it is the third time this summer . . . Have a good time!"[33]

Rosa suffered from acute sleeplessness and was exhausted to the point where she had to stop in a bar for a shot of Schnapps before teaching a class. Torn between defeat and passion, she could find no way out. Hans Diefenbach, whom she had hitherto barely tolerated—a bore and a nuisance, as she often said in her letters to Costia—became her steady companion. Good-humored, intelligent, and dashingly handsome, the young doctor genuinely admired and liked Rosa. But he got on her nerves, perhaps because, as a contemporary of Costia's, he had combined a successful medical career with broad intellectual interests, perhaps because she was jealous of the friendship between the two men. His innocent remarks about Costia, "our little Cherub," as Diefenbach jokingly called him, set her teeth on edge.

Hans Diefenbach, who may have suspected the truth about Rosa and Costia, became a daily guest, escorted her to concerts and theaters, brought books, and looked after Mimi. Luxemburg accepted his courtship out of loneliness and vanity. "When she learned that Diefenbach traced his origin back to Justinus Kerner, Rosa was electrified," recalled Luise Kautsky.[34] Diefenbach's noble pedigree, reflected in his looks and manners, and his taste for literature and music finally won him Luxemburg's appreciation, but no more. She might have been hurt by his lack of interest in her as a woman, though it seems there were no women in his life. His "constantly cold hands" and his *"semmelblondes Temperament"* (lukewarm disposition) annoyed her, as did his totally incomprehensible reverence of Jews and interest in their cause, for which he left a sum in his will.

The final showdown between Rosa and Costia came three years after the first break, almost to the day, in August 1912. Zetkin's weakness for attractive women was bound to surface sooner or later. Aware of Luxemburg's sensitivity, he had always tried to spare her feelings, but they moved in the same circles and gossip reached her easily. Since April Luxemburg had been planning that they would go back to Corsica, where they had spent a vacation together in October 1911, but Costia procrastinated and the trip collapsed. To make matters worse, a young woman friend of his seems to have appeared on the scene. This time Luxemburg wrote him a brief note saying that there was no place for her in his life and that she could bear his "ambiguous" attitude toward her no longer. Though his recent behavior caused her pain she did not wish to reproach him or to burden his personal life, which "belongs only to you."[35]

Costia was now even more afraid to lose her than he had been three years earlier. At twenty-seven, still drifting, he had grown still more dependent on Rosa. Once more he begged for her friendship. She continued to write him friendly though often melancholy letters centered around his mother, Mimi, her work, and his future. Since the rift in 1909, Luxemburg increasingly identified with Clara Zetkin in her perception of Costia. "Your mother and I" was a recurring motif. He was their unhappy child dissatisfied with himself and the entire world. "Your melancholy is really a disease," she impatiently complained, apparently drawing no parallel with her reproaches to Jogiches a decade earlier about his "self-destructive streak" leading to "spiritual suicide." If Jogiches deserved compassion solely on account of his mother's death, Costia had "no real reason to be depressed" except for his "mother's condition."[36] And his mother suffered mostly because he was unhappy, she wrote him, fully aware that it was the breakdown of her marriage to Zundel and not her son that devastated Clara.

If there is a discernible pattern in Luxemburg's attitude toward Costia, it is a lack of consistency that must have been exasperating and confusing to him. Depending on his behavior, she would praise him extravagantly or scold him harshly. At one point she told him not to bother about money—"I'll have enough money for both of us"—or waste his talent working for *Die Gleichheit* because he could become a scholar or a great artist and "write exactly like Tolstoy."[37] At another point she told him to stick it out at *Die Gleichheit*. When it seemed likely that she would keep Costia, Rosa showered him with compliments and encouraged his unrealistic dreams. When he began to drift away, the indulgent mistress became a stern mother.

After Costia's defection in 1909, she urged him to accept a teaching position at the Party School and told him bluntly that at last people would stop saying "What will become of Costia?"[38] To help him perform at his best she prepared an outline of twenty-four lectures on the history of socialism in western Europe, Russia, and the United States. Before the SPD board had the chance to turn him down, Zetkin backed out. Luxemburg chided him, although she was undoubtedly as aware as he was of his dubious credentials. He should either stop complaining, she said, or else he should have accepted the position. Had the position actually been offered and had he accepted it, he would have had to move to Berlin and perforce work closely with her. Then perhaps she might have gotten him back. When several months later Zetkin turned down the job as a science editor on a party newspaper in Dortmund, for which he was incomparably better suited, she applauded his decision: "I want to spare you anything that's unpleasant and difficult."[39] No doubt that was true, and it was the root of her conflict. She knew that he should grow up, but once he did he might leave her. As long as he dabbled in philosophy or the arts, read novels and climbed mountains, he depended on her for spiritual and material support; as long as he lived in his dream world, she remained part of the dream. Therefore, everything that she condemned in Jogiches—indecisiveness, a disorderly life, the waste of time, the waste of his mind—she praised in Costia. For fifteen years she had tried to change Jogiches because she wanted a man and a husband; for the next seven years she nurtured Zetkin's weakness because she wanted a lover and a child.

Luxemburg had been at the height of fame when she met Costia Zetkin. Yet public success had given her no confidence in her private life. If she ever entertained the idea of living openly with Costia, there is no evidence of it. Since it had always been easier for her to reveal herself in writing than face to face, such thoughts would have appeared in her correspondence with Zetkin. Perhaps she did not dare suggest it for fear of a rebuff, or perhaps the image of him as a child canceled out that of a husband. Jogiches's claims on her during the first two happy years with Costia may have influenced her attitude as well; Jogiches had retained a certain power over her and she may have had a vague sense of still belonging to him. In any case, she was unable to break with convention. She might revolutionize social conditions, but her personal values remained traditional, as evidenced also by her taste in literature, music, and the arts. Her powerful intellect could not break through the limits of her own existence. Her longing to "capture the act of creation" might have been another reason for making Costia her "son" rather than a full-fledged partner. Had she had the child she so wanted, that longing might have been satisfied. Just as a fulfilled personal life remained unattainable, so did the act of creation. As a little girl she had wanted to observe a rose open, she once wrote to Costia, and she waited and waited till she was told to go to bed, and when she got up in the morning the rose had already opened.

It would be difficult to pinpoint the time when either Luxemburg or Costia came to realize that the two people who had dominated their lives before they met were there to stay. Though their motives differed, they shared the urge to escape. Dreams of running away together to some distant land were a recurring theme in their correspondence. They studied maps and planned routes and gave each other travel books, but they never went farther than on a brief vacation in Europe. And finally they returned—Luxemburg to Jogiches and Costia to his mother.

Luxemburg's passion for Zetkin was not purely sensual. He personified Germany—the strong Nordic type and Goethe's sentimental Werther. In breaking away from Jogiches, she was trying to break away not only from the man who "did not know how to love" but also from that part of her history she had never come to terms with. No matter how fiercely she criticized the "Prussian philistines," she yearned after sentimental love, admired efficiency, and felt close to German romantic poets. With Zetkin she shared not her unwanted Jewish heritage but the spirit of German culture. They spoke and corresponded in German, his native tongue, whereas she spoke with Jogiches in Russian and wrote to him in Polish sprinkled with Yiddish. She responded enthusiastically to everything that was German in Zetkin: his communion with nature, his remoteness from reality, his excessive emotions—the canon of German romanticism. His ecstasies, particularly if she was the object, his longings, and even the incoherence of his life were as irresistible then as Jogiches's Dostoevskian darkness had been fifteen years earlier. Zetkin took her back to poetry, while in Jogiches's rational world there was little place for beauty. In her letters to Jogiches she mentioned in passing a concert she had attended; to Zetkin she described at length the profundity of Bach's *St. Matthew Passion* or the lyric drama of Beethoven's symphonies. What Jogiches tried to separate in her—the prose and poetry of life—Zetkin let her bring together.

The two men were the children of two cultures Luxemburg both admired and despised. She wanted nothing more than to read Goethe with Jogiches and Tolstoy with Zetkin. Zetkin's dislike of the city struck her not as escapism or an inability to deal with ordinary problems but as a romantic longing that Jogiches sadly lacked. Zetkin's *Weltschmerz*, which she fostered, was in fact no less destructive than Jogiches's "spiritual suicide," which she scorned. She deplored Jogiches's "savagery" and adored Zetkin's "gentleness," unaware that these qualities were born of a sense of inferiority. Both men were sired by Russian Jewish fathers whom they had erased from their lives; both were scarred by being left fatherless in childhood; both idolized their mothers. In Luxemburg they sought the strength they lacked, and she failed them, unable to give what she did not have herself—a strong sense of identity rooted in acceptance of her past. Rosa tried to exorcise the symptoms of their inner turmoil without comprehending its source. Capable of effecting change in the consciousness of the workers, she believed she could also change an unhappy man into a happy one. The difference between the amorphous crowds she so easily swayed and the individual escaped her. So did the distinctions inherent in divergent cultures and social conditions; she saw humanity but not the individual human being. "Contact with the masses gives me inner courage and tranquility," she said, but Jogiches or Zetkin seldom evoked these sensations.[40] With them she felt unloved, unappreciated, and unneeded, or at best was constantly afraid of not being loved, appreciated, or needed. Lonely and sick at heart, she increasingly sought in humanity the wholeness and security that her parental home and her lovers had failed to give her.

Rosa Luxemburg with Costia Zetkin
in front of her apartment building

Clara Zetkin

Costia Zetkin accompanies
his half-blind mother to the
Reichstag, Berlin 1930

Rosa Luxemburg with Costia Zetkin
in front of her apartment building

Clara Zetkin

Costia Zetkin accompanies
his half-blind mother to the
Reichstag, Berlin 1930

Rosa Luxemburg in 1907

Leo Jogiches, probably 1908

Rosa Luxemburg delivers a speech at the Congress of the Second
International, Stuttgart, 1907. Clara Zetkin sits on her right.

Rosa Luxemburg and Karl Kautsky, Jr., hold her charcoal drawing of Karl, Christmas 1907

Rosa Luxemburg in her apartment, 1909

Rosa Luxemburg's self-portrait,
painted about 1911

12 | *Other Fires, Other Fights*
1908–1913

AS HER LIAISON with Zetkin deteriorated, Luxemburg's attitude toward Jogiches slowly and subtly changed. Her rebellion abated, her dependence increased. After her first rift with Costia in 1909 the suppressed anger, the clipped words, and the quarrelsome ring in her letters gave way to a muted deference. She remained haughty and remote in varying degrees but, after the final break with Zetkin in 1912, the uneasy truce was replaced by peace.

Unlike her loving and sentimental letters to Zetkin, in which Luxemburg often played a magnanimous friend and tried to hide her disappointments, the somber and unembellished letters to Jogiches exposed her distress. The 1908–1914 correspondence covers a very trying period in Luxemburg's personal and public life. That period seems to fall naturally into two parts: the first when she made every effort to eradicate Jogiches from her life, the second when she came to understand that she never would.

In 1908 Luxemburg wrote Jogiches eight letters; in 1909 she wrote him about twenty before Zetkin demanded his freedom in August and about forty afterward. In 1910 she wrote Jogiches close to ninety letters, in 1911 sixty, in 1912 over forty, and in 1913, over seventy. More than sheer numbers, the tone and content of the letters reflected her moods. During the first two years she avoided even addressing Jogiches. One might be tempted to write that off as indifference; but a close reading of her words in Polish shows a strenuous struggle for language that would serve as a barrier between them. Had Rosa indeed become indifferent to Leo she would not have gone to such pains. It would have been much easier to write formally than to invent a style exclusively for him. These letters were in a sense more intimate than those written before the break, for only Jogiches could easily understand her. She wrote, "Steglitz should make sure" or "Steglitz should write the details"—Steglitz being the district where Jogiches lived—but she would not put "you" on paper.[1] His bemused reaction is evidence that her labor was not lost on him.

Significantly, until August 1909 Luxemburg discussed only business in her letters to Jogiches. In September the colorless letters she wrote to Zetkin were offset by the intensely emotional plea to Jogiches not to intrude on her home. After Zetkin's retreat she complained to Jogiches of depression and exhaustion and kept him informed about her mood—but only when it was bad.

Mostly it was bad. Luxemburg was now forty years old and her personal life was a shambles. The platonic friendship with Hans Diefenbach came at the wrong time; it was a reminder of her aging and of Zetkin's betrayal. The realization that no man could replace Jogiches, that he remained the rock he had been from the time she met him, the only human being who understood her and cared about her, made matters worse. She did not consider going back to him, not because of Zetkin or even out of pride, but because she was not prepared to become merely a comrade. She did not know that Jogiches had acquired a mistress, a young salesgirl with no intellectual claims. The ungrammatical letters she wrote to him indicate that this was not a partnership of equals. But Jogiches preferred his sexual life on the periphery, and that was utterly alien to Luxemburg's nature.

After the break with Zetkin in 1912, when Luxemburg needed it most, Jogiches brought an element of stability to her life. The return of shared everyday matters—money, clothes, vacations—gave her a foothold. Even his occasionally crude criticism, the prodding and commands, were proof that he was the same, that nothing had changed, and paradoxically it was a relief. His request for an article *"at the latest"* within forty-eight hours allowed her to tell him how sick she was and to get his immediate attention. So did his criticism: "If my writing is poor, there's nothing I can do about it. I *cannot* write better in such a hurry and being so exhausted. Yesterday I suffered again . . . from chest pains and immediately had to go to bed."[2] Or she was "so depressed" that she could not fall asleep or so nervous that she could not work. True to form, he responded with concern but without indulgence.

Luxemburg's family never learned about the break with Jogiches. For the sake of appearances Leo was present at her apartment when Rosa's brother Maksymilian brought his wife and children to Berlin in 1910 to introduce them to her. "That was when I first met uncle Leo," Rosa's niece, Halina Luxemburg-Więckowska, remembered.[3] Whether Luxemburg did not want to initiate her family into her personal affairs or to admit failure (she often dispatched newspaper clippings to Warsaw praising her professional triumphs), Jogiches understood and complied. Reminded by Luxemburg of her sister's forthcoming wedding anniversary,* he sent congratulations; at her request he sent a birthday present to Rosa's little nephew in Warsaw; as instructed by Rosa he dropped a few "warm" lines to her brother and looked up her sister-in-law who was visiting Berlin. For the first seven years of their life together her family had not known of his existence; she then invented the marriage ceremony in Switzerland and finally pretended conjugal life when it did not exist.

Officially Jogiches never moved out of their flat in Cranachstrasse. To maintain the fiction that he still lived there, he rented a room in the Schlosspark Hotel under the name of K. Krzyształowicz. Along with most others, his tailor, C. Wiethölter, believed that Jogiches still lived on Cranachstrasse. He delivered his suits and bills there and settled the complicated accounts with Luxemburg. The tailor was paid in monthly installments, but at times Jogiches lagged behind. "Wiethölter is on my back," Luxemburg told him calmly in 1910, aware that the delay was due to financial difficulties. Or Jogiches could not find his suit, lost somewhere en route: "Wiethölter swears he has no suit. If he did, he delivered it a long time ago. Perhaps it is in the wardrobe? Perhaps it is the same one I sent . . . to Steglitz?" Or he wanted his coat repaired: "I found only the raincoat . . . ; Wiethölter asks what he is supposed to do with it since it is in perfect condition. There are no other clothes in the wardrobe."[4]

*Anna Luksenburg (1858–1932) married in 1909 at the age of fifty-one.

At first, whenever she broached a personal subject in her letters Luxemburg would then move abruptly to the business at hand as though to blur the distinction. With time she became less concerned with form. In December 1910, she advised Jogiches "not to give up a vacation, no matter what." The work would not suffer since she would adjust her vacation to his. "Even Marchlewski asked me to persuade you to take time off," she added, as though to disclaim personal concern.[5] A brief note she sent Jogiches in August 1910 from her Swiss vacation is a measure of the progress of the rapprochement. "A request—have Krakus [a comrade] send me a few Polish novels *immediately*. I don't have a single work of fiction." Within two days Jogiches wrote from Berlin to Feliks Dzierżyński in Kraków: "Would you [send] two or three works of fiction (I'll tell you which) . . . to Rosa in Switzerland. I'll be happy to cover the expense, of course."[6]

Another bond was money. Jogiches's entire income came from his family's business in Wilno. Whether because the business fell on hard times or because the health of Leo's brother, Pavel, was failing, Jogiches had financial difficulties in 1909. His income was sent from Wilno to Maksymilian Luksenburg in Warsaw, who forwarded it to Rosa, so she knew how much Jogiches received and when. In November 1909, without telling him, she asked her brother to urge Pavel Jogiches to increase Leo's allowance. Maksymilian, who owed Leo money, then repaid the loan—or so Luxemburg told Jogiches. Since she also asked Leo not to mention it to Maksymilian, Jogiches suspected that she had repaid her brother's debt herself. He returned the money with a note which infuriated Luxemburg. "I don't understand what's going on," she fumed. "If you don't want your money, send it back to Munio [Maksymilian]." Jogiches answered: "In that case let me have the postal receipt, please." Luxemburg fired back: "I cannot search the trash barrel for the receipt. Kindly get in touch with Munio and do not bother me."[7]

It does not matter whether Luxemburg paid off her brother's debt. Evident in the dialogue about money are the care and the feeling of responsibility. That exchange took place in 1909, three months after Zetkin's withdrawal. Perhaps for the first time, Luxemburg compared the behavior of the man with that of the boy.

The return to the past, limited though it was, restored Rosa's balance, which the affair with Costia Zetkin had upset. Jogiches's singlemindedness, his exclusive concentration on the movement, so painful when she lived with him, now helped her deal with a number of political setbacks.

⟶

While the 1905 revolution strengthened Luxemburg's militant position, the German Social Democratic Party (SPD) was increasingly apprehensive of a revolution in the Russian style, or for that matter an insurrection Polish-style. Revolution was something to be discussed, not to be made. The task at hand was to gain more power in the Reichstag, the SPD leadership felt. The more openly Luxemburg pressed for "revolutionary Marxism," the more isolated she became. The Polish tradition of heroism and martyrdom and the German tradition of conformity and conservatism were irreconcilable.

Although she glorified the 1905 Russian revolution to her German comrades, it did not follow that she was in accord with the Russians. Their internal party struggles bewildered the Germans and enraged Luxemburg. "I was simply ashamed to tell Kautsky about it," she wrote to a Russian comrade in 1909, referring to a successive split within the Bolshevik faction.[8] Maxim Gorkij, at odds with Lenin's views, refused to publish his *Materialism and Empirio-criticism* in the St. Petersburg–based *Znanie (Knowledge)*. Lenin asked Luxemburg to write a notice about this work for *Die Neue Zeit,* which she did; but the friendly gesture could not halt the Russians' infighting. Invited to lecture at the Russian Social Democratic Workers' Party School on Capri, organized under Gorkij's aegis, she was not sure, she wrote to Jogiches, whether she should accept "in view of the hostility between the Capri colony and Lenin." The tug-of-war persisting among the Russians steadily undermined their authority in western Europe. Their "Tatar Marxism . . . creates a psychological pressure to curb their arrogance," Luxemburg claimed. Discussing the strategy of the Polish Social Democracy (SDKPiL) with Jogiches, she wrote: "Whether the Bolsheviks are now indeed undermining party unity and are too bossy is hard for me to say; I have not yet noticed it . . . I don't see any reason for us to withdraw from the Central Committee [of the Russian Social Democratic Workers' Party] . . . Instead we should be using *that platform* for counteraction. In general, an open war with the Bolsheviks seems to me very difficult for *us* . . . A split between us and the Bolsheviks is bound to bring the chaos in the party to a peak, and that will play into the hands of the Mensheviks who are the most dangerous plague."[9]

To balance the "Mongolian savagery" of the Russians, the careful practicability of the Germans, and the tensions in the International between socialists of various nationalities, Luxemburg needed Jogiches's political expertise and his moral support. At the beginning of her career, she needed him because she was unknown and overawed by the powerful German Social Democratic Party; now she needed him because she was known and determined to fight that party. She had created her own socialism together with Jogiches, and he alone understood why it fit neither the German nor the Russian party line.

Luxemburg's concept of socialism emerged from her differences with Marx, the SPD, and Lenin. Its main tenets were elaborated, however fragmentarily, in her 1918 assessment of the Russian Revolution and were interspersed throughout her entire work. The common denominator in Rosa's concept of socialism was freedom to "think differently." Her commitment to revolution was fundamentally a moral matter—an obligation to fight for a more humane social system. Humanity's progress was inevitably linked to moral virtue. *Realpolitik*, whether conceived by Marx, Kautsky, or Lenin, was immoral and therefore worthless. She stressed an ethical dimension and the idealism of workers while Marx stressed the inexorable laws of history, Kautsky the welfare of the workers, and Lenin the dictatorship of the proletariat. Because she did not create a comprehensive work on social change, she was largely discounted as a theorist or an innovative political thinker. Yet her contribution to the national question was no less valid theoretically than that of Lenin; and it was certainly a consistent deduction from Marx's teaching.

Her ideas appear in various publications and statements. The 1904 article "Organizational Questions of the Russian Social Democrats" refuted Lenin's basic doctrines, which in her view distorted "revolutionary Marxism." In 1906, "The Mass Strike, the Political Party and the Trade Unions" expanded her criticism of "central party authority" in contrast to spontaneous mass strikes—the expression of the workers' readiness to determine their fate by themselves. In a speech delivered in London at the Fifth Congress of the Russian Social Democratic Workers' Party in 1907, she argued against armed insurrection and artificial means to "unleash" a revolution. And the 1908 "The National Question and Autonomy" condemned nationalism as a divisive force.

According to scientific socialism, Luxemburg argued, "revolution is above all a profound radical change in social class relations" which affects the consciousness and attitudes of the people.[10] "Marxism contains two crucial elements: the element of analysis and critique, and the element of the active will of the working class . . . A Marxist . . . should assess conditions from the summit of theory, not from the lowest depth of a passing day and temporary circumstances." Marx's theory, she maintained, was reduced by his interpreters to "shapeless pulp," and she took it upon herself to continue his work as she understood it.[11] She conceived of Marxism as a humanistic philosophy capable of restoring wholeness to people. The "Marxist jargon," which supplied fuel for demogogues and corrupted the intellect, she found deceptive and dangerous. "Rosa Luxemburg," wrote György Lukács, "was the only disciple of Marx who effectively continued his life work in both economic theory and economic method."[12]

It can be argued that Luxemburg's ideas were not original, that anarchists had advocated mass strike earlier, that she took from Marx the idea of internationalism and from Moses the idea of social justice. She readily acknowledged her debts to thinkers and philosophers, to the entire Western tradition, and often used historical analysis as a point of departure. Yet she created a concept of socialism that was her own, socialism the people themselves demanded, as reflected in the spontaneous revolutions in Hungary in 1956, Czechoslovakia in 1968, and Poland in 1980.

While the International was confronted by increasing nationalism, while the German socialists were backing the growing power of the Prussian state, and Lenin was arguing for national self-determination, Luxemburg was working on "The National Question and Autonomy," published in Polish in 1908 as a series of articles in the *Social-Democratic Review*. Luxemburg was not alone in the belief that nationalism in Europe was on the decline. "No influential thinker . . . foresaw its future—at any rate, no one clearly foretold it," Isaiah Berlin wrote in 1972. "Nationalism was, by and large, regarded in Europe as a passing phase."[13] Luxemburg was of course aware that people have a need to belong to a group. That group, in her view, was to be the international proletariat, shaped by a common way of life and defined in terms not of nation, race, or heredity but of a community of interests. Her idea stemmed from Marx's proletarians—people with no national allegiance.

That her articles on the national question rather aggressively defied Lenin did not cloud Luxemburg's personal relations with him.

Lenin was conscious of Luxemburg's position in the German Social Democratic Party and her influence with Kautsky, who had not yet earned the distinction of being the "renegade Kautsky" he became to generations of Soviet-educated people. The SPD had influence and money, both badly needed by the Bolsheviks, and in addition Luxemburg was in the leadership of the Polish Social Democratic Party (SDKPiL), whose support they also needed. But Lenin's respectful attitude toward Luxemburg was not motivated by self-interest alone—he recognized her fine mind. He visited her together with his wife, Krupskaja, when Luxemburg was putting the final touches on "The National Question," and after its publication in 1909 sent her his *Materialism and Empirio-criticism* with a friendly inscription.

Nationalism preoccupied Luxemburg all her life. The very reason for creating the SDKPiL was her disagreement with the Polish Socialist Party on the question of Poland's independence. Her first articles on that issue were published in 1893, and her doctoral dissertation provided the economic rationale against separation from Russia. In "The National Question" she attempted to give universal validity to her argument against nationalism. The international socialist revolution would end national domination, as it would end exploitation, gender inequality, and racial oppression. Just as the "right to work" would cease to be an empty phrase once capitalism, with its chronic unemployment, was abolished, so would the "right to freedom" of a nation. "In a class society 'the nation' as a homogeneous socio-political entity does not exist." Only classes exist within one nation, "with antagonistic interests and 'rights.' "[14]

Though the starting point of Luxemburg's deliberations was invariably Poland, where, she argued, the interests of the proletariat clashed with the nationalism of the gentry and the petite bourgeoisie, the butt of her criticism was Social Democracy. Social Democracy, she said, was obligated to "realize not the right of nations to self-determination but only the right of the working class . . . to self-determination."[15] The analogy drawn between the right to national self-determination and the right to free speech, free press, and free association and assembly was fallacious, she maintaineed; the two had a "certain superficial similarity," but lay on "different historical levels." The latter group of rights were "legal forms of existence in a mature bourgeois society," while the right to self-determination was a "metaphysical formulation of an idea that in bourgeois society is completely nonexistent and can be realized only under a socialist regime."[16] That Marx advocated Poland's independence only showed "how deeply Marx was in error," for he also predicted the disappearance of the Czechs, "whose vitality the Austrians find so troublesome today." But then "Marx never claimed to be infallible."[17]

A socialist regime in which individuals are tied together "by harmony and solidarity" would create a "nation" by common consensus. The concept of a nation's right to self-determination is abstract, for we do not know who constitutes that "nation" or who has the authority and the right to speak for it. "How can we find out what the 'nation' actually wants? Is there even one political party that would claim that it alone . . . truly expresses the will of the 'nation'?" Even the German Social Democracy "is not and does not claim to be the embodiment of the will of the majority. It expresses only the will and the consciousness of the most advanced and most revolutionary section of the urban-industrial proletariat." Although that party, with its three and a quarter million voters, was the most powerful in Germany, it was "a minority compared to the eight million voters for bourgeois parties and the thirty million who have the right to vote . . . The German nation then 'determines itself' by electing a majority of conservatives, clerics, and freethinkers, and puts its political fate into their hands."[18]

It is sufficient to look at the long list of Russian socialist parties represented at a conference in Paris in 1904 to understand why Luxemburg opposed Lenin's concept of the right to national self-determination. The participants were the Lithuanian Social Democracy, the Ukranian Socialist Party, the Georgian Social Revolutionary Federalists, the Armenian Social Democracy, the Belorussian Hromada, and the Armenian Revolutionary Federation. Many other nationalities and ethnic groups within the Russian Empire were absent. At the other end of the ethnic spectrum, Luxemburg explained, was the United States of America, where a "loose and voluntary union" was transformed by the 1787 Constitution into "a unified state with a central legislative authority and a central executive."[19]

Differing motives have been attributed to Luxemburg's extreme antinationalism. Long before Stalin invented the phenomenon of the "rootless cosmopolitan"—a Jew hostile to the national feelings of the working class—some people pointed to Luxemburg's Jewish origin, some to her stateless status (there was no Polish state), and some to her mixed heritage. Luxemburg considered herself a citizen of the world and wanted socialism without nationalism. This was consistent with her adolescent faith in Adam Mickiewicz's ideals, which matured when geopolitical reality called for concrete solutions. If there was a hope of ending exploitation and bloodshed, it lay with the international brotherhood of workers. Her lack of sympathy for national aspirations may have stemmed from her experience as a Pole and as a Jew. Still, Julian Marchlewski, who was half-German, and Feliks Dzierżyński, a Lithuanian Pole, also did not support Poland's independence. For Germans, Frenchmen, or Russians, internationalism was a theoretical concept; it did not involve renunciation of national independence. Marx or Kautsky, Lenin or Jaurès could engage in philosophical discussions about the advantages of internationalism without implicating their own status or that of their countries. Not so with Luxemburg.

Of course Luxemburg, along with others, underestimated the force of nationalist sentiment and overestimated the solidarity of the workers. However, in 1918 when Stalin declared that "the principle of self-determination must be an instrument in the struggle for socialism and must be subordinated to the principles of socialism," she was sadly vindicated.[20]

Until the outbreak of World War I, Luxemburg's stature continued to grow—"It must be a peculiar feeling to be in the center of history," someone remarked to her.[21] Her fame spread throughout Europe and reached the United States. She had friends and comrades, a rich social life, a nicely furnished apartment complete with maid and pet, and financial security. Italy and Switzerland were her favorite vacationing places, painting and gardening her favorite pastimes. She skated and studied English, visited museums and exhibitions, delighted in reading novels and poetry in five languages, enjoyed the company of artists and intellectuals, and liked automobile trips. Elegantly dressed, she attended concerts, theater, and the opera, escorted by Hans Diefenbach, the painter Hans Kautsky (Karl's brother), or another of her artist friends. No one was as popular with the workers as she was; no one drew such large crowds. The position in the Party School enhanced her prestige and provided a handsome income and another group of admirers—the students. Her journalism enjoyed a wide readership, her speeches enthusiastic audiences. Her life, private and public, to all appearances was happy and fulfilled.

It was yet another of the illusions Luxemburg was so adept at creating for the outside world. Immense energy went into building that image. She paid for it with sleepless nights, bouts of depression, and a loneliness that grew inside her like a weed. Role-playing was an enormous drain on her psychic and physical health; except with Jogiches, she was always on stage, in costume and makeup, perfect.

Perhaps most painful was the realization that after all these years she did not belong anywhere. She had made her home in a country where she remained an outsider. Goethe and Bach might carry her away, but the Germans did not. At a Beethoven concert, "the reaction of the audience made me shudder . . . I was sick to my stomach"; her suggestion to discuss *Anna Karenina* with her students elicited a remark that there was "too much about love" in the novel. Tolstoy has nothing in common with culture or art, she was told by "these 'heirs of the classical philosophy.' "[22] And their attitude to social change was similar. For the Poles no great idea was too unrealistic, no great cause unworthy of sacrifice. She was repelled by the German socialist leaders, who were unwilling to exchange their comfortable houses for the barricades. Distraught because of her alienation, anguished by her unfulfilled dreams, Luxemburg was becoming more uncompromising and more belligerent.

The sheer number of battles Luxemburg waged in the years 1910–1913 indicates her mood. Kautsky and Bebel, Lenin and Radek, the German Social Democracy and the Russian Social Democratic Workers' Party, the opposition within the Polish Social Democracy, and the Polish nationalists—each individual or group that crossed her she dealt with ruthlessly and sometimes viciously.

Although Karl Kautsky was her promoter and personal friend, Luxemburg seemed to share Marx's opinion of the renowned theorist: "a small-minded mediocrity," Marx observed, "too clever by half, industrious in a certain way, busying himself with statistics from which he does not derive anything intelligent, belonging by nature to the tribe of Philistines."[23] Yet early in her German career she and Kautsky were the sole defenders of the extreme left, and their common political platform drew them together. Kautsky played a crucial role in her success, and his friendship eased her way to the top. It was on his recommendation that she was offered the professorship in 1907 at the Party School—the only woman on the distinguished faculty.

The polemic with Kautsky that ended their relationship began with his refusal to publish Luxemburg's article on mass strike in *Die*

Neue Zeit unless she deleted a passage urging the establishment of a republic in Germany. The article, "What Next?," was turned down by *Vorwärts* and finally appeared in March 1910 in *Dortmunder Arbeiterzeitung* without the offending passage. Kautsky wounded her not because he refused to publish the article—this had happened before—but because he disagreed with her political stance. "I'm contemplating," she wrote to Luise Kautsky, "whether I should next drop the school and move into the country"; in fact, she was contemplating how to return the blow.[24] In the polemic that ensued, Luxemburg was at her poisonous best. That she was vindicated by the popularity among the workers of her idea of mass strike did not appease her.* As evidenced by her letters to Jogiches and to Costia Zetkin, she spent days and nights preparing ripostes. Her "What Next?" was answered by Kautsky's "What Now?," his "Road to Power" by her "Attrition or Fight?" Kautsky then responded with "Between Baden and Luxemburg," making a pun on her name.

The battle was not over words, however, it was over the redefinition of roles. In her articles Luxemburg maintained that workers should be encouraged to take charge of their own destinies, with mass strike their main tool. The party leadership should yield their power and, as the vanguard of the workers, help them to end the domination of the economic and political forces that manipulated them. The SPD should redefine itself; it still failed to demand a republic, thus playing into the hands of a united front of bourgeois parties.

Luxemburg openly challenged the SPD establishment, and she paid for it. Editors who had solicited her articles were now turning her down. "I'm in a fine mess," she wrote to Jogiches. "*Vorwärts* refused to publish my article . . . *Neue Zeit* refused to publish my response." And a few days later: "*Dortmunder* [*Arbeiterzeitung*] turned down my article . . . and sent it to Bremen. Whether Bremen will accept it devil only knows."[25]

The Luxemburg-Kautsky polemic went down in party history less because of its intellectual depth or the merits or demerits of mass strike

---

*Rosa dispatched the following clipping to her family in Warsaw: "If the mere appearance of comrade Luxemburg was greeted by enthusiastic cheers and her statements were often interrupted by stormy applause, the end of her speech was met with a thunderous ovation. . . . Even on the street she was loudly cheered and her way back to the hotel turned into a triumphant procession. The meeting and the mood of the audience proved that the Hagen workers allowed themselves to hold a view on mass strike different from that . . . held in some circles of the Party leadership." Luksemburg, *Listy* 3:176.

than because of its vindictiveness. For several months it was the *coup de théâtre* whose every successive act raised a flurry. Luxemburg's old-time foes reveled. "Have a look now at your dear Rosa," Austrian socialist leader Victor Adler wrote to August Bebel, "how Karl [Kautsky] is suffering at the hands of his good friend . . . the poisonous bitch will do a lot of damage yet, all the more serious because she is dangerously shrewd."²⁶ Luxemburg protested to Luise Kautsky that her husband stabbed her, Rosa, in the back, and Kautsky wrote his mother that the "heaviest cannons" are just about to be rolled out, while Bebel told Kautsky that the entire polemic was nothing but grist for the enemy's mill. "I have the impression that you're overwrought," Bebel wrote to him. "The entire story with Rosa would have taken a different turn but for your nervousness . . . you should have told Rosa: all right, I'll take your article but *when* I consider it *suitable*. She could then complain, but not lament about partiality, and we would have had peace for the next few months."²⁷ But there was no going back, and Luxemburg could rightfully "lament" that her own Party was trying to silence her. In fairness Bebel admitted that although the world was having a good laugh over the conflict, Rosa was essential to the party and certainly to the Party School, where she was the best teacher. Kautsky, for his part, was pleased that the world would no longer see him and Luxemburg as "Siamese twins."²⁸

The storm abated when Kautsky suffered a nervous breakdown in August 1910 and spent several months in a sanatorium. "Some people gave me to understand it was my fault," Luxemburg wrote to Jogiches.²⁹ At that point Bebel wrote to Luise Kautsky claiming that her husband's condition was due to Luxemburg's attempt, two years earlier, to wreck their marriage.* Although the timing and the circumstances fail to bear out Bebel's imputation, it is possible that Kautsky broke down under Luxemburg's vitriolic attacks. She might have seen him as a symbol of the decay in the SPD, and he bore the brunt of her love-hate attitude toward Germans and Germany. They were not on speaking terms until the last meeting of the International, in July 1914.

---

*Early in 1908 Luise Kautsky left her family and went to Vienna. Her letters to her husband reveal that she was contemplating leaving him for his brother Hans. She pleaded with her husband to let her have their youngest son, Benedikt. Eventually, however, Luise Kautsky returned to her family. Her letters prove that not Luxemburg but Luise's personal conflict caused the temporary breakdown in the Kautskys' marriage. (International Institute of Social History, Amsterdam, Kautsky Collection.)

With the Kautsky polemic still in the air, Luxemburg had a bitter falling-out with the venerable August Bebel. The issue was the "Morocco crisis." The appearance of the German cruiser *Panther* in Agadir, Morocco, in July 1911 was regarded by a segment of European opinion as a provocation against France, possibly leading to war. The International Socialist Bureau considered the situation dangerous enough to call an emergency meeting. On the eve of the Reichstag election, the SPD was more eager to canvass votes than to inflate the incident. On behalf of the SPD, Hermann Molkenbuhr informed the Bureau by letter that a Morocco conference had a low priority at that point. The meeting did not take place, and the crisis blew over; but not so Luxemburg's outrage. First, she was dismayed by the SPD's growing efforts to be represented in the Reichstag; second, she disapproved of playing down a potentially explosive international incident for the sake of domestic policy; and third, she objected to important decisions being made by the SPD leadership without consulting the workers. After much soul-searching, she published Molkenbuhr's letter along with a terse criticism. Bebel was indignant. At the Jena Party Congress in September 1911 he publicly accused Luxemburg of "serious indiscretion" and dishonorable behavior, clearly aiming at destroying her political credibility. Her unshakable rebuttal and the antiwar sentiment that was running high saved Luxemburg from being ostracized. But she did not forget Bebel's attack. Several months later she wrote to Costia Zetkin: "I won't let up on this gang and stand by idly. At yesterday's gigantic meeting . . . I spoke harshly of Bebel, and the people were with me. Next week I'll speak in the same spirit in the first electoral district in Berlin, and if I can manage I'll speak still more harshly."[30]

However harshly she spoke of Bebel, a trusted old friend, she certainly did not restrain herself at all over the notorious "Radek case." A young Polish Jew and an unusually gifted journalist and orator, Karl Radek (his real name was Sobelson) was a devoted follower of Luxemburg. His pen drew her attention as early as 1905. "Watch out for this Radek," she alerted Jogiches, "he writes for us [the SDKPiL] superbly."[31] "You'll certainly like him," she wrote, "he looks very original, slightly resembling Trotsky with those 'curls' of his." She herself treated the twenty-year-old youth "pretty coolly, or rather with reserve," in her words, but she asked Jogiches to be "lenient" with him.[32] She disliked Radek's "coarse" argumentative voice and manners, and although she did not want to antagonize the new acquisition of a party chronically short of good writers, she kept him at arm's length. In 1910 he was still "very obedient" but was becoming too "self-important."[33] A year later came the split within the SDKPiL and with it Radek's downfall.

Political friction kept the SDKPiL on the brink of division for years. "The main cause of dissatisfaction and opposition to the policy of the party's leadership, in which the dominant influence of Tyszka [Jogiches] consolidated after the [1910] August conference . . . was and is the method employed by the leadership," wrote Zdzisław Leder, Jogiches's close collaborator.[34] The lack of strong ties between the leadership in Berlin that issued the orders and the rank and file in Warsaw that was expected to carry them out exacerbated the antagonism. Even his close comrades balked at Jogiches's iron hand. Julian Marchlewski refused to work with him. "I cannot go on," he wrote to Feliks Dzierżyński, "and feel that the dam is going to break open any time. I can't help it—Leo has his work style, I have mine."[35] "You should try to control yourself," Luxemburg cautioned Jogiches, "you're humiliating Adolf [Warszawski] and treating him like dirt . . . and he too may get bitter."[36] However unpleasant, these troubles were trivial compared with the political differences between Berlin and Warsaw that surfaced around 1908 and triggered a split within the SKDPiL in 1912.

Radek joined the "splitters," that is, the opposition centered in the Warsaw Committee and directed against the Berlin-based Central Committee of the SKDPiL. The amount of time and energy Luxemburg put into destroying Radek seemed puzzling. He was not influential in the Polish or German movement, nor was he an irreplaceable asset or a potential danger. Yet the anti-Radek campaign Luxemburg launched was unique in the annals of both parties. Having expelled him from the SDKPiL, she wanted the SPD to follow suit. For more than a year Radek was a fixture in her letters to Jogiches. "Let me know immediately what steps should be taken against Radek; should a response of mine be published in *V[orwärts]* or will the party respond also on my behalf?" she wrote in September 1912. "If we could prove Radek's guilt to the Germans beyond a reasonable doubt, it would be our salvation," ran another message. "Read carefully the enclosed report concerning R.!! Naturally, we must react immediately," she pressed. "It would be a great victory if the [SPD Executive Committee] wrote the promised letter . . . which, published by us, will be a new slap in the face for R."³⁷ And so it went in letter after letter, breathlessly, urgently, mercilessly. An SDKPiL commission was convened in Paris in September 1913; the Russian Social Democratic Workers' Party (RSDRP), the Bund, and the Latvian Social Democracy participated in the investigation of Radek's case. The accusations against Radek ranged from the alleged theft of a coat while he was a student in Kraków to the embezzlement of party monies and failure to pay party dues. Technicalities, such as Radek's neglect in properly applying for membership in the German Social Democratic Party, were used to close the doors to any socialist party to him. None of the charges touched on the genuine reason—Radek's defection from Luxemburg's camp.

In his well-known *Meine Abrechnung* [*My Reckoning*] Radek repudiated all the charges, in vain. Finally he was saved by the Bolshevik revolution and became Lenin's expert on German affairs, a member of the Central Committee of the Bolshevik Party, and a major force in the Third (Communist) International. He was obedient to Lenin, to Trotsky, and to Stalin, in that order. He stood trial in 1936 and disappeared in 1939, a perfect example of the adage "He who lives by the sword perishes by the sword." After their breach Luxemburg met him once, in 1918, when Lenin sent him to Berlin to make contact with the German Left. She required a great deal of persuasion to shake hands with him. The meeting was cool and ineffective—its main subject was terrorism. "After all, terrorism never defeated us," Luxemburg said upon hearing that Feliks Dzierżyński headed the Cheka.* "Why should *we* have to depend on it?" Radek, from his new heights, presented a deft argument in defense of the use of terror.³⁸

Some scholars have found Luxemburg's attitude toward Radek irrational at best and paranoid at worst. As often happens, however, her behavior was examined in a vacuum or interpreted to fit the preconceived notion of the quarrelsome female. Her vehement reaction to Radek's betrayal may have been triggered by her sense of being betrayed by everyone. By joining the defectors, Radek had stabbed Jogiches in the back. Revenging herself on Radek, she retaliated for all the disillusions, private and public, she had suffered over the years. For

---

*Russian acronym for All-Russian Extraordinary Commission to Combat Counterrevolution, Sabotage, and Blackmarketeering; the forerunner of the GPU, NKVD, and KGB.

once she could make a show of strength, and she did. She cared little about Radek himself. But she cared for Jogiches and he had been betrayed; and she cared for the unity of the party, both Polish and Russian, and it was constantly being ripped apart. In her eyes Radek represented a symbol of disloyalty, corruption, and treachery.

As her political isolation grew, words like "crush" or "destroy" became more frequent in her letters to Jogiches. Used with reference to the opposition within the Polish Social Democracy, to the German Social Democracy, or to individuals, the terms aptly reflect her frame of mind. Nor did she stop at words. "I have a certain idea I'm *almost* sure about but not entirely," she wrote to Jogiches on the eve of the split in the SDKPiL in 1912. "The Central Committee [the Berlin-based leadership of the SDKPiL] should respond to the sedition of the Warsaw Committee [the "splitters"] . . . with an immediate public statement that the W[arsaw] C[ommittee] is in the hands of *agents provocateurs;* that names cannot yet be named but the C.C. [Central Committee] is on their track; that the C.C., reluctant to hurt members who are in [the Warsaw Committee's] hands out of blindness or ignorance, exhausted all means available . . . to fight that plague. Now, however, party *duty* requires action. The C.C. has no right to procrastinate lest the Azev monster corrupt the spirit of the party. One blow deserves another. One ought to act and fear nothing." Luxemburg thought that Jogiches might object to her "idea" which amounted to a monstrous character assassination of a group of socialists guilty only of political differences; for no crime was more hideous than that committed by Evno Azev, the notorious *agent provocateur* who infiltrated the Russian revolutionary movement on the orders of the tsarist police. "There'll be a hue and cry, but one mustn't be afraid," Luxemburg warned Jogiches, anticipating his reservations.[39] In fact, of course, the issue was one of ethics, not of fear; but Luxemburg had pushed the right button. Jogiches consented, as did other members of the leadership, and Luxemburg's "certain idea"—one that became Stalin's favorite means of destroying political opponents—was put into practice. There can be no justification for Luxemburg's act, the false accusation that tsarist agents infiltrated the Warsaw Committee. As Joseph Conrad said: "Principles won't do." Luxemburg was gradually becoming part of the machine that devours its own children.

Luxemburg and Jogiches crusaded for unity within the Russian Social Democratic Workers' Party (RSDRP), a concern Lenin did not share, and they were unequivocally opposed to any relations with the Polish Socialist Party. The strife within the Russian and Polish parties, causing factions within factions and warring splinter groups, left the International so perplexed that the SDKPiL asked Lenin to clarify the matter for the sake of "foreigners unfamiliar with conditions in Russia" and in Poland.[40]

After the 1912 split in the Polish Social Democracy (the factions reunited in 1916), the feud between Jogiches and Lenin, with Luxemburg in the middle, came into the open. The SDKPiL was conspicuously absent from the Russian Social Democratic Workers' Party conference in Prague in 1912. The press organ of the SDKPiL, *The Red Banner*, called the conference a "farcical Leninist lark" and said: "Already in 1904 comrade Luxemburg . . . severely criticized Lenin's anti-Marxist and purely bourgeois idea of a political party in which the leader is everything and the masses are nothing."[41]

Lenin paid little heed to such epithets but he could ill afford to ignore a more substantial vengeance Jogiches had in store for him. Money, Jogiches knew, was a powerful weapon; and money was Lenin's perennial need. A wealthy Russian socialist sympathizer, N. P. Schmit, had left a considerable bequest to the Russian Social Democratic Workers' Party. The inheritance, despite Lenin's protests, was deposited with the German Social Democratic Party in 1910. Clara Zetkin, Karl Kautsky, and Franz Mehring were authorized to disburse funds at their discretion to factions within the RSDRP and to the member parties. In 1911 and 1912 Lenin went to Berlin several times to negotiate with Clara Zetkin and Kautsky for the allotment of money to the Bolshevik faction of the RSDRP. Aware of Jogiches's hostility and his influence on Luxemburg and also of her friendship with the trustees, Lenin paid Luxemburg four visits in February 1912, doubtless to gain her support.

In a letter to Costia Zetkin, Luxemburg denied that money was used to blackmail the Bolsheviks into coming to terms with the Mensheviks. "You're wrong with regard to the Russians," she wrote. "No one wants to keep them together merely by means of money; the *majority* of the party wants unity."[42] But earlier she had written to Jogiches: "Quite frankly I do not at all like the idea of snatching away from [the Bolsheviks] their part of the legacy . . . This business smacks, pardon the expression, of blackmail or even robbery. I think that the Bolsheviks will finally feel as if they have leeches sucking their blood, and would prefer an open fight with the Mensheviks to a forced unity

178

with us. Should the matter explode into a scandal, our position in the Russian party will be seriously undermined."[43] Yet she yielded to Jogiches's pressure and perhaps underwent a change of heart herself, for her subsequent letters to Jogiches suggest that she was trying to manipulate the trustees to the disadvantage of the Bolsheviks.

Rosa Luxemburg was alone; she was fighting Kautsky and Bebel, Lenin and Radek, the socialist parties, the bourgeois governments, capitalism, nationalism, and militarism. Besieged, she seemed more satisfied with life and with herself than in the bland years following her return from the rebellious city of Warsaw. She no longer fought for Costia Zetkin or against Leo Jogiches. She fought to kill the emptiness of her personal life, eager for the world to see that she was unvanquished. Her frenzy was fueled by the attacks of the radical, nationalistic Polish intelligentsia. Its Warsaw-based organ, *Myśl Niepodległa (Independent Thought),* was edited and published by Andrzej Niemojewski, a well-known Polish writer and journalist vehemently opposed to the Social Democracy of the Kingdom of Poland and Lithuania. The SDKPiL, composed of agitator-Jews, the journal claimed, "is tied by race and family to the rest of the Jews; these purely anthropological ties are so strong that one who dares to question the ideology of any Jew is immediately confronted by an alliance of a Talmud Jew, a socialist Jew, and a liberal Jew."[44] Accusations that Jews had deliberately fomented strikes in 1905 in order to shed the blood of Polish workers were an almost perfect parallel to charges of ritual murder.

In 1910 *Independent Thought* carried a series of articles attacking Luxemburg. Her physical disability was an example of the degeneration of the Jews, the journal maintained. "Rosa Luxemburg does not even know what national feelings are," wrote Niemojewski. "She misses no opportunity to trample upon them and shows nothing but derision for them. The reason is simple. It is a category of feelings alien to her . . . But then, what can Poles mean to her?"[45] Another attack stated: "The ancestors of the lady assiduously supplied the common Polish people with vodka. Rosa Luxemburg is beyond the stage of selling vodka, but what she gives the common people to drink, in the guise of articles and pamphlets, has all the qualities of a literary alcoholic beverage . . . The kikes . . . question Poland's independence . . . Poland and the Polish worker can do without masters . . . who bestow upon us their Semitic hysteria and their hereditary hatred of our mother country."[46]

The intellectual level of the arguments hardly merited attention, but the SDKPiL was up in arms. This episode showed that Luxemburg was not impervious to racial abuse, as had often been maintained. Indeed, her reaction in the past had been different; she took particular pains to ignore racial slurs. During the Lübeck Party Congress in 1901 a deputy, Richard Fischer, had accused her of "falsifying" and "twisting" the opinions of some comrades. Wolfgang Heine followed suit, declaring that Polish and Russian Jews—he was referring to Rosa Luxemburg and Alexander Parvus-Helphand—had abused German hospitality. "If someone comes to us as a guest," he said, "and spits in our parlor," he cannot but be objectionable.[47] Luxemburg ignored Heine; but in a written declaration, which Kautsky refused to publish, she challenged Fischer to prove his charges.

This time she took her defense into her own hands. First, the leadership of the SDKPiL asked August Bebel, Karl Kautsky, Franz Mehring, Otto Bauer, and Jean Jaurès to take a public stand, and they obliged. Their articles denouncing anti-Semitism without mentioning Luxemburg by name were published in the fall of 1910 in *Młot (The Hammer)*, the SDKPiL paper edited by Jogiches. And then, between September and December Luxemburg herself published at least ten unsigned articles in the Polish and German press in response to Niemojewski.

Although in her letters to Jogiches Luxemburg emphasized that she did not identify her personal affairs with those of the party, she herself directed the rebuttal. In the first round, statements had to be obtained: "To obtain and publish ten or twelve letters [to the editor] in *The Hammer* is wrong in my opinion," she wrote to Jogiches in October 1910. "To publish, let's say, articles by Jaurès, Vandervelde, Bebel and Bauer is a different matter . . . This is . . . proof enough that the International is behind us."[48] Julian Marchlewski was to solicit an article from Kautsky and was dispatched to Paris to solicit another from Jaurès. The second round concerned logistics. "*The Hammer* is overloaded," Luxemburg wrote to Jogiches, referring to the 8 October issue carrying three articles devoted to Niemojewski. The next issue, of 15 October, contained two articles on the same subject, both written by her. "In my view that should be avoided," she told Jogiches. "*One* article per issue will do, otherwise the reader will simply get tired." And she added, "*Monotony* is of no advantage; the readers should be won over, not terrorized."[49] Writing anonymously, Luxemburg referred to herself in the third person—as Mrs. Rosa Luxemburg—lending a slightly amusing air to the deadly serious battle.

The European Social Democrats were genuinely concerned with the attacks on Luxemburg and on the Polish Social Democracy and were dismayed by the blatant anti-Semitism. It was one thing for August Bebel to confess privately to Kautsky that Luxemburg aroused anti-Semitic sentiments and another to see her vilified on account of her origins. Luxemburg herself had accused the Bund publicly (at the Fifth Congress of the Russian Social Democratic Workers' Party in London in 1907) of behaving like hucksters, only to find herself lumped together with them.

In her correspondence with Jogiches, frequent and animated during the anti-Niemojewski campaign, terms such as "Jew" or "anti-Semitism" are conspicuously absent. *The Hammer* is mentioned; so are Niemojewski and *Independent Thought;* and strategy and tactics are discussed. But Luxemburg's letters, which after all were strictly personal, in no way reveal that the subject of the "Niemojewski polemic" was anything other than an ideological difference between *Independent Thought* and the SDKPiL. The pains she took to avoid writing the word *Jew,* so ominous-sounding when Niemojewski used it to describe her, disclose the depth of her fears. At the time of the Dreyfus affair, she went out of her way to prove that the matter concerned the French bourgeoisie and should be used by socialists to consolidate their power. Ironically, Jaurès invoked the Dreyfus affair in his plea to stop the anti-Semitic campaign in Poland, pointing out that in France during that "nationalistic orgy . . . pseudo-patriotism and anti-Semitic savagery . . . unleashed . . . atrocity and a dangerously licentious reaction."[50] That the same reactionary forces stood against Dreyfus and Luxemburg she could not admit even to herself.

Not for a moment did Luxemburg slow the frantic pace of her life while she was conducting her battles. If anything, the strife seemed to recharge her energies. She had time for leisure and entertainment, for Costia Zetkin and Hans Diefenbach, for letters to Jogiches and her family in Warsaw, for writing two books and about 270 articles; she attended congresses, toured Germany making speeches, and taught in the Party School.

The Party School had been founded in 1906 to provide a solid education to party and trade union activists. Luxemburg's position was well paid—3,000 marks per semester—but demanding. From October to March, she lectured for two hours four times a week on political economy, Marxist theory, and the history of trade unions. Preparation took several hours, usually in the evening, and school exhausted her. A former student, Mrs. Rose Frölich, remembered the lectures as an intellectual feast.[51] Luxemburg's incorporation of the classics of world literature—Shakespeare, Tolstoy, Dostoevsky, Mickiewicz, Goethe, Kleist, de Maupassant, Stendhal—gave her lectures a new dimension. Had Luxemburg conformed to the constraints of the accepted educational system, her lectures would have been lumps of dry data and statistics washed down with propaganda sauce. Literature was to her a source of beauty, a reflection of life. She presented power struggles portrayed by Shakespeare, the corruption of the bourgeoisie depicted by Balzac, and the hypocrisy of the propertied classes described by Tolstoy as examples of an amoral system, dehumanizing and degrading, that socialism would wipe from the face of the earth. Luxemburg forbade taking notes in class lest it distract the students' attention; but she rigorously required careful study of assigned reading and warmly encouraged discussion with her. August Bebel's opinion that Luxemburg was the best teacher in the Party School was not unfounded. Although the teaching staff included well-educated men such as socialist theorists Franz Mehring and August Bebel and outstanding lawyers such as Kurt Rosenfeld and Arthur Stadthagen, no one matched Luxemburg in creativity and inspiration.

Her lectures on political economy were slowly turning into a book that occupied most of her time apart from teaching. Costia Zetkin and Jogiches were kept abreast of its progress. In early spring 1910 she informed Jogiches that the work would be published under the title *Introduction to Political Economy,* both in book form and in eight pamphlets. The manuscript was to be finished in June, and negotiations for a German and a Russian edition were under way. The German publisher forwarded an advance, and now and then Luxemburg told Costia that the money the book would earn would free them from financial concerns. In October the manuscript was ready, and she was checking the quotations and footnotes, although she was still dissatisfied with Marx's analysis of expanded reproduction. "At the end of the second volume of *Das Kapital* I came across Marx's formulations which have long sounded strange to me," she wrote to Costia a year later, in October 1911, and announced her intention of working on a "new, strictly scientific analysis of imperialism and its contradictions."[52] This intellectual exercise was sheer pleasure, she declared, but extremely laborious and time-consuming.

Eventually, the manuscript of *Introduction* was put aside, and Luxemburg embarked instead on research that resulted in her magnum opus, *The Accumulation of Capital,* published in January 1913. Here she advanced the following theory: accumulation can take place only through capitalist expansion into foreign markets or in less-developed parts of the same country. Noncapitalist markets are necessary for capitalism to function and ultimately to survive, yet they are being destroyed as independent entities; thus the capitalist system deprives itself of demand through which to realize the surplus value—a condition for continued accumulation of capital—and inevitably collapses because of the contradiction inherent in the laws governing accumulation. "The time when I worked on *Accumulation* was the happiest in my life," she later wrote to Hans Diefenbach. "I was intoxicated, saw and heard nothing day and night when the problem unraveled so beautifully, and I no longer know what gave me more pleasure, the process of thinking . . . or of creation . . . At one stroke, I wrote [the whole work] within four months—unbelievable!—and without looking at the draft a single time gave it to the publisher."[53]

When the book was published Luxemburg was immediately accused of numerous heresies by the right and by the left in the German Social Democratic Party. The chief accusation was that she had prophesied the inevitable, automatic collapse of capitalism. Indeed, she argued that the disappearance of noncapitalist markets must lead to a deep crisis of capitalism which would make a victorious socialist revolution inevitable. But this "inevitability," according to her, was not merely a mechanistic, "natural," "objective," "automatic" necessity; on the contrary, it would also require the conscious revolutionary activity of the working class.

In the ensuing polemical reviews she was alternately accused of having misinterpreted or distorted Marx and hailed, by Mehring and Marchlewski, as the most knowledgeable interpreter of Marx since Engels. Jogiches pressed her to respond to her critics. As behooved a scholar, she accepted criticism from Franz Mehring, to whom she said: "I was fully aware that . . . the book would at first meet with resistance. Our mandatory 'Marxism,' like a rheumatic elderly uncle, is afraid, unfortunately, of any gust of fresh air, and I know that I'll have to argue quite a lot."[54] About Miron I. Nachimson, an economist and active Bundist, she felt no such constraints. "To defend my [work] against that kike N[achimson] would be ... a disgrace."[55] The controversy stirred by the book prompted Luxemburg to write *Anti-Critique*, considered to be the sequel to *The Accumulation of Capital*.[56]

During World War I Luxemburg began to work on *Anti-Critique*, "which will certainly outlive me," she wrote to Diefenbach. "It is much more mature than *Accumulation*." A model of clarity and simplicity, it was " 'naked' like a block of marble," she felt, unlike Marx's writing in the first volume of *Das Kapital*. "Overloaded with rococo ornaments in Hegel's style," it struck her as "abominable"—a crime, she joked, punishable by the party with five years in prison and ten years loss of civil rights.[57] In *Anti-Critique* Luxemburg pointed out that "Marx himself only posed the question of the accumulation of gross capital" but he went no further.[58] She showed that there were no "experts" on Marxism and that "Marx himself certainly was no 'expert.' " In other words, she defended creativity against dogma. "It has always been the privilege of the 'epigones' to take fertile hypotheses, turn them into rigid dogma, and be smugly satisfied, where a pioneering mind is filled with creative doubt."[59]

13 | *War on War*
1914

IN AUGUST 1911 Luxemburg moved to what became her last home. For a long time she had wanted to get away from Cranachstrasse and painful memories. The move from the Friedenau section to Südende meant saying good-bye to the Kautskys, who had been her family for ten years but whose house was now closed to her. She was leaving a home she had shared with Jogiches. Here also she and Costia Zetkin had become lovers. Once again she was starting a new life.

The apartment at Lindenstrasse No. 2, in a quiet, tree-lined neighborhood on the outskirts of Berlin, was the most spacious Luxemburg had ever had—five rooms and a kitchen. It was pleasantly furnished and later equipped with a telephone. The household and the cat, Mimi, were cared for by Gertrud Zlottko, the maid who stayed with Rosa from 1909 till 1915. Zlottko was more interested in painting and botany than in cooking and cleaning, and she soon became the subject of Luxemburg's private theory on the emancipation of women. Luxemburg insisted that Zlottko learn typing and accounting to qualify for a more appropriate job and, characteristically, urged her to read and improve her mind.

Jogiches had keys to the new aparment, at least when Luxemburg was away. More of the old ties were restored. She asked him to "produce ideas" that she would then elaborate and to read the galleys of *The Accumulation of Capital*, as she had done with her first book fifteen years earlier. Squabbles over the layout or contents of the Polish party journals were less vehement and less acrimonious than in the past. "I do not think a newspaper should be symmetrical, trimmed like an English lawn," Luxemburg wrote to Jogiches. "Rather, it should be somewhat untamed, like a wild orchard, should bristle with life and shine with young talents."[1]

Luxemburg carried on her battles, on the German and the Russian fronts, more assertively than ever. At best there were periods of relative tranquility, at worst harsh polemics. Toward the end of 1913, after a protracted fight, Luxemburg, Mehring, and Marchlewski quit *Leipziger Volkszeitung*, whose editorial policy clashed with their extreme left views, and founded *Sozialdemokratische Korrespondenz*, the forerunner of *Spartakusbriefe* (*Spartacus Letters*).

This event was but a symptom of the deepening division within the German Social Democratic Party (SPD). In the summer of 1913 the SPD deputies to the Reichstag voted for a property tax undisguisedly earmarked for armaments. Luxemburg responded with a series of articles entitled "The Parliamentary Faction in the Reichstag and the Military Estimate," a sharp attack on the SPD for its support of military expenditures. "You don't have to push me," she wrote to Jogiches, who as usual found her pace too slow. "I'm as impatient to see the articles published as you are."[2]

At the meeting of the Bureau of the International in London in December 1913, the never-ending problem of the unity of the Russian Social Democratic Workers' Party was put on the agenda, mainly because of Luxemburg's insistence. "It seems we suffered a complete defeat," she wrote to Jogiches. "Plekhanov didn't come, and neither did Lenin. The Bolsheviks were represented by a complete idiot [M. M. Litvinov], while the Mensheviks came in droves. Kautsky (on behalf of the German Executive Committee) immediately introduced a resolution recommending that the Executive of the Bureau reach an agreement with 'all who consider themselves Social Democrats!' I opposed the resolution but was completely isolated." Eventually two motions emerged: Kautsky's, calling for a meeting of all Russian Social Democratic factions, and Luxemburg's, calling for a congress aimed at unifying Bolsheviks and Mensheviks. Her defeat consisted not merely in having her motion turned down, she explained to Jogiches, but rather in the acceptance of Kautsky's motion. "The old Party is dead," Kautsky declared, "and we can not resurrect it."[3] Luxemburg, for one, believed that they should and they could.

Earlier in 1913, in September Luxemburg had delivered a speech near Frankfurt/Main, urging the German workers not to take up arms against workers of other nationalities. Five months later, on 20 February 1914, she stood trial at the Second Criminal Court in Frankfurt for inciting public disobedience, was convicted, and was sentenced to one year's imprisonment, which she appealed. Her defense attorneys were Paul Levi, a thirty-year-old lawyer from Frankfurt, and Kurt Rosenfeld, a distinguished Berlin jurist. She addressed the court in her own defense, in effect putting the Prussian court on trial and transforming it into a forum for Social Democracy. Published as "Militarism, War and the Working Class," her speech was a brilliant piece of oratory on war and peace and the right of people to determine their destiny.

"Sir," Luxemburg addressed the prosecutor, "if I could assume that you have the . . . capacity to understand how a Social Democrat thinks, and a somewhat nobler view of history, then I would explain to you what I successfully explain at every meeting with the working people—that mass strikes . . . can no more be 'made' than a revolution can be 'made.' Mass strikes are a *stage in the class struggle* that our present development inevitably leads to. Our role, the role of Social Democrats, consists in *clarifying* [this] *to the working class* . . . in order to have them rise to the occasion as an educated, disciplined, mature, determined, and effective class of people." Contrasting the government's policy with that of Social Democrats, she said: "Wars can be conducted only if the working people see them as just and necessary, or at least accept them passively. But once the majority of the working people concludes—and it is precisely the task of Social Democracy to arouse that consciousness and lead them to this conclusion—. . . that wars are barbaric, deeply immoral, reactionary, and against the interests of the people, then wars will become impossible . . . According to the . . . prosecution, the party at war is the *army;* according to us it is *the entire people.* It is the people on whom the decision must rest whether or not to make a war . . . working men and women, old and young, and not the small section of the people wearing the so-called King's uniform." In closing, she spoke in defense of her honor: "The public prosecutor said . . . that I should be imprisoned immediately since 'it would be incomprehensible if the defendant did not attempt flight.' In other words, if I, the public prosecutor, had to serve a year in prison, I would try to escape. *Sir, I do believe that you would run away. A Social Democrat never does. A Social Democrat stands by his deeds and laughs at your judgments.*"[4]

Overnight Luxemburg became a celebrity. Her courage, her defiance, and her wit struck the right chord—some were inspired, some stimulated, some shamed. If she had dreamed of the sweet taste of revenge—for the virtual ban imposed on her articles, for the interpretation of her opinions as treason, and for the abuse heaped upon her—she could now savor it. The SPD newspapers outdid each other in vying for her work. And her public success was underscored by a different kind of conquest—she and Paul Levi, her attorney, became lovers.

The love affair with Levi was brief and intense. It started in the shadow of the trial in February 1914 and lasted for about six months. An abrupt change in the tone and content of Luxemburg's letter to Levi after July 1914 indicates that the intimacy had ended; the friendship survived until her death.

Levi played an unusual role in Luxemburg's life, unlike that played by Jogiches or Zetkin. In taking him as her lover she chose to have an adult relationship with an adult man. She accepted him for what he was: mature, strong, an equal in every respect. She never attempted to educate, shape, or influence Levi. Her letters to him, written between February and November 1914, differ enormously from those she wrote to her former lovers. Private, invented endearments gave place to standard German expressions—*Liebling* (Darling), often with an exclamation mark at the end of the letter, and occasionally *Geliebter* (Beloved). Her letters to him are never seductive or flirtatious, a means of control or a weapon; even in moments of ecstasy they retain the crispness of dry wine.

Paul Levi was born in 1886 in Hechingen, near Stuttgart, into a well-to-do Jewish family. While still a student in the Stuttgart Gymnasium, his interest in politics and the law made him a socialist. His wide-ranging, inquiring mind led him to study the Greek and Roman cultures as well as such seemingly disparate subjects as French and English statesmanship and literature. "Levi, that psychological puzzle," Kark Radek said about him, "a man full of contradictions, a collector of antique vases, interested in Cheops' pyramids . . . he brought to the party barren sceptisim and faithlessness."[5] He read law at the universities of Berlin and Grenoble, earned his degree at Heidelberg University, set up a practice in Frankfurt, and became active in the radical left of the SPD.

Two photographs are preserved that capture his rise and fall. The first, taken in Berlin in 1914, shows a tall, lanky, well-dressed man with an angular, expressive face, a full mouth, and bespectacled eyes under bushy eyebrows. Walking beside him is a woman with a mass of dark hair under a wide-brimmed hat, who barely reaches his shoulder. In the other picture, taken in Moscow in 1920, the same man, now aged and balding, is sitting behind a table piled high with papers, absorbed in thought, seemingly oblivious to three men standing next to him engaged in conversation: Lenin, Bukharin, and Zinovjev. Luxemburg shared in his rise; Lenin caused his fall.

For Levi the relationship with Luxemburg shaped the rest of his life. He never married, though he had women companions, known for their intellect, beauty, and elegance. He devoted his life to carrying on Luxemburg's work. For Luxemburg the brief romance with Levi changed nothing in her personal life. However, he became an important political ally at a time when her uncompromising radicalism left her almost in a void.

In 1914 Luxemburg was still on the warpath within and outside the SPD. She seemed to be proud of her isolation, perhaps because Paul Levi admired and supported her, perhaps because her popularity among the workers was steadily increasing. That it was decreasing among the party elite did not bother her. Her friends remained faithful—Luise Kautsky and Clara Zetkin, Hans Diefenbach and Costia—though only Clara was in a position to give political support. Never kindly disposed toward the women's movement, Luxemburg had seldom written for Clara's magazine. "A Russian woman . . . asked me to write an article about the Woman's Day . . . for *Pravda*," she wrote to Jogiches. "Is it worth my while? Hadn't I better give it to [Clara] Zetkin?"[6] But in 1912, when she had had difficulties placing her work, five out of nine of her articles written in German appeared in Zetkin's *Die Gleichheit*. One was devoted to women, "Women's Voting Rights and the Class Struggle," as was the article "The Proletarian Woman," published in 1914 in *Sozialdemokratische Korrespondenz*. Although she was deeply attached to some women, she retained a slightly patronizing attitude toward women in general; her respect was reserved mainly for men. She endured a Miss Twining, a socialist from Colorado, because it enabled her to brush up on her English, she said. That lady, she wrote to Costia, regretted Germany's small size and asked whether it wouldn't be better for the movement "if Germany were bigger?!"[7] Luxemburg's unique success and the support of Jogiches, Costia, and Paul Levi had spared her the common lot of her female contemporaries, and she saw herself in a world apart. The war, it seems, would somewhat change her perception. She realized then that women were fighting not their inferior status but its result—the lack of power. With no political influence, they were unable to make decisions about themselves, their children, or their country. In 1915 she decided to participate in an International Women's Conference in Bern, but incarceration thwarted her plans.

With the Frankfurt appeal pending, Luxemburg, in a public speech made in Freiburg in March 1914, accused the German military of maltreating soldiers and abusing them psychically and physically. The Minister of War, General von Falkenhayn, had her indicted for insulting military men. Once more Kurt Rosenfeld and Paul Levi acted as her defense attorneys. At the outset Luxemburg's chances did not look bright. Witnesses were slow in coming forward. But two weeks before the opening of the trial she informed Jogiches, "We have 145 and can count on some 200."[8] Both parties were caught by surprise: 1,013 victims of military abuse volunteered to testify for the defense.

The trial, which opened on 29 June 1914 in Berlin, became one of Luxemburg's greatest victories. It was adjourned after two days because in the same month three editors of *Vorwärts* who had published a story about corruption among high-ranking officers were taken to court, and the two interlinked trials were certain to produce adverse publicity. Reopened on 3 July, Luxemburg's trial was again suspended over her vehement protests, this time permanently. It left her triumphant; the prosecution, unwilling to put such a vast number of soldiers on the witness stand, tacitly admitted defeat. Again, Luxemburg had reversed the roles in the courtroom. A satirical magazine carried a cartoon showing a petite woman trying a mammoth general in the prisoner's dock while uniformed skeletons sat on the witness benches.

Though she had been sentenced to one year in prison in the earlier Frankfurt trial, she was nevertheless able to spread her ideas since the appeal procedure took many months. But celebrity inevitably bred hostility. That the "scandalous behavior" of that "impertinent female" was tolerated by the authorities offended the conservatives. She had had the temerity to speak about the "future German republic," a subversive idea if there ever was one. It was not in a mood of hopelessness or despair that, on the eve of the outbreak of the war, Luxemburg was fighting armaments in Germany, exposing the growing naval rivalry between Germany and England, and inciting public disobedience. Her belief in the international solidarity of workers was as firm as her faith in the moral strength and authority of the International. It had been buttressed for several years by the resolution on war jointly amended by Luxemburg and Lenin and adopted at the Congress of the International in Stuttgart in 1907. That resolution stipulated that in case of war the working class was duty-bound to rouse the people and thereby hasten the abolition of capitalist rule. Unlike August Bebel, who recognized the limitations of ideals, theories, and resolutions, Luxemburg could not bring herself to acknowledge that resolutions do not prevent wars. War was unpopular, as the Morocco crisis in 1911 had proved, and Luxemburg was convinced that a general strike on an international scale could avert war. If standing armies were abolished, if workers, conscious of their power, refused to fight, there would be no war.

The ineffectiveness of the International and the unwillingness or inability of its members to recognize their impotence had been eloquently exposed at the Congress in Copenhagen in 1910. When the Serbian delegate bitterly reproached the International for taking no action and only making vague protests after Austria annexed Bosnia two years earlier, the assembly merely listened. The annexation was not even an item on the agenda. In a letter to Costia Zetkin, Luxemburg dismissed the congress as a "waste of time," while to Jogiches she mentioned a variety of subjects that were discussed but passed over in silence the one that four years later would trigger the First World War.[9]

The German Social Democratic Party continued to be looked upon by European socialists as a formidable force, perhaps a savior in need. That its power, achievements, and influence were placed increasingly at the service of the government rather than of the International, as Luxemburg frequently pointed out, seemed not to bother the party leadership greatly. In 1912 there were 110 SPD deputies to the Reichstag; that is, one elector in three voted socialist, giving the party a power unrivaled in any country. But as August Bebel succinctly put it: "The heart of the people turns toward us because we take up the cause of their daily needs."[10] Still Luxemburg believed in the worker, "for whom the highest good, life itself—not to mention material well-being—is worth little compared to the ideals he is fighting for."[11]

The First Balkan War in the summer of 1912 once again demonstrated the unfounded confidence of the International in its ability to effectively prevent war. At the emergency Congress called by the Bureau of the International in Basel in November, there were speeches and resolutions, appeals, declarations and proclamations, marches and demonstrations. "War on war, peace for the world," ran the slogan. Ravaged by illness, August Bebel made his last appearance. He was one of the few seriously alarmed by the prospect of a large-scale international conflict, which he thought was inevitable. Jean Jaurès's spirited oration was long remembered for its forceful defense of universal human values against barbaric warmongers. It easily drowned out the unpleasant truth voiced by Victor Adler: "We do not know how the proletariat will respond when a war breaks out," the Austrian socialist said, "whether it will, like mute sheep, let itself be led to the slaughter."[12]

The Russo-Japanese war of 1905, the Austrian annexation of Bosnia and Herzegovina in 1908, the Italian seizure of Tripoli in 1911, and the two Balkan Wars in 1912 and 1913—ten years of "contained" international conflicts—had inured people to the use of violence, to its relative harmlessness, and to the impunity of its instigators. That and the optimism generated by the International so lulled public opinion that most people were totally unprepared for the 1914 outbreak of war.

With her one-year prison sentence awaiting appeal and the Berlin trial set to open in June, Rosa Luxemburg arrived in Clarens in April 1914 for what was to be her last vacation. She probably spent this vacation with Paul Levi in the same small village on the Lake of Geneva which twenty years before had been a refuge for her and Jogiches. An inveterate letter writer, she sent one postcard to her maid and one letter to Jogiches to caution him against the police, who had arrested Julian Marchlewski. She was being showered with invitations to speak in various districts in Berlin, she reported, "a veritable palace revolution."[13] Indeed, in May and June of 1914 Luxemburg delivered a series of speeches concentrating on militarism, warming up for her courtroom confrontation with the highest German military authorities.

One day before the trial opened in Berlin, on 28 June 1914, Austrian Archduke Franz Ferdinand and his wife were assassinated in

Sarajevo. Assassinations of royalty and prominent figures were not uncommon at the time, and the murder produced no more than short-lived shock. More than three weeks were to elapse before Austria gave an ultimatum to Serbia. June turned into July, Rosa's friends left for the summer holidays, but she was "chained to hot, sweltering Berlin," she wrote to Luise Kautsky on 11 July, "like Prometheus to the rock, although I stole nothing from anyone."[14] Luise, hospitalized in Rome with a bad case of typhoid, received Rosa's next letter, dated 18 July, from Brussels, where Luxemburg was attending a meeting of the Bureau of the International called to discuss the unification of the Russian Social Democrats. On 19 July she returned to Berlin, to be urgently summoned back to Brussels nine days later, on 28 July, when Austria declared war on Serbia. Mobilization in Austria had begun, but "the Executive remained unconvinced throughout our [the International's] deliberations that war between Austria and Serbia meant a general international war," Angelica Balabanoff, the prominent Russian socialist, later recalled. "Our feeling of hopelessness and despair mounted steadily," the more so since the Austrian socialist leader Victor Adler "failed to utter a single word to indicate that we could hope for an uprising of the Austrian masses . . . He made no effort to conceal his deep pessimism. The passivity of the workers was taken for granted!"[15] As Balabanoff was to discover, workers, regardless of nationality, were far from being passive. Instead they turned into implacable enemies overnight, donned their uniforms, and, singing patriotic songs, set off to defend the honor of their mother country. The one thing the soldiers expected of their socialist leaders was to vote for war appropriations. "In retrospect," Balabanoff wrote, "Jean Jaurès and Rosa Luxemburg seem to me the only delegates who, like Adler, fully realized the inevitability of the World War."[16]

Accounts of Luxemburg's reaction to the outbreak of the war differ. Some delegates remembered her as being as outspoken as ever, others as being dumbfounded. Clara Zetkin is said to have confessed that they were both on the verge of suicide. It took three years and the solitude of a prison cell for Luxemburg to admit to her despair in those July days, when her mystical faith in the "intuitive wisdom" and idealism of the proletariat crumbled. Her helplessness, her "shameful weakness," she ironically wrote to Hans Diefenbach in 1917, turned a ten-year-long hostile relationship with the prominent Belgian socialist Camille Huysmans into a friendship of sorts. Huysmans had never been able to tolerate Luxemburg's strength and independence. But for once "he finally saw me weak." At the Brussels meeting, Huysmans showered her with attention, treated her in his house to "*un petit concert Schubertien*," saw her off on the train (she left Brussels by the last train before Germany invaded Belgium), sighing, "*Mais il est impossible de vous laisser voyager seule!*" (But it is impossible to let you travel alone!).[17]

If Luxemburg was ever heroic it was not so much in revolutionary Warsaw in 1906 or later in vanquished Berlin in 1918 as it was in the months following the declaration of World War I. A born fighter, she was in her element fighting; to go on defeated was an act of unmatched bravery. "There is no doubt that the Party and the International are *kaput*, completely *kaput*," she wrote to Diefenbach in November 1914. But now that the force of the initial blow was wearing off, she was ready to start "a new life," she said somewhat wryly: to go back to the manuscript of *Introduction to Political Economy*, write something about the war, take care of Mimi and the household. With the Party School closed, her income dwindled and Diefenbach offered to supply 100 marks a month. She said she would prefer that he give the money to "a very talented young man who wants to study but is without means."[18] In all probability she meant Costia Zetkin.

Once the war broke out, Social Democrats—German, French, and Austrian (Lenin did not attend the Brussels meeting and disassociated himself from his government's actions)—declared their support of the war and of their governments by voting for war appropriations. The brotherhood of workers, the supranational alliance, ceased to exist. Luxemburg now wanted one thing: to separate herself officially from the German Social Democratic Party. On 30 October 1914, a Swiss newspaper, the *Berner Tagwacht*, carried a "Declaration" signed by Clara Zetkin, Franz Mehring, Karl Liebknecht and Rosa Luxemburg. In one brief paragraph they disclaimed their allegiance to the official party line and assured foreign comrades that they, like many other German Social Democrats, held a view on "the war, its origin and character" different from that of the SPD. Kautsky's caustic remark that Luxemburg preferred "to be the first in the village rather than the second in Rome" was a poorly concealed justification of his pro-war stand.[19]

Luxemburg's wrath at the country where she had always been a "foreigner" now turned full circle. Comical moments were not entirely absent. She went to bookstores, eyed the empty shelves, and innocently asked for French and English books, which of course had been hastily removed—"the salesgirl looked as if she wanted to slap my face." Listening to a Beethoven concerto, she felt nothing but cold hatred. "I keep thinking that somebody should write a book about what's going on here . . . a book that like a red-hot iron would brand their stupidity."[20] This "mindless pack, this cannon fodder," made her tremble with rage, and she was already planning to leave Germany after the war and move to Italy—"but first, of course, we must settle accounts."[21] Reading Cervantes, she thought about the slavish souls of the Germans, their deadly sense of obedience, and compared them with people endowed with independent minds and spirits. Fiction and reality were never far apart, not for the teenager in the Warsaw Gymnasium or for the forty-five-year-old woman on the Berlin frontier.

Luxemburg's time was running out. The Frankfurt prison sentence was due to start in December. She was not looking forward to the enforced inaction; seething inside, she wanted to blow up the enemy camp—the SPD. On 4 August a small group met in her apartment—Leo Jogiches, Franz Mehring, Julian Marchlewski, Käthe and Hermann Duncker, Wilhelm Pick, and a few others, the nucleus of what became the Gruppe Internationale and subsequently, in 1916, the *Spartakusbund* (Spartacus League). They discussed means of preventing the SPD deputies from voting for war appropriations, but their appeal, directed to some three hundred leading socialists, remained unanswered except by Clara Zetkin. The only weapons Luxemburg had were her oratory and her pen. She rushed from one meeting to another, convinced, as she wrote to Camille Huysmans, "that the working masses would take our side if it were possible to present our case."[22] But she was wrong. The German army scored its first victories, and national pride was running high. Yet just as Luxemburg hung on to the tiny Polish Social Democratic Party (SDKPiL) that was not at all representative of Poland's aspirations, she was now determined to build up the opposition, representative or not. Karl Liebknecht went to Liège in October, met with the secretary of the International, Huysmans, saw the devastation wrought by his countrymen, and departed saying: "Now I know what has happened and I shall do my duty."[23] In December he voted, a lone voice, against renewal of war appropriations. Contacts were made with antiwar groups abroad with the vague hope that the carnage might somehow still be stopped.

After the war broke out Luxemburg had told the Russian socialist Alexandra Kollontaj that conspiratorial work was premature, but in a few months there was no alternative except to go underground. "The first shipment [of a foreign trade union publication] duly arrived and is at Karl Liebknecht's," Luxemburg wrote in January 1915 to Marta Rosenbaum, who was to become a good friend. "From him it will go to Mehring, then to you, and from you to Kurt [Rosenfeld] . . . and since I won't be here, would you be good enough to keep the operation under control and take over the finances?"[24] The instructions she dispatched before entering prison, not unlike those Jogiches used to shower on her, were intended to ensure continuity of the work she had started. Most important was the new organ of the group, *Die Internationale*, which replaced the *Sozialdemokratische Korrespondenz*, a favorite target of the censors. Luxemburg was the moving spirit behind this venture, starting everything from scratch, obtaining money, paper, and printers—an experience perhaps reminding her of the Paris days twenty-two years ago when she put together the Polish organ *The Workers' Cause*. The first and last issue of *Die Internationale* appeared in April 1915. It contained an article by Luxemburg, "The Reconstruction of the International," in which she suggested an amended version of the appeal ending *The Communist Manifesto:* "Workers of all countries unite in peacetime, but in war—slit one another's throats!"[25]

The frantic activity, the constant presence of people Luxemburg both loathed and needed, were a defense against the most tragic defeat she suffered in her life. Stubbornly, she was turning the defeat into victory, albeit spiritual and not material, because defeated she was unable to breathe. She believed, as she had since she was a child, that no matter how insurmountable the obstacle, ultimately she would prevail.

In December Luxemburg was hospitalized with extreme nervous and physical exhaustion. The prison sentence that was to start in December was postponed until 31 March 1915, but on 18 February two officers of the criminal police appeared at her apartment and took her by car to police headquarters in Alexanderplatz. The formalities duly executed, she was put in a green van and taken to the Royal Prussian Prison for Women in Berlin.

14 | *In and Out*
of Prison
1915–1918

PRISON WAS AN INTEGRAL PART of the life of a
socialist. Some left it broken or discouraged, others came out more
determined and better educated than when they went in. Serving
inordinately long sentences in remote Russian prisons, one could study
the old masters, Marx and Engels, and devise new strategies for
conducting the fight. After the old world and international socialism
crumbled in the First World War, prison became a real calamity for
political offenders; but until then, it was a measure of revolutionary
spirit and was regarded as a university of sorts. In 1907 the
following exchange took place at the Congress of the International in
Stuttgart:

> *Gustave Hervé:* I love the good German people, placid and
> benevolent. I admire your science, your organization, your
> great fighters. But you are no more than an admirable
> machine to vote and collect fees. You have no revolutionary
> conception. You can reach far into the mysteries of the
> mind, but confronted with the government you recoil, you
> try to avoid issues. You are afraid of prison.
> *Rosa Luxemburg:* No.
> *Hervé:* Not you, it's true.[1]

Luxemburg's brief imprisonment in Warsaw a year earlier, in 1906, was well remembered; it had given her special status in peacetime. But in a time of war her incarceration was of little concern except to her and the small circle of her friends and comrades. Her imprisonment in 1915 was unlike any of her former prison terms—not the baptism of fire, rather exciting in 1904, nor the proudly endured arrest in 1906 in Warsaw, to which Hervé referred. Then life held many hopes; now all hope was dashed.

During the war Luxemburg spent three years and four months in prison: a one-year sentence for inciting public disobedience in 1914 and the rest in protective custody, which had no time limit. Her year's sentence ended on 18 February 1916; five months later Luxemburg was detained and kept in jail without trial for the duration of the war. She kept a diary in prison in which she haphazardly jotted down her weight, letters sent and received, quotations from books, and remarks about birds, plants, and the weather. During her year's imprisonment she marked off the days, weeks, and months and recorded the passage of time in various other ways. On 18 April 1915 it was "two months, 1/6," on 18 August, "one half," on 19 August, "26 weeks," and so forth. These entries reflect her impatience and above all her certainty that an end was in sight; there are no such entries in the calendars covering the years 1917 and 1918.

Several collections of Luxemburg's letters, containing many written from prison, have been published. They are incomplete, for both the recipients and the editors exercised their discretion; many were in code and were destroyed. Those that remain attest to the importance letters had for Rosa while she was in isolation. Always conscious of the power of her pen, she resorted to writing when spoken words seemed treacherous or inadequate; now that letters replaced personal contact she transformed her gift into an art. The elaborately composed yet seemingly effortless letters drew their recipients into her cell. Her friends readily responded to her intellect, her friendliness, and nostalgia. In many lives, she asserted herself even more forcefully than she had in person. The letters were statements of pride and resolve, a challenge to weakness—always a dreaded threat. Prison did not matter, ran the underlying message; she was strong enough to support and protect her friends, to cheer them up and laugh with them. Yet between the lines, whether lyrical, angry, merry, or sad, underneath the involvement in nature, art, and literature was a despair that she could not suppress.

The people to whom Luxemburg now turned were mostly new friends. Whether she felt more at ease with people who knew her slightly or whether she needed confirmation of her power to attract admirers, she carried on her war correspondence mainly with people she had recently met. Luxemburg met Sonja Liebknecht, the wife of Karl, a prosperous lawyer and the son of the cofounder of the German Social Democratic Party (SPD), in 1912.* She had known Mathilde Jacob, whom she had occasionally employed as a typist, since 1913; Marta Rosenbaum, since 1914. Hans Diefenbach was an old friend, but his status changed entirely in Rosa's letters to him in 1917. She corresponded with Clara Zetkin, Luise Kautsky, Mathilde Wurm, Franz Mehring, and Jogiches, but it was not these old and intimately known friends that she wanted to captivate.

Each of her correspondents knew a different Rosa Luxemburg. To Sonja Liebknecht she was a devoted, older friend, protective, undemanding; to Mathilde Jacob, a stern mistress, used to giving orders and seeing them followed, yet vulnerable and often despondent; to Marta Rosenbaum, a loving, modest person devoted to humanity; to Hans Diefenbach, an appealing woman, emotional and generous, a woman he had not known before. Chameleonlike, Luxemburg adjusted herself to the needs and expectations of others. Each of them was assigned a certain role in her drama, and each was a lifeline. She made an effort to be less domineering—"I've no need to play the schoolmaster with people who are dear to me," she wrote, "I *like* them, *just as they* are"—but it was not very successful.[2] Old and new friends alike were subjected to endless lectures on the art of living, given ceaseless advice on what books to read, what concerts to attend, how to discover beauty in flowers and insects, how to escape the trap of depression. The more distraught she was herself, the more aggressively she pressed upon others her own cheerful image, admitting her true mood only at moments of acute crises. By persuading her friends of the bright side of life and the virtue of endurance, she kept herself from drowning.

Distorted as Rosa Luxemburg may emerge from the incomplete prison correspondence, her letters and the somewhat unreliable mem-

---

*Sophie (Sonja) Ryss (1884–1964), of Russian-Jewish origin, studied the history of art in Germany. In 1912 she married the forty-one-year-old Karl Liebknecht, recently widowed and the father of three young children.

ory of Mathilde Jacob are the main sources from which Luxemburg's life in the years 1915–1918 can be reconstructed.

Mathilde Jacob was Luxemburg's main link to the outside world throughout her imprisonment, and far more letters were addressed to her than to anyone else. Franz Mehring recommended Mathilde Jacob as an efficient typist to Luxemburg in 1913, and the encounter was a turning point in Mathilde's life. "The first time Rosa Luxemburg came to me to dictate an article . . . she made a deep impression on me," Jacob wrote in her memoir. "Her big, shining eyes, which seemed to understand everything, made my heart beat faster."[3] Three years younger than Luxemburg, Mathilde Jacob had grayish, thinning hair, a withered, pale complexion, and unassuming looks. She came from an assimilated Jewish family left without means after the premature death of her father. The older of two daughters, Mathilde had to give up her dreams of a higher education to build an existence for her mother and sister. The small typing office she set up with one employee was the family's sole source of income.

Mathilde Jacob left behind a memoir, ostensibly a recollection of Luxemburg and in fact a touching, awkward confession of an emotion that overpowered her. Typed and retyped, the unpublished memoir survived in two versions. In the end, Jacob could not bring herself to destroy this proof of her repressed love for Rosa; before she was shipped off to a Nazi concentration camp, the old woman managed to smuggle out of Germany her memoir and the letters Luxemburg wrote to her.

Luxemburg's imprisonment transformed the life of the modest typist. At Jogiches's suggestion she represented herself as Luxemburg's secretary to the prison administration, which greatly facilitated her access to the convict. Overnight the utterly apolitical Jacob turned into an active participant in illegal work; she passed on to Luxemburg Jogiches's oral messages and smuggled coded letters and Luxemburg's manuscripts in and out. She was accepted into the circle of Luxemburg's friends, a great distinction: Clara Zetkin, Luise Kautsky, Hans Diefenbach, Paul Levi, and others communicated with Luxemburg through her. Jacob saw to Luxemburg's personal needs—clothes, diet, books—and was entrusted with Mimi, the cat, "the highest honor I could bestow," in Rosa's words.[4] "Our daughter," as Luxemburg referred to Mimi, was a fixture in their correspondence until the cat died in 1917. No one but Mimi could arouse Luxemburg's scorn toward Mathilde. "To bring Mimi in a basket . . . and carry her back! As if she were an ordinary creature of the species *felis domestica!*" she greeted Jacob's innocent suggestion to bring the cat to visit her. "Mimi is a tiny mimosa, a hypernervous little princess . . . When I, her own mother, once used force to carry her out of the house she was seized by nervous cramps and lay all stiff in my arms . . . You've no idea what my mother's heart went through."[5]

Luxemburg called Jacob her guardian angel, but for all her devotion she remained a subordinate. It is doubtful that she had higher aspirations than to type Luxemburg's articles and smuggle her messages. An existence in Luxemburg's shadow, a right to divine her wishes and shower her with presents were compensation enough. There was also the pleasure of Luxemburg's interest in her: "I hope you're taking walks rain or shine"; "did you finally go to the Botanical Garden?"; "do read something good in every free minute."[6] But Luxemburg's attention did not suggest equality. Luxemburg never criticized her friends to Jacob as she criticized Sonja Liebknecht to Luise Kautsky, Clara Zetkin to Diefenbach, or Diefenbach to Costia Zetkin. The boundaries were clear, and if Jacob attempted to overstep them she was promptly called to order.

During the first prison term (February 1915 to February 1916) Luxemburg wrote twenty-two letters to Jacob, nine to Clara Zetkin, three to Marta Rosenbaum, and two to Luise Kautsky. Those to Jacob are more relaxed than those to her friends and free from play-acting. Jacob did not have to be wooed and was, like Jogiches, privy to Luxemburg's moments of weakness. It is possible that Jogiches read Luxemburg's letters to Jacob and that Luxemburg was aware of it. Her pleas for warmth and affection, descriptions of her sad and dreary life and of her emotional and physical afflictions are reminiscent of her early letters to him. When she observes that "a woman's character shows not when love begins but when it ends," she might have imagined Jogiches reading over Jacob's shoulder.[7]

Mathilde Jacob was the perfect intermediary for Luxemburg and Jogiches. She eased their reconciliation. She revered both of them and, knowing no details, took for granted their great love for one another. So compelling is the picture of their mutual devotion painted in her memoir that no one unfamiliar with their barely ended seven-year war would guess at any conflict. And they responded to this idealized image. Jacob was unaware that she bridged past and present for them, but by talking to her and through her they were finally able to accept the human weaknesses in each other.

Mathilde Jacob and Leo Jogiches developed a curious relationship. She was one of the few people neither frightened nor mystified by him, and with her he talked about his life with Luxemburg. "I'll tell you something about Rosa that will make you laugh," he interrupted a nightly session with Jacob, who was encoding his report to Luxemburg. "When we lived in Paris, we once visited friends who lived far away. On the way home Rosa was tired, so she hailed a fiacre and asked how much it cost to get home. The price was high, we couldn't afford it. *O, Monsieur,* Rosa cried, *nous sommes pauvres!* [we are poor!] The cabman answered, *Ce n'est pas ma faute, Madame!* [It's not my fault, Madame!] His answer amused Rosa so much that she sat down on the pavement, laughed unrestrainedly and showed no trace of fatigue during the walk home."[8] The anecdote is less revealing than is Jogiches's willingness to talk openly about living with Luxemburg, traveling together, sharing friends, accommodations, and expenses. His secretiveness about their liaison evaporated in Jacob's presence. The Jogiches who emerges from her memoir, kind, generous, witty, and open, bears little resemblance to the man everyone else knew. Whether he was really so changed in Luxemburg's absence or Jacob's presence is a matter for conjecture. In any event, no one in that unconventional trio felt threatened.

" 'To do without life's little ornaments,' Lady Kennedy said to Maria Stuart as the Queen's trinkets were taken from her, is harder than to endure big trials."[9] With her usual poignancy Luxemburg quoted these words from Schiller's drama in her first letter from prison (written in February 1915) to Mathilde Jacob, indicating that she was not losing heart. "May God punish England and forgive me for comparing myself to the English Queen," she joked. She had been hastily taken from her apartment, without a nightgown, soap, or comb, had twice undergone a body search, and had had difficulty holding back the tears. "Life's little ornaments" were promptly delivered to her. The big trials were still ahead.

Shortly after Luxemburg was imprisoned, the court granted her two free days to arrange her personal affairs. Paul Levi came from

Frankfurt to be with her; Jogiches, Liebknecht, Mehring, and Jacob were also at hand. The brief reunion was confused and joyless. Instructions and information were exchanged, channels of communication established, financial matters settled. "I did not know at that point that Rosa Luxemburg was impecunious," reminisced Mathilde Jacob.[10] A fee of 60 marks, exacted from prisoners for the privilege of doing their own work instead of assigned labor, was covered by the SPD; the rent for her apartment was paid, according to Jacob, by a well-to-do friend, probably Hans Diefenbach.

A strict regimen was the best way, Rosa knew, to survive the year that lay ahead. In accordance with prison rules, she rose at 5:40 and retired at 9:00 at night, a considerable change in her habits that she said she did not mind. The day was devoted to reading and writing and tending the tiny garden in front of her cell. She resumed botanizing, a hobby she had acquired two years earlier when for four months "I did literally nothing else," she wrote to Luise Kautsky. "I must always have something that absorbs me completely."[11] Being permitted to work and to have her own books was a great relief. She was writing the *Anti-Critique,* a reply to the critics of *The Accumulation of Capital;* "do soothe Gross [Jogiches]," she told Jacob, "my work is primarily theoretical, not economic or historical."[12] Jogiches was worried that without his supervision her rebuttal would not be worthy of a leading Marxist theorist.

By April 1915, Luxemburg had finished her most forceful statement against war and militarism, "The Crisis of the Social Democracy," signed "Junius" and known as the *Junius Pamphlet.* "The spectacle is over," Luxemburg wrote. "The trains carrying the reservists now leave in silence without the enthusiastic farewells of fair maidens . . . The crisp atmosphere of the pale rising day is filled with the voices of a different chorus—the hoarse clamor of the hawks and hyenas of the battlefields. Ten thousand tents, regulation size, guaranteed! One hundred thousand kilograms of bacon, cocoa powder, ersatz coffee, immediate delivery, cash only! Grenades, drills, ammunition bags, matchmakers for war widows . . . serious offers only! The hurray-patriotically glorified cannon fodder . . . is already rotting on the battlefields . . . Disgraced, shameful, bloodstained, filthy—that is the true face of bourgeois society . . . The well-groomed, cosmetic mask of virtue—culture, philosophy, and ethics, order, peace, and constitution—slips and its real, naked self is exposed. During this witches' sabbat a disaster of world-wide magnitude occurred—the capitulation of the International Social Democracy."[13]

The *Junius Pamphlet* was Luxemburg's sharpest indictment of the German Social Democracy, the "brain" and the "vanguard" of the International. Since the 1870s, when the center of gravity of the European workers' movement shifted from France to Germany, "the German Social Democracy," Luxemburg quoted Engels, "occupies a particular place and . . . has therefore a particular role to play." Indeed, she elaborated, "the German vanguard played a decisive role [in the Second International]. At congresses and meetings of the International Socialist Bureau everyone waited for the Germans to express their opinion . . . Blindly confident, the International submitted to the leadership of the revered, powerful German Social Democracy, the pride of every socialist and the terror of the ruling classes in the whole world." But when the historical test came, the SPD broke down completely and ignominiously. "Nowhere is a proletarian organization so totally subservient to imperialism; nowhere is the state of siege tolerated so uncomplainingly; nowhere is the press so thoroughly gagged and public opinion so completely stifled."[14] Yet only the German Social Democracy, the greatest hope and greatest disillusionment of the international proletariat, Luxemburg maintained, could rescue socialism, through serious analysis of its errors and unsparing criticism of its shortcomings. This was the highest duty of the fallen leader of the proletariat.

For all her criticism of the SPD, Luxemburg adamantly opposed a formal split. "A splintering of Marxists (not to be confused with differences of opinion) is fatal," she had told her friend, the Dutch socialist Henriette Roland Holst in 1908.[15] The split within the Russian Social Democracy and the split within the Polish Social Democracy strengthened her conviction. But unification was not uniformity; the former was fruitful, the latter lethal. The phrase "not to be confused with differences of opinion" was as important as the main clause. The small, radical Gruppe Internationale (later Spartacus League) worked within the SPD precisely to prevent the "fatal" splintering.

The political line Luxemburg took in the aftermath of the defeat of the International was expounded in articles published in 1916–1918 in the *Spartakusbriefe (Spartacus Letters)* and in a document called "Theses Concerning the Tasks of International Social Democracy," which was smuggled out of prison in December 1915. The twelve theses *(Leitsätze)* and six propositions, written in crisp, terse language, imparted the essence of the *Junius Pamphlet* and provided guiding principles for the reconstruction of the international workers' movement. Assessing World War I, Luxemburg said: "The present World War, whether it brings victory or defeat for anyone . . . means the defeat of socialism and democracy. Whatever its end—excepting revolutionary intervention of the international proletariat—it leads to the intensification of militarism, of international contradictions, and of economic rivalries. . . . Today's World War is thus developing all preconditions for new wars."[16]

Unlike Lenin, who accepted war as a means toward revolution, Luxemburg considered war, regardless of the results, as a return to barbarism. The theses also discussed the creation of a new International. The question had been addressed in September 1915 at a meeting in Zimmerwald, Switzerland. Luxemburg had worked out a blueprint, but it did not reach the conference in time. She envisaged a supreme authoritative body that determined the tactics of the national sections in questions of general and economic policy and armaments. It was to rise from the ashes of the old International, purged of its weakness and proof against national aspirations. Once again Luxemburg was at odds with Lenin. Lenin's proposal to turn an imperialist war into a civil war and to create a new International, presented at the conference, was dismissed by most of the participants, including Adolf Warszawski and Bertha Thalheimer, representatives of the Gruppe Internationale. "I deeply regret," Jogiches quoted Luxemburg in his letter to Thalheimer, "that I was not informed in time about the Zimmerwald plans. I consider this entire idea not just off target but a catastrophic error, a false start before it got off the ground."[17] It was not unusual for Luxemburg and Jogiches to speak in one voice in matters of party policy. It was unusual for Jogiches to represent Luxemburg openly on the German forum.

Luxemburg's imprisonment meant Jogiches's freedom. It was the ultimate irony of their entangled destinies that it took a war to set Jogiches free.

After Luxemburg left him in 1907, Jogiches was alone and was condemned to a marginal existence in a country in which he remained a stranger and a nonentity. Nearing fifty at the outbreak of the war, he was resigned to his failure. Then it became clear that the radical opposition must go underground; his hour struck. Conspiracy, the daily bread of Russians and Poles, had always been suspect to the legalistic Germans; it offended their code of honor and respect for order. Thus Jogiches had no competition on German soil. Age and the barren years might have tempered him somewhat, or perhaps the Germans admired him for the authoritarian bent the Poles could not abide. At any rate the Germans accorded him the recognition he had missed for so long.

The radical opposition, which in 1916 became known as *Spartakusbund*, needed a publication to disseminate its political views. On 27 January, a "political letter" signed *Spartakus* appeared, a few hundred typed copies, the first feeble effort of people unfamiliar with illegal work. After Jogiches took over the underground operation, the September issue of *Spartakusbriefe* was published, with several thousand copies circulated, and later issues had a circulation of as many as 30,000 copies. Although in 1915 Luxemburg still despaired over Jogiches's "criminal" waste of time, once left alone in the field he worked day and night. Under his editorship *Spartacus Letters* "became the best political organ of the war period . . . and a spiritual center, while the distribution network provided the organizational link for the left opposition."[18]

Nothing changed in Jogiches's style. He never appeared publicly, and his role was known to a few—Mehring, Liebknecht, and Paul Levi among others. Mathilde Jacob was in charge of his contacts. "Jogiches . . . used to phone me every day to let me know that nothing had happened to him. Besides, I had to know where to reach him because everyone who wanted to speak with him reported to me, and I arranged the connection."[19] Usually he met with one person at a time, preferably by daylight in a well-frequented place. A dashing man, with deep-sunken eyes and graying hair, nonchalantly waving his ever-present umbrella, he attracted the attention of women rather than of the police. He was known under different names—Krumbügel, Kraft, Krzyształowicz—and, except for Franz Mehring and Mathilde Jacob, no one knew his address. Living incognito, he knew, was his biggest asset.

Right under the eye of the police, who were becoming increasingly nervous about the dangerously spreading publication, Jogiches built an impressive underground network. He often spent the night dictating a report for Luxemburg or supervising the printers, to emerge at noon, fresh and elegant, in a fashionable café, meet his contact, and disappear.

During the war Jogiches's personal life took a different turn as well. He moved out of the Schlosspark Hotel in Steglitz and sublet a room in the apartment of a German war widow. The young housewife fell in love with Jogiches. According to Mathilde Jacob, apparently the one person who knew about the liaison, Jogiches's mistress, though devotedly loyal, was extremely inquisitive and jealous. She spied on him, Jacob relates, made scenes, opened his correspondence, and asked the owner of the neighboring tobacco store, where Jogiches often used the telephone, to keep his ears open. "Since Leo Jogiches addressed me as Mathilde when he called . . . the woman would not rest until she found out who I was," Jacob wrote in her memoir. "Triumphantly, she told him one day that she knew to whom he made all these phone calls . . . Since then, he has made no calls from there . . . When I came . . . she asked whether I was the wife of the old man with the white beard [Franz Mehring]." Evidently his mistress's behavior did not bother Jogiches. Repeatedly, he told Jacob: "Should anything happen to me, get in touch with my landlady. She would do anything for me."[20]

The five months between Luxemburg's release from prison on 18 February 1916 and her arrest on 10 July were the last in which she lived a normal life. The day she was released, a huge crowd of women socialists and well-wishers gathered in front of the prison, but Luxemburg, accompanied by Mathilde Jacob and Karl Liebknecht, left through a back exit. The crowd caught up with her and left her house at nightfall only after she had accepted homemade bread and cakes. At last she could enjoy her apartment and Mimi. She was in much worse physical condition than they had realized, Jacob remembered. "Yet she worked without allowing herself any rest . . . often while racked by severe pains. I'd say to her, 'Rosa, perhaps you should rest a little,' and she'd answer, 'I pay no attention to pain. I pretend that I'm all right and then I work very well.' "[21] In the spring Luxemburg went to visit Clara Zetkin, also recently released from prison, and spent a few days in her country house; it was to be the last time she saw Clara. She went to Königstein to see Paul Levi, who was on sick leave from the army.

Hans Diefenbach obtained leave to come see her. Her condition gradually improved, and she made some trips to attend illegal meetings of comrades and workers. In Berlin Jogiches and Liebknecht were constantly at her side. Although her ties with Liebknecht became closer, Rosa remained critical of his ill-considered actions, which, though spectacular, she sometimes thought ineffective, if not outright harmful. "I must guard myself constantly against Karl L[iebknecht]," she wrote to Costia Zetkin in 1915, "who, guided by the best intentions, tries to drag me every day to every possible place, to take care of every possible thing, which is time-consuming and has little or no effect."[22] Asked to behave with more caution, Liebknecht cited his parliamentary immunity; still it irritated Luxemburg that he endangered people who did not enjoy this privilege. But "do not compare him with Leo Jogiches, as you always do," she defended Liebknecht. "Compare him with German comrades and you will see he is superior to all of them."[23]

The Spartacists put enormous effort into the May Day celebration in 1916. Luxemburg wrote the leaflets distributed in factories, and 10,000 antiwar demonstrators gathered in Potsdam Square. The demonstration was led by Liebknecht, dressed up in a soldier's uniform, shouting, "Down with the war! Down with the government!" Luxemburg marched at his side. Arrested on the spot, he was stripped of his immunity, and was sentenced to four years and one month of penal servitude. Thereafter, Luxemburg was under constant police surveillance.

On Sunday, 9 July 1916, two plainclothesmen came to Rosa Luxemburg's apartment and introduced themselves to Mathilde Jacob as comrades from the Berlin Neukölln district. Luxemburg was expected back from Leipzig late at night, Jacob informed them. The next morning Luxemburg was still asleep when Jacob admitted the men. She helped Luxemburg to dress, served breakfast, and accompanied her by suburban train to Potsdam Square, where she had to leave her with the police. Luxemburg was taken to the women's prison on Barnimstrasse that she had left in February.

For lack of incriminating evidence, she was held in protective custody, which had some advantages; she could receive food, books, flowers, and letters. Jacob could visit Luxemburg once a week for an hour. During one such visit, in September, the officer in attendance declared after ten minutes that the hour was over and kept interrupting the conversation. Luxemburg lost control, threw a chocolate bar at him and called him *"dreckiger Spitzel"* (filthy spy). Late that night she was taken to the police headquarters at Alexanderplatz and put into a dark, tiny cell. "The month and a half I spent there," she wrote later to Hans Diefenbach, "turned my hair gray and left me with nerves wrecked so badly that I'll never be the same."²⁴ With no artificial light and with darkness falling in the early afternoon, she lay on an iron bunk, right under passing trains whose "devilish concerto" shattered the silence. At the end of October 1916 she was transferred to Wronki near Poznań, in Prussian-annexed Poland. It was the fourth prison she had been in within a year.

Wronki, a forbidding, huge compound, was located in beautiful country. In a separate small house on the grounds, Luxemburg was allotted a bedroom and sitting room. A corridor opened to a little garden, an unexpected gift. The nearness of nature, the trees, the birds, and the open sky made Luxemburg feel alive again. Contact with nature had always been necessary to her, a refuge from nagging problems, personal and public. She resumed botanizing and immersed herself in studying plant life.

In her first letter from Wronki to Mathilde Jacob, dated 31 October 1916, she requested money to pay for her own and her two guards' transportation and her upkeep (4.20 marks a day) and asked that her books, clothes, soap, and a flower vase be sent to her. Jogiches suggested that Jacob visit Rosa. "She'll be happy when you come and see how she is; in fact, she'll be waiting."²⁵ She was. "I've hoped somebody would soon come to see me," she exclaimed. Embracing Jacob through the barrier in the visiting room, she whispered, "Didn't you bring me something from Leo?"²⁶ Mathilde slipped a letter into her hand.

Both the director of the prison, Dr. Dossmar, and his assistant in charge of women prisoners, Else Schrick, were friendly. Wartime economy measures were relaxed, and a fence was built to separate Luxemburg's garden from the prison yard; soon Clara Zetkin was sending bird food for Luxemburg's pets. Else Schrick, deeply impressed with Luxemburg, went out of her way to make her life easier. Though she left her job two months after Luxemburg's arrival, Schrick kept in touch with Mathilde Jacob, unable, she wrote, to forget Luxemburg.

Protective custody, Luxemburg rightly assumed, was a temporary measure, and she kept hoping she would be released. Custody was indeed limited by law to three months but could be extended at the discretion of the authorities. Barely three weeks after she was imprisoned, Rosa thought freedom was around the corner; and in March 1917 she hoped to be home by the end of April. The uncertainty was devastating. Each extension was a new blow, and utter helplessness was slowly dragging her into depression. Never before had she been a victim of forces she could not control or even fight.

Now she knew what it meant to be a pariah, with no law to defend her. Sometimes her thoughts turned to the distant past and her parents; she had never had time for her father because she had been so busy with humankind, she told Hans Diefenbach. Once it had amused her that her mother believed King Solomon understood the speech of birds, she wrote to Sonja Liebknecht; now she identified with her mother—she too understood the birds. At other times, it seemed to her that she was losing her mind: "I'm suffering from spiritual depression," she wrote to Mathilde Jacob. "It gets so bad sometimes that I fear the worst." Most of all she feared her inability to reach people: "I sometimes have an urge to get in touch immediately with the outside world, and I want to telephone, to cable, to mail a special delivery letter."[27] Nightmares tormented her. "I dreamt I was to sing a song . . . and play my own accompaniment on the piano . . . at a concert arranged by Faisst.* Suddenly at seven o'clock in the evening, I realize that I cannot play the piano. Who will accompany me? I cut my finger till blood flows to have an excuse . . . No, for heaven's sake! I scream. Faisst would be so angry he'll never see me again. I must quickly fetch my niece to accompany me! Then I remember that my niece does not play the piano but the violin, and in horror I wake up."[28]

The purpose of the protective custody was clear—to destroy Luxemburg's psychic resistance. Officially, Luxemburg was a subversive "with no regard for the interests of the fatherland," a "danger to the safety of the Reich," the more so as she was a "skilled . . . and particularly influential agitator."[29] Indeed, the punishment was effective. "When I came to visit her," Mathilde Jacob wrote in her memoir, "Rosa would sit in my lap, put her head on my shoulder and let herself be caressed, something she could never stand before. She was sick and helpless."[30]

*Hugo Faisst, Luxemburg's singer friend, died in 1914.

But Luxemburg mobilized all her resources. She would not allow her weary spirit and her sick body to slip out of her control, she would spare no effort to end her captivity and failing that, try to blunt its effects. Twelve years earlier Rosa refused an amnesty; ten years earlier she forbade her family to ask the German government to release her from prison in Warsaw; in 1914 she protested against having her trial dismissed. Now her attorneys bombarded the government with petitions for her release; her friends devised a scheme to have her released on medical grounds, and she reluctantly cooperated—"precisely because I am a woman I resent making a fuss over my physical weakness."[31] Though she would not feign sickness, she requested a brief leave and lodged a formal complaint over the prolonged protective custody; both were turned down. And, after the 1917 February revolution in Russia, she considered reclaiming her Russian citizenship and having herself deported. Once she had said in the Prussian court: "A Social Democrat stands by his deeds and laughs at your judgments." The time of laughter was over.

Only her pen could break the isolation. More strenuously, more stubbornly and daringly than during the 1915–1916 imprisonment, she used it to rally friends, to draw them into her life. If they fell short of her expectations, she laid the guilt squarely at their doorsteps. "In such a mood I naturally crave an affectionate, warm letter, but unfortunately my friends always wait for the . . . inspiration to come from me," she complained, not quite justifiably, to Luise Kautsky.[32] Or else she appealed to her friends' better selves: "I hope to see by turns you, Mathilde, Luise K. . . . and Sonja," she wrote to Marta Rosenbaum in April 1917. "I'm certainly asking a great sacrifice of you . . . but left alone for a long time I feel completely down, and I bless every minute I can spend with my friends."[33] *Sehnsucht* (yearning) is a word that appears again and again in her letters; the longing to see, to touch, and to confirm the link between herself and life was the mainspring in the relationships she now developed. But she did not want to be in debt to her friends. From her distant cell she persuaded them that they needed her as much as she needed them.

Hans Diefenbach felt Luxemburg's thirst for life more poignantly than others. For two years he wrote to her without getting a reply. Then, on 7 January 1917, she broke the silence to start her last romantic affair. She was hardly moved by compassion for the lonely soldier. Her letters, suffused with erotic innuendos, attest to something different.

Shakespeare, Goethe, and Mörike served as messengers in this amorous game. Why did she choose the restrained young man—"your court jester," he called himself—for the role of knight-errant?[34] The scion of a distinguished German family, Diefenbach could give her a sense of belonging and a hope for the future. He could sustain her faith in herself and make her feel like a woman, a need intensified by age and loneliness. That he had no verve or imagination, had "constantly cold hands" and a dispassionate nature, mattered little in an affair confined to paper. What mattered was the admiration and acceptance by one of the German elite. "So you are a descendant of Justinus Kerner? By God, a distinguished ancestor!"* Rosa wrote to Diefenbach.[35] It was typical of the contradictions in her nature to be impressed by a name while languishing in prison for the nameless masses.

"Hänschen, are you asleep?" she wrote. "I'm coming with a long straw to tickle you behind the ear.† I need company, I am sad, I want to make a confession."[36] If Diefenbach was puzzled or embarrassed, he must still have responded to the new Luxemburg in a way that left her free to "tickle" him. Whether she quoted Anacreon's lyrics—"I love you, I am yours"—or discussed *As You Like It*, her exquisite pen traced titillating images of carnal intimacy.[37] In a "beautiful, exciting dream" she touched with her finger the lips of someone close and dear and asked, "Whose mouth is it?" The answer was " 'Mine,'—Oh, no, I cried laughing, that mouth belongs to *me!*"[38] Or she remembered a bitter critic of her work whose remarks were "nothing but a vengeance for long and vain attempts" to become her friend and who on one occasion, alluding to her "Lilliputian figure . . . softly sang a song by Wolf: 'Small things too can bewitch us.' "[39]

Literature was their trysting place; here she met with Diefenbach, gave him a look, teased, and flirted. The essay, she wrote to Diefenbach, a splendid achievement of the French and English mind, is sorely missing in German letters because of the Germans' pedantry and lack of spiritual grace. Since Hänschen, as she lovingly called him, possessed that grace, he was simply made to introduce the essay into German letters. He should immediately order the Tauchnitz edition of Macaulay and study it. He owed it to his eminent ancestors to become

---

*Justinus Kerner (1786–1862), prominent medical doctor, poet, and fiction writer.
†Luxemburg always addressed Diefenbach formally, *Sie*. By contrast, she addressed Jogiches, Costia Zetkin, and Paul Levi informally, *du*.

somebody. *She* was destined to write a book on Tolstoy, he responded, but the idea did not appeal to her. "For whom? . . . Everyone can read Tolstoy's books, and if they don't get a strong breath of life from them, they won't get it from my commentaries. Can the music of Mozart be 'explained'? Can the miracle of life?"[40] Romain Rolland? "I'm afraid to upset you, but I must be honest as usual." No, Rolland's *Jean Christophe* was "not a true work of art," but "a pamphlet rather than a novel . . . the most beautiful tendentious literature cannot replace the divine spark."[41] That letter, dated 27 August 1917, was the last to find Diefenbach alive. To Luise Kautsky she later wrote: "Hannes adored Romain Rolland . . . I too learned to love him and suggested to Hannesle that we go to Paris after the war to meet Romain Rolland or invite him to Germany."[42] Diefenbach never knew of Luxemburg's change of heart or of her plans. That was immaterial—the real and the unreal intermingled in death as they had in life. Admiration for a writer transcended reality and materialized in a common trip to Paris.

Distance allowed her to paint herself in pastel colors. Diefenbach was aware of her tempestuous nature; now she revealed her other side. Infinitely patient and tactful, she listened to Diefenbach's complaints. "Seriously, Hänschen, your depression . . . genuinely worries me," she responded to a complaint that had made her squirm when voiced by Jogiches and later by Costia Zetkin.[43] Even Diefenbach's lack of passion was now a virtue. "Blessed are those without passion if that means they would never claw like a panther at the happiness and freedom of others. That has nothing to do with passion, though," she promptly retracted. "You know I possess enough of it to set a prairie on fire, and still I hold sacred the freedom and the simple wishes of other people."[44] The last segment of the sentence, which most of Luxemburg's friends would have found somewhat difficult to accept, suggested the image of herself she wished to impress on Diefenbach.

Diefenbach was intimidated by Luxemburg and despite his reserve he evidently alluded to her power in one of his letters. "If, as you wrote in your last letter, the stronger sex is mostly attracted to women who appear weak, by now you must rave about me," she responded half in jest. "I am oh so weak, more than I'd like to be."[45] Openly, she told him how much she wanted him to come and see her (he did) and implored him to be "loving and patient with me even if I'm not worth it." Diefenbach extolled her youthfulness and zest, but much as she yearned for his compliments, she also wanted his sympathy. "Every day I must endure grows into a small mountain that I climb with the utmost effort."[46] As the year wore on she increasingly needed his reassurance and adulation: "Hänschen, good morning, here I am again, I feel so lonely today."[47]

Diefenbach was killed in battle in October 1917. Within ten months Rosa had written him nineteen letters—a lyric testimony to her longings. His death was a tremendous blow to her. Though physically absent, Diefenbach made her feel like an appealing woman.

It was rumored that Diefenbach was sent to the front because of his close contact with the political convict; thus the blame for his death was placed on Luxemburg. If the rumor reached her, she never alluded to it. But she did confide to Luise Kautsky, after Diefenbach's death, that they "had a thousand plans for after the war."[48] He was her dearest friend, she told Mrs. Kautsky, who understood and shared every single mood of hers, like no one else.

Reticent as Luxemburg had always been about Jogiches, she now broke the silence. Jogiches does not know "how to love," she wrote to Luise Kautsky.[49] Jogiches returned the Christmas present she sent him from prison, a print of a painting by Turner, with a comment that it was "vandalism" to remove it from its album (the album was a present from Costia Zetkin), and an order to put it back where it belonged. "That's genuine Leo, isn't it?" Rosa burst out.[50]

Although Luxemburg had hardly ever discussed Jogiches with Luise Kautsky, it was nevertheless unnatural for Luise to assume that Diefenbach "was closer to Rosa than almost any other human being."[51] Luise Kautsky perpetrated the myth of the prominent role Diefenbach played in Luxemburg's life just as she perpetrated that of Luxemburg's youth and family. In her recollection of Rosa she devoted disproportionately more space to Hans Diefenbach than to Leo Jogiches.

The romantic affair had an incongruous postscript. In his will Hans Diefenbach bequeathed to Luxemburg 50,000 marks in his sister's trust. His brilliant friend, he said, did not manage her personal affairs with the mastery she demonstrated in solving economic problems on a world scale. He "feared that I might use the money for the Party," Luxemburg said, a bit defensively, in interpreting the restriction.[52] All she received was 4 percent interest for life on the principal, and this was barely sufficient, she pointed out, to cover half of her budget—her expenses in prison and the rent for her apartment. She did not appreciate Diefenbach's caution. When she gave, she gave lavishly, with no reservations.

Rosa Luxemburg's relationship with Luise Kautsky changed further, as Luxemburg's urge to influence her friends' lives intensified. When Luise had contemplated leaving her husband for her brother-in-law, Luxemburg steadfastly denied exercising pressure on Luise. But now, in writing, she invariably linked Luise and Hans Kautsky. She invited them to visit her (they did) and dwelled on the experiences they shared and interests they had in common. She discussed their situation at great length, insisting that it was Luise's duty to remain at Hans's side and to impart a spiritual dimension to his petit bourgeois existence.

There was, it seems, a connection between Luxemburg's bond with Diefenbach and Luise Kautsky's with Hans Kautsky, and the connection was created by Luxemburg. Luise was to give higher meaning to Hans Kautsky's life, and Luxemburg would help Diefenbach overcome his fear of gruesome reality. The women would enrich the quality of the two men's lives, perhaps change their destinies. Many years earlier Luxemburg had been eager for Luise to emulate her intellectually; now her relationship with Diefenbach could serve as a model for Luise trapped in a conventional marriage.

Luise Kautsky became for her a "haven," a refuge from the blow the war dealt to her faith. Luise's role as mother and wife stirred Rosa's sense of loss, more poignant in the face of the political debacle. "I must have *someone* who will believe that I am whirling in the maelstrom of world history only by mistake," she wrote, "and was in fact born to tend geese."[53] Prison, she knew, did not leave her unscathed. "This psychology," she told Luise in July 1918, describing "thoughts and ghosts" that haunted her, "develops unconsciously when one sits long in prison."[54] This was her last letter to Luise. They never met again.

After Hans Diefenbach was killed in battle, Rosa wrote to Sonja Liebknecht, "I am feeling so well in spite of the pain over Hans," adding that she lived in a dream world in which he was still alive.[55] To Luise Kautsky she wrote about the ordeal of sleepless nights and the nightmares; to Sonja, "in darkness I am smiling at life . . . and searching for the reason for that happiness . . . The deep nocturnal darkness is so beautiful and soft as velvet if one knows how to look at it." While some of Rosa's friends knew of her growing despondency, she impressed on Sonja toward the end of 1917 that "with each passing day . . . I grow calmer and stronger."[56]

"Poor Sonja," as Luxemburg referred to her, the young, beautiful wife of the imprisoned Karl Liebknecht, was the recipient of little masterpieces of epistolary art, filled with descriptions of nature and imbued with compassion for the suffering of all its creatures. The letters showed the author's unique strength in the face of adversity and an admirable tolerance. "I like you so much in your role of housewife," the legendary figure wrote to the "little woman."[57] Explaining her own attitude toward the trials of life, she advised Sonja: "One must always take everything that belongs to [life] and find *everything* beautiful and good. At least that is what I do, not guided by reason or wisdom but simply following my nature. I feel instinctively that this is the right way to live, and therefore I feel really happy under any circumstances."[58] Luxemburg was not happy "under any circumstances" and at the time of writing, in the spring of 1917, she was fighting a bout of depression. But Sonja Liebknecht remained to Rosa a slightly spoiled, pretty doll, an acquaintance to whom she generously gave solace and affection but whom she would not treat as an equal. Underneath the compassion there was unintentional yet transparent condescension. Still Luxemburg sometimes put aside the lyric essays and treated Sonja like a friend. "Clara [Zetkin] shared with me her enthusiasm about [John Galsworthy's] *The Man of Property*," Luxemburg wrote to Sonja. "But how harsh and puritan is her judgment of our Irene, yours and mine, of this adorable creature who is too weak to use her elbows . . . and who lies in the road—a crushed flower. Clara has no understanding of these 'ladies' who are to her mere 'sexual and digestible machines.' As though every woman could become an 'agitator,' a typist, a telephonist or otherwise 'useful.' And as though beautiful women—beauty is not just a pretty face but also inner fineness and grace—were not a gift from heaven merely because they please our eyes! . . . I am for luxury in all its forms."[59] Luxemburg could find no better way to say that it is not the Claras who make life beautiful.

The year 1917 was critical for Rosa Luxemburg in many respects. The news from Russia, exhilarating in April, began to worry her toward the end of the year. The medical release she expected was not granted and, worse, she was transferred from the relative comfort of Wronki to yet another prison, in Breslau (Wrocław). She suffered from violent changes of mood; ecstatic over a blossoming flower one day, she brooded the next over its short life. As she was bitterly complaining to Luise Kautsky over her friends' silence, those same friends wrote letters, sent books, food, sweets, and flowers. Her family sent tea and soap from Warsaw. But she was not easy to please. Sonja's letters sounded like "cracked glass"; Luise's were "suspiciously morose"; everyone who wrote to her was just "moaning and groaning"; no one had or even strived for Goethe's concept of life—the universality of interests and inner harmony. Inner harmony, the unattainable dream, seemed more within reach for her than for her friends; she contrasted her strength with their weakness and her rich inner life with their spiritual poverty. The longer the confinement lasted, the more defensive she grew.

In July 1917 the district attorney informed Luxemburg about her impending transfer to another prison. There were two female prisons in Germany, she was told, and her cell was needed for another woman. The decision came as an unpleasant surprise. During the eight months at Wronki, Luxemburg had become accustomed to the cell filled with her books and bric-a-brac and especially to the garden, which she loved. Also, she regularly saw a private doctor in Poznań for psychological and physical treatment, and the trips to the city provided a welcome change. Now the modicum of stability, essential for her mental balance, was shattered. She had to pack, leave, and start anew.

Mathilde Jacob was at Wronki when the news came. As was her habit, she was spending her vacation near the prison, to be closer to Rosa. In fact, the authorities, alarmed by Luxemburg's depressed mood, had allowed Jacob to see her more frequently. This immediately roused Luxemburg's suspicions. Fearing that Jacob had requested special privileges on her behalf, she refused at one point to see Jacob and relented only after she made sure that her suspicions were unfounded.

Initially, Luxemburg was not told the new location or the date of the transfer. But the prudent Jacob started at once to gather food supplies, more readily available in the country, and enlisted the help of a guard and some Russian prisoners of war to obtain crates and pack books, clothes, kitchenware and to have everything moved as quickly as possible; a bare cell, she knew, would affect Luxemburg adversely. Shortly before leaving Luxemburg was told she was going to Breslau. The time of departure was kept secret lest Jacob board the same train, as Luxemburg anxiously begged her to do. The district attorney was ready to reveal the time if Jacob promised not to come to the station. Jacob retorted that she would rather go there twice a day and check every train than be deprived of seeing Luxemburg off. Eventually, in the afternoon of 22 July 1917, Luxemburg was seen off by both the district attorney and Mathilde Jacob.

Jacob followed Luxemburg by the next train and was in a hotel in Breslau to receive Luxemburg's first letter. It was a desperate letter. The trip itself was an ordeal; the people, the noise, the traffic left Rosa completely bewildered. Three years earlier, almost to the day, Luxemburg had traveled from the last Congress of the International in Brussels amidst the clamor of war trumpets and trainloads of boisterous soldiers, and had arrived in Berlin ready for action. Now the mere sight of strangers and the sounds of the city unnerved her. Her worst suspicions were confirmed; the new prison, she wrote, was dreadful. "I'll perish here," she told Mathilde when she first saw her.[60] She was ready to petition for a transfer.

The Breslau prison was to be the last stage of Luxemburg's captivity. She remained there one year and four months, the longest time she spent in any prison. The conditions proved not to be as bad as she feared. Jacob found the wife of a laborer, Selma Schlich, who agreed to cook and deliver meals to the prison. Luxemburg was allotted two rooms. "Two rooms of course sounds nice, provided one has access to them," she wrote to Jacob. "But I'm locked in, and to get into my other cell I have to knock . . . and get the guard."[61] A commission summoned from Berlin agreed that this was an undue hardship, and a wall was torn down to connect the rooms. Furnished with her possessions, pictures, a rug, and an armchair, the rooms acquired a personal character. Luxemburg could receive visitors in her cell, and Jacob recalled that she felt "like a hostess."[62] She was allowed to walk in the yard for as long as she liked. The prison doctor, an admirer of Goethe and subsequently of Luxemburg, obtained borrowing privileges for her at the university library. She now could read the Russian writer Vladimir Korolenko, whose autobiography she was translating into German. In his stories Korolenko depicted Jews; in life he fought for their rights. Inadvertently she was drawn into their world.

During her years in prison Luxemburg's attitude toward Jews became more complex. There may be several reasons for this, ranging from Korolenko's interest in Jews to an overabundance of time for contemplation. Both a letter Luxemburg wrote on 16 February 1917 to

Mathilde Wurm, her German friend and party comrade, and her preface to Korolenko's autobiography reveal the depth of her conflict. The letter contains a passage frequently quoted to prove either Luxemburg's ambivalence about Jews or her blatant anti-Semitism. It reads as follows: "Why do you dwell on this special suffering of the Jews? The poor victims of the rubber plantations in Putumayo, the Negroes in Africa, whose bodies the Europeans use to play a game of ball, are just as close to me."[63]

In an earlier letter to Mathilde Wurm, Luxemburg described the German Social Democrats as "miserable creatures, with the souls of small shopkeepers, ready to sell a little 'heroism' but only 'for cash' . . . as long as the 'profit' is lying right on the counter."[64] Mathilde Wurm, perhaps resentful of this allusion to a Jewish stereotype, responded by sending Luxemburg a fictionalized biography of the excommunicated Jewish philosopher Spinoza. Luxemburg, in turn, might have interpreted this present, which she branded *Kitsch,* as an attempt to teach her a lesson, and angrily reacted to the "special suffering of the Jews."

That Luxemburg reacted vehemently when confronted with her Jewishness is attested to by a Polish socialist, Tadeusz Radwański, who remembered that she burst out in anger when he mentioned that he taught himself Yiddish in order to communicate with Jewish workers. " 'Here is another madman, another *goy* who learned the Yiddish jargon,' she cried. 'Literature in jargon! That's sheer mockery! And in particular [I. L.] Peretz, that lunatic, who has the temerity to insult Heine with his translation from the beautiful German language to that old-Swabian dialect corrupted by a smattering of Hebrew words and garbled vernacular Polish.' "[65]

In the preface to Korolenko's autobiography, *The History of My Contemporary,* Luxemburg wrote: "Oppression, insecurity, injustice, poverty and dependence . . . mold the souls of people in a certain manner."[66] Whether or not she was referring to herself, the remark is revealing in light of the material she discussed. Describing Korolenko's fight for justice, Luxemburg mentioned the notorious 1911 Kiev trial of a Jewish bricklayer, Mendel Beylis, accused of ritual murder. But she referred to it as the "Kishinev ritual murder," evidently confusing the 1903 Kishinev pogrom and the Beylis trial in Kiev. In the entire civilized world both incidents stood as symbols of the persecution of Jews; yet Rosa Luxemburg confused the facts. One may dismiss this as an oversight or regard it as symptomatic of her ambivalence.

No less intriguing is Luxemburg's interpretation in the preface of "the scapegoat phenomenon," which she regarded as a product of modern civilization. In the United States the Negroes served as scapegoats; in western Europe, the Italians. An example of the latter, Luxemburg wrote, was "a small Italian pogrom" near Zurich which occurred at the turn of the century in the wake of the murder of a child. She also mentions that in Russia seven savage, heathen Votjak peasants were accused of ritual murder and were prosecuted.[67]

The order in which Luxemburg listed the minorities—Negroes, Italians, Votjaks, Jews—is revealing; so is her application of the word "pogrom," normally associated with an assault on Jews, to Italian workers. It is also symptomatic that she singled out the Italians, not the Jews, as the scapegoats in western Europe, while saying that the Jews served as the focus of people's discontent in eastern Europe. And, significantly, she invoked the Dreyfus affair in the context of the Votjaks' case rather than that of the Beylis trial, though the parallel between the Dreyfus and Beylis cases was self-evident.

Most of Luxemburg's time at Wronki was devoted to the Korolenko translation. Transported from the German prison to nineteenth-century Russia, she relived the hopes and dreams of the Russians. In the preface she outlined the development of literature in Russia in a popular, simplistic, and inaccurate way. She suggested that Russian literature burst out "overnight" from darkness and barbarism "like Minerva from Jupiter's head."[68] Her exaggerated view of Russia, where miracles occur and backwardness turns overnight into progress, had a political underpinning. Her frequent allusions to German complacency and slave psychology, as opposed to the Russians' need for self-analysis, in effect showed German spiritual development on the decline and Russia rising to monumental spiritual heights. On the canvas of literature, Luxemburg embroidered the words that ten years earlier she had flung into the face of the Germans: When will you finally learn from the Russians!

The technique of translation became a new challenge. Always a little concerned about her German, she had first Hans Diefenbach and after his death Luise Kautsky correct her language, until she realized that even in a translation the language must be her own. She learned that in order to translate into idiomatic German she must gain distance from the original text, so she would put aside the first draft and let some time elapse before revising it. A translator, like a creative writer, has a constant gnawing feeling of dissatisfaction; in this way she justified the slow pace of her work. In fact, she worked anything but slowly; toward the end of August 1917 she had eighty pages of the manuscript ready, in mid-September another hundred pages. Since the prison censors were her first readers, it took a long time before the manuscript reached Mathilde Jacob, who typed it. The delays irritated Rosa and she often worried that the single, handwritten copy might get lost. But the work gave her much pleasure and she was proud that her friends praised her German language.

By Christmas 1917, the third and last she would spend in prison, Luxemburg was looking forward to the yearly holiday ritual. Jacob was entrusted with buying a book on Egyptian art for Clara Zetkin, books for Sonja Liebknecht and Marta Rosenbaum, and "a Christmas gift for me," W. R. Eckhart's work on climate.[69] It was Rosa's way of saying that life was still normal.

In March 1918, when Luxemburg learned of Jogiches's arrest, she showed no emotion. Throughout the years of his clandestine activities in the Spartacus League she had trembled for his safety, Jacob recalled, but once he was caught, Luxemburg turned to practical matters. Every bit of food that friends gave her was to be sent to Jogiches, she instructed Jacob, and she checked whether her orders were strictly followed. "You know that prison fare is inedible, and Leo lives almost exclusively on what you bring him," she reminded Jacob.[70] Should Jogiches need towels, her linen could be used; but Jogiches badly wanted cigarettes. Luxemburg produced them. Mathilde Jacob, now with two prisoners in her charge, traveled between Moabit prison in Berlin, where Jogiches was incarcerated, and Breslau, delivered Luxemburg's gifts, and transmitted messages.

Jogiches was in good spirits, Rosa knew from Jacob. She had no doubt he could outwit his captors, which he did. Confronted with a fellow member of the Spartacus League, Jogiches remarked: "Too bad we haven't met before." Presented with evidence—the last issue of *Spartacus Letters,* which he himself had edited—he asked the judge to let him read it and with feigned curiosity inquired how many issues had appeared.[71]

After his imprisonment Luxemburg did not mention Jogiches in letters to her German friends. It was a pain she had to live with alone.

But she knew that life behind bars was deadly for Jogiches and desperately wanted him to be free. The separate peace treaty signed in March 1918 between Germany and Russia opened a possibility for the exchange of prisoners. Jogiches, a Russian subject, was a likely candidate. So in letters to Polish comrades in Russia, Luxemburg pleaded again and again: "Save Leo!"

After the 1917 February revolution in Russia, Luxemburg remarked that the "comic *change de places*"—her old Russian friends were let out of prison while she was behind bars—pleased her, although her own chances of getting out were diminished.[72] By April she appeared less self-absorbed. "The wonderful events in Russia affect me like a life-giving elixir," she wrote to Marta Rosenbaum, at the same time expressing her apprehension that the change in Russia was not sufficiently appreciated and understood in Germany. "It *must*, it *will* have a redeeming effect in the whole world, it *must* radiate all over Europe. I am absolutely convinced that this is the beginning of a new epoch." Still, "one cannot count on a lasting success over there," she cautioned, unless the international, and especially the German, proletariat actively supported the Russians.[73] At the end of November, after the October Revolution put the Bolsheviks in power, she wrote to Luise Kautsky: "Are you happy about the Russians? Of course, they cannot last long in this witches' sabbat," not because of their backward economy but because the Social Democracy in the West consisted of miserable cowards who would look on as the Russians bled to death.[74]

Luxemburg scanned the papers closely for the fragmentary and confusing news from Russia, and in December 1917 she became upset over the Bolsheviks' determination to make peace with Germany. Prison became torture as doubts began to creep in, doubts over what was going on in Russia. "It occurred to me today, while I was classifying the flowers," she wrote in July 1918, "that I am consciously . . . deluding myself into thinking that I still live a normal life, while in fact all around me there is a pervasive atmosphere of universal doom. Yesterday I read in the papers about the 200 'expiatory executions' in Moscow, and perhaps that is what did me in."*[75]

*Luxemburg referred to the punishment meted out to the left Social Revolutionaries, who attempted the overthrow of the Soviet government.

There is no doubt that in their clandestine correspondence Luxemburg discussed the events in Russia with Jogiches. He defined his own position bluntly: "Most important, under no circumstances should we appear publicly as an offshoot of Russian Bolshevism; rather, we should be examining the situation in Russia from our radical Marxist point of view," he wrote in November 1917 to the editor of the Stuttgart-based *Sozialdemokrat*. "Indeed, the latter will not correspond in certain points with the radicalism of Lenin and his comrades. They are of course good comrades and honest revolutionaries, but the specific conditions in Russia push them toward certain conclusions that we may not be able to underwrite."[76]

Luxemburg, less concerned with appearances and more with world revolution, continued to observe the Russian scene. A series of articles, published mainly in *Spartacus Letters* between April 1917 and September 1918, reflected her views. Her admiration was reserved, as usual, for the Russian workers, their indomitable spirit, and their devotion to socialism. It was the leadership that troubled her. The Peace Treaty of Brest-Litovsk signed by Soviet Russia and the Central Powers was "nothing but the capitulation of the Russian revolutionary proletariat to German imperialism."[77] Called "The Russian Tragedy," Luxemburg's article was published in September 1918 and carried an editorial footnote: although the editors of the *Spartacus Letters* shared the author's apprehensions, they were concerned with the *objective* situation of the Bolsheviks, not with their *subjective* conduct. Thus a form of logic was born which in time became an instrument of Soviet party policy. It was three decades before Arthur Koestler made it clear to the world: whoever disagrees with the Soviet leadership can be *objectively* proven to be an agent of Fascism even if *subjectively* he happened to have his kidneys smashed by the Fascists.

In the summer of 1918 Luxemburg wrote an article about the Russian Revolution. Friends pleaded with her to refrain from publishing it, arguing that public criticism of the beleaguered, fragile Bolshevik regime was not in the interest of the revolution. This was possibly the first time the argument was used that to openly criticize Soviet Russia was to join forces with Russia's enemies. Luxemburg insisted on publication. In September Paul Levi visited her in prison to persuade her to change her mind, and after a long discussion she agreed. But the discussion convinced her that she must clarify her position; she started a longer work that remained unfinished. She communicated its contents to Levi through a "trusted friend," he recalled, certainly Mathilde Jacob. That Levi and Luxemburg differed in their assessment of the Russian Revolution is borne out by her message to him: "I am writing this pamphlet for you, and should I manage to convince only you, I will not have worked in vain."[78]

The fate of this slim volume, some sixty pages long, is an almost perfect symbol of the fate of its author. It never ceased to embarrass both socialists and Bolsheviks; it is interpreted either as the work of a Marxist heretic or that of an orthodox Marxist who is betraying or apologizing for the Russian Revolution. Even before the unfinished pamphlet was published, strings were being pulled to suppress it. After Levi had it published in 1922, he was accused by the Communist Parties in Moscow and Berlin of falsifying Luxemburg's work. In the West it was largely ignored by the public-spirited young generation that was looking to the Soviet Union for a remedy for Fascism.

Luxemburg's analysis of the October Revolution, dismissed as a momentary delusion by some and hailed as prophetic by others, is neither. It is a logical continuation of her theory, based on the concept of the development of history toward a more advanced, more democratic society. She welcomed the Revolution as "the most significant event of the World War," stating that Lenin's was "the sole Party in Russia that grasped the true interests of the revolution in that first period." But she believed that Lenin's and Trotsky's method, the complete elimination of democracy, was catastrophic.

Point by point, she discussed the failures of the Soviet government: the seizure and distribution of land was bound to create a powerful mass of new property owners, potential foes of the Revolution; the right to national self-determination and the right to secede from Russia enhanced nationalistic sentiments, thus undermining the unification of the proletariat; the dissolution of the Constituent Assembly deprived the masses of a fundamental democratic institution; the abolition of universal suffrage and the destruction of the most important democratic guarantees—freedom of the press and the right of association and assembly—prevented the development of a healthy public life.

With hindsight, Luxemburg's criticism of the Bolsheviks' agrarian policy and of national self-determination was of course pointless because neither was implemented. But it is a tribute to Luxemburg's faith in the moral standards of revolutionaries that she took their words seriously. In her mind's eye she saw masses of new property owners—the Russian peasants and one nation after another—seceding from revolutionary Russia. Although she decried the "terror and suppression of democracy," she did not think the cause was lost. Lenin, Trotsky, and their supporters were the first to set an example for the world proletariat, the first who could proudly say, "I have dared!" They had advanced the dispute between capital and labor in the entire world. But, she said, the problem could only be posed in Russia; it could not be solved in Russia.

With a few master strokes she illuminated her point. "Socialism, by its very nature, cannot be dictated, introduced by command . . . [Lenin] is completely mistaken in the means he employs: decree, the dictatorial power of a factory overseer, Draconian penalties, rule by terror . . . Without general elections, without unrestricted freedom of press and assembly, without a free exchange of opinions, life dies out in every public institution and only bureaucracy remains active . . . Slowly, public life falls asleep, and a few dozen party leaders . . . command and rule . . . In reality power is executed by a dozen outstanding minds while the elite of the working class are now and then invited to meetings in order to applaud the speeches of the leaders and to approve unanimously proposed resolutions. In fact, then, it is a clique—certainly a dictatorship, not the dictatorship of the proletariat, however, but that of a handful of politicians." Lenin and his comrades "have contributed to the cause of international socialism whatever could possibly have been contributed under such fiendishly difficult conditions. The danger begins, when they make a virtue of necessity . . . Freedom only for the supporters of the government," she said, "only for the members of one Party, no matter how numerous, is no freedom. Freedom is always for the one who thinks differently."⁷⁹

Nothing was ever so painful to write as her assessment of the Russian Revolution—nothing ever would be.

Would Jogiches, had he been free, dissuade Luxemburg from making public her opinion of the Revolution as Levi did? Certainly not. Had her criticism been published, the events in postwar Germany might have taken a different course. Luxemburg had always believed that well-informed workers were capable of making decisions, that it was the duty of the leadership to keep them informed. Now she agreed to withhold the truth. She let herself be swayed by Levi, who had good intentions but little knowledge or experience. Without Jogiches she was all alone, confronted with a dilemma whose magnitude she could not fathom.

The following postscript sheds some light on the avalanche that Luxemburg's pamphlet set in motion after her death.

In the fall of 1921 Clara Zetkin brought from Moscow a recommendation from Lenin to have Luxemburg's collected works published. In spite of "Luxemburg's errors," Lenin publicly called her "the eagle of the revolution."* But Zetkin also brought instructions to burn Luxemburg's manuscript on the Russian Revolution. Allegedly Luxemburg had withdrawn her criticism of the Revolution, had had a change of heart before she died. Clara Zetkin said that she knew this from Jogiches, but since Jogiches was dead too, there was no one to verify her statement. Zetkin wrote to Paul Levi to ask him to refrain from publishing the disputed manuscript. Levi replied that he was not interested in what "Radek says" or "Zinovjev says," or "Bukharin says," a clear indication that all three had pressed Clara Zetkin to prevent the publication. "You . . . still believe that we must continue to be silent," Levi wrote in response to her request. "Myself, I wonder whether we were right to keep silent so long." Luxemburg had been criticizing Lenin's concepts for twenty years, he said, and the work in question was but a continuation of her arguments. "Dear comrade Clara," he maintained, was doing Rosa as much harm as Lenin or more by trying to reduce Luxemburg's views to "a misunderstanding, the wrong information—Rosa was very well informed—or simply her bad mood." "In certain questions Rosa was in opposition to the Bolsheviks . . . and these are precisely the questions that the course of the Russian Revolution pushed to the forefront . . . To publish her literary legacy and pass over her opposition in silence . . . would mean, first, to renounce any criticism once and for all as long as Russia stands alone . . . ; second, to renounce the course . . . Rosa pointed out to us while she was still alive, which . . . history has justified; and third, to destroy Rosa's wonderfully complete *Weltanschauung*."[80]

Clara Zetkin did not give in, and neither did Levi. She published a book, *Rosa Luxemburgs Stellung zur russischen Revolution (Rosa Luxemburg's Position on the Russian Revolution)*, and Levi published an

---

*Lenin maintained that Luxemburg "erred" over the question of Poland's independence; in her evaluation of Menshevism in 1903; in her theory of the accumulation of capital; in her demand in 1914 that the Bolsheviks unify with the Mensheviks; and in her writings from prison in 1918.

introduction to *The Russian Revolution,* as the work became known, almost as long as the text itself. Zetkin argued that Lenin and Luxemburg never had any major differences; Levi argued the opposite. Taking as a point of departure Luxemburg's 1904 article, where differences were first spelled out, Levi demonstrated the consistency of Luxemburg's opposition down to the program of the Spartacus League.

Levi was fully aware of the storm the publication would cause: "Some will reproach me with publishing it too *late,* others with publishing it too *early* or publishing it at all."[81] He prepared *The Russian Revolution* for publication after the uprising in Kronstadt in 1921—the first revolt of the people against the Bolshevik regime. At that point he had his own irreconcilable differences with Lenin and was accused of using Luxemburg to square his personal accounts. The Kronstadt revolt and the ruthless way it was quashed prompted his difficult decision. Any illusions he might still have harbored about the course adopted by the Bolsheviks were gone. That the *"most faithful sons of the revolution,* the most devoted supporters of the Bolsheviks . . . the elite of the revolutionary fighters,*" tested in a hundred battles, he wrote, rose up in arms against the government was an indication of a profound crisis in Russia.[82]

Luxemburg's diary for 1918 bears an inscription in Mathilde Jacob's handwriting: "Prosit Neujahr, Rosa. With best wishes for 1918, hope to see you at home soon."[83] It was the last of three diaries Luxemburg kept in prison and the most cryptic. Days, weeks, months were passing her by, indifferent and uncontrollable. The entries are scattered and monotonous—a letter to Mathilde, a letter from Mathilde, a parcel to Costia Zetkin, nice weather, a singing bird. In April the style changed. After Jogiches was arrested, she remembered how much he had disapproved of her lack of discipline and tried to impose some on herself. On 1 April she noted that she saw a small fox, on 2 April the temperature was 22 degrees in the shade at 4 o'clock, on 3 April she mailed two letters to Mathilde, on the fourth and on the sixth special delivery letters to Mathilde, on the seventh "3 × to Mathilde"; spread over the rest of the month there are six similar entries. In May there are two entries, in June one. In July, her weight was 51.1 kilos, in August she paid the dentist 39 marks, 17 September was a hot summer day, in

October she sent a letter to the prison administration. On 6 November an amnesty for political offenders was granted. On 8 November she made a big cross in blue ink and wrote, "10 o'clock at night."[84] At 10:00 P.M. she was told she was free.

She left the prison immediately and spent the night in the offices of the railroad workers' union preparing for a demonstration the following day, where she addressed the cheering crowds from the balcony of the City Hall.

She returned to Berlin alone, sitting on her suitcase in the aisle of a train packed with soldiers returning home. Jogiches, released on 9 November, had dispatched Mathilde Jacob to fetch Rosa in a car since train transport was uncertain, but they missed each other. Luxemburg descended from the train in Berlin on 10 November 1918. She had come to that city twenty years earlier ready to change the world. Now, gray-haired and frail, she stood at its gates—the same city and the same dream.

15 | *The End and the Beginning*
1919

ON 29 OCTOBER 1918, the German Emperor and King of Prussia Wilhelm II, impervious to pressure for his abdication, left Berlin for the military headquarters in Spa to seek the protection of the army. On the same day, the navy, the pride and glory of his empire, revolted. The mutiny of the sailors in Kiel turned into a general uprising after six hundred sailors were imprisoned on 4 November. By 6 November red flags were flying in the Hansa cities, Lübeck, Hamburg, and Bremen, and the next day the revolutionary movement spread throughout the country. In Munich, the most stolid of the German cities, the Bavarian Republic was proclaimed, and councils of workers, peasants, and soldiers were formed. The troops joined the rebelling workers.

The German summer offensive had collapsed, and the High Command, conceding defeat, recommended ending the war. Nevertheless, Field Marshal Paul von Hindenburg demanded continued resistance, even after armistice negotiations had begun in early October. Bent on fighting to the last man—Hitler's defense of Berlin comes to mind—the military kept the fearful and hungry population in line. Käthe Kollwitz's drawings of starving German children shook the conscience of the world but not that of the generals. The "turnip winter" of 1917, when even coffee, beer, and cigarettes were made of turnips, had turned the prospect of yet another year of war into a nightmare.

The stability and security of peacetime had ill prepared the people for the horrors of war. Though not a parliamentary democracy, Germany still gave its subjects a measure of freedom and optimism. The economic situation of workers and peasants had been steadily improving. The 1884 Health Insurance Act and the Social Democrats' rise to power demonstrated the state's interest in its citizens' welfare. When war came, it was regarded largely as an invitation to heroism, unification as a *Volk,* and a display of manhood and patriotism, not as a war of conquest. The proclamation of Wilhelm I, King of Prussia, as German Emperor, in the Hall of Mirrors at the Palace of Versailles in 1871 was within living memory. The Germans believed what they had been told for generations: that their armies, indeed superb, were unconquerable. The population came to know deprivation and disease during the World War but it had experienced no gunfire, no trenches, and no battlefields. With no concept of the real dimensions of the military catastrophe, people fell easy victims to propaganda that victory was certain. Therefore, after the war ended, they readily believed the reasons the army gave for the defeat.

For several decades the Junker military caste had looked on with anger and revulsion as industrialization and all that goes with it— business, money, workers, socialists—poisoned the soul of the people and undermined the power of the country's legitimate masters. The war provided a chance not only to show the world that the spirit of the Iron Chancellor was alive but to stamp out the vermin at home. Victory would put the power back where it belonged. The tide would be reversed, the old values reinstated. No one would dare, as the Jewess Luxemburg had, to abuse what was sacred—the men in uniform. The defeat, when it came, was a complete surprise; it would never have happened had it not been for a bunch of foreign degenerates. For years they had been turning honest, patriotic Germans against their own country, and now they were plotting to deliver the country to the Bolsheviks.

The armistice brought an end to hostilities without and a beginning of hostilities within Germany. No sooner had the truce been signed than the army aired its famous stab-in-the-back *(Dolchstoss)* theory: the socialists, communists, liberals, pacifists, and above all the

Jews, had dealt Germany the fatal blow by undermining morale at home and among the soldiers. "The Jew," Dr. Joseph Goebbels was to say in 1930, "is the real cause of our losing the Great War."[1]

The events on the ninth of November—dramatic, but not without elements of farce—were symptomatic of the chaos into which the unexpected and unaccepted defeat plunged Germany. Wilhelm II insisted on leading his troops to Berlin to restore order and lift the spirits of his subjects; they, however, were loudly demanding his abdication. The chancellor, Prince Max von Baden, urged the Emperor to abdicate in favor of his eldest grandson. "In this way, with the help of the socialists, we could save the situation," he told the emperor. "Otherwise there will be a republic."[2] Around noon, Prince Max forced the emperor's hand by making the abdication public; only then did Wilhelm II agree to resign as German emperor, though not as king of Prussia. Finally persuaded that the army "no longer stands behind Your Majesty," he boarded the train which carried him into exile in Holland.[3]

Prince Max appointed a Social Democratic chancellor, Friedrich Ebert, in a last attempt to save the monarchy. During the reign of the monarchy the Social Democrats had gained considerable political leverage and now contemplated a parliamentary monarchy rather than total abolition of the old order. Within two hours, however, they were faced with an accomplished fact—the proclamation of the German Republic. While Ebert conferred with his colleagues, a rumor reached the Reichstag that Karl Liebknecht was about to proclaim a German soviet republic. Allegedly in response, Philipp Scheidemann, a Social Democrat and member of the new government, appeared on the balcony of the Reichstag at 2:00 P.M. and, without consulting Ebert, proclaimed the German Republic. At 4:00 P.M., Liebknecht, perhaps in response to Scheidemann, proclaimed not a soviet but a "free, socialist German Republic."[4] The speed of events, compounded by confusion both in government circles and in the streets, makes it virtually impossible to reconstruct coherently the day's events. One thing is certain: the birth of the Republic was a reaction rather than a deliberate action. And its survival was to depend on the army who loathed it.

Events were forced by hunger and disastrous military losses, not by a desire for democracy. Prince Max von Baden entrusted Ebert with the chancellorship in order to preserve the monarchy, not to abolish it. Ebert then entered into an alliance with Hindenburg. By not making a clean break with the past, the Republic carried the germs of its own destruction. War was easier than peace. As long as the war lasted, there was the kaiser and the legend of Bismarck and absolute faith in an unconquerable Germany. Peace launched a period of national destruction that ended only in 1945.

Berlin reflected the turbulence that had seized the country. The streets teemed with armed civilians. Sailors and soldiers invaded the Reichstag building and made themselves comfortable in elegant armchairs; they slept on antique tables and benches and stamped out their cigarettes on Oriental rugs. Unshaven, with bloodshot eyes and guns slung over their shoulders, they evoked unpleasant associations. "It was like a film from the Russian Revolution," Count Kessler noted in his diary.[5]

The Russian Revolution! The seeds of the red scare were sown. "The Danger of Bolshevism!" ran the legend under a poster showing a skull with a knife between its bared teeth and a gallows in the background. "German Women! Do you know what Bolshevism and Spartacism threaten? . . . women will become the property of the people . . . any man who wants to use that communal property needs a permit from the Workers' Committee . . . everyone is duty-bound to report on women who refuse." "Come to us," appealed the Union to Combat Bolshevism, "we shall show you how you can help."[6]

Yet the trams in Berlin ran regularly, the telephones worked, the stores were open, and the fate of the country was debated in crowded cafés to the sound of machine gun fire and whistling bullets. Now and then, orderly steel-helmeted troops passed through, showing where the power lay.

The power lay on the side of the government. On 10 November, the chief of staff, Major General Wilhelm Groener, and Chancellor Friedrich Ebert conducted a telephone conversation. In effect they entered into an alliance, supported by Field Marshal von Hindenburg, to combat the revolution. "As a first measure," Groener testified in the so-called stab-in-the-back trial, in 1925, "we established a line of communication between Headquarters and the Reich chancellory. Every night from eleven to one o'clock we were to consult on a secret telephone line . . . Then . . . a plan was drawn up to bring ten divisions to Berlin. Ebert expressed his agreement."[7] A contemporary put it bluntly: "If Scheidemann proclaimed the Republic on the 9th of November, Ebert finished it off on the 10th."[8]

On 10 November, the day Rosa Luxemburg returned to Berlin, her death warrant was virtually signed. She had sixty-seven days to live. Luxemburg arrived in Berlin four days after the revolution had swept over the country and one day after the proclamation of the Republic. The city she had last seen in July 1916, before hunger and defeat had changed its face, was in commotion; streets abounded with boisterous crowds, red flags flew everywhere. It was an awesome sight that could not but affect her deeply. But the crowds were deceptive, she knew, and like the flags could change with the wind. Within a few hours she was to witness those shifting currents.

Rosa telephoned Mathilde Jacob from the railroad station only to learn from her mother about Mathilde's trip to Breslau. Mrs. Jacob invited Luxemburg to her apartment, and after checking her luggage she went there. She barely had time to wash and change after the exhausting trip when Jogiches, Liebknecht, and Paul Levi came and immediately took her to the editorial office of the *Berliner Lokalanzeiger*. The previous night a group of workers had occupied the offices of the right-wing newspaper, a favorite of the emperor's, and declared it the property of the proletariat. The first issue of what was to become the official organ of the Spartacus League and later of the Communist Party of Germany, *Die Rote Fahne (The Red Flag)*, carried the date 9 November. "Berlin Under the Red Flag," ran the huge headline. The second issue was published on 10 November. When Luxemburg arrived, it fell to her to negotiate with the printers—her first though by no means last unsuccessful effort on behalf of the revolution. The printers refused to set the paper, and the guards who had volunteered to protect the safety of the Spartacists now pointed guns at their heads. Acting on the orders of Scherl-Verlag, the owner of the requisitioned newspaper, the guards threatened the Spartacists with death should they try to leave the premises. On the third day of the revolution, Paul Levi later recalled, they were contemplating the fate of a revolution whose soldiers changed sides between breakfast and lunch. After protracted negotiations, Luxemburg and her friends were released and proceeded to the Hotel Excelsior. When Mathilde Jacob arrived late that night with Luxemburg's luggage, she found them in a somber mood, debating what to do next.

The following week Luxemburg stayed at the Hotel Excelsior. Her room became a headquarters of sorts where the Spartacist leaders were in constant session, reviewing events and devising strategies. The most urgent matter was the acquisition of a newspaper. Without its own daily paper, the Spartacist League was cut off from the people and rendered totally ineffective. Further talks with Scherl-Verlag were futile; the company had been granted an injunction. Day after day Luxemburg looked for a printer. "Oh, *The Red Flag* will be flying on my grave," she sighed after yet another failure.[9] Finally a magazine called *The Little Journal* was acquired, and the third issue of *The Red Flag* appeared on 18 November. That same day, Luxemburg wrote to Clara Zetkin from Hotel Moltke (the Excelsior had asked her to leave) that the hunt was over and the nerve-wracking question "Will it come out or won't it?" was solved.[10] Officially Luxemburg and Karl Liebknecht coedited the paper; in fact, with Liebknecht away at meetings and conferences, she edited it alone. There were no experienced journalists, no writers, no editors to count on. The situation at the Spartacist paper mirrored the isolation of its leadership and the division that had occurred within the German Social Democratic Party: the older Social Democrats almost invariably stayed in the SPD or joined the Independent Social Democratic Party of Germany (USPD) founded in 1917. Therefore, the rank and file of the Spartacist League consisted mostly of young men and women, less seasoned but more impetuous than their leaders.

Protective and proud of her newborn—"the only socialist paper in Berlin," she pointed out—Luxemburg was well aware of its shortcomings and spared no effort to make each issue better than the last.[11] She spent almost every hour of the day in the editorial offices and sometimes, too exhausted to walk, had to be carried to a cab at night. "I'll sleep well," she would say to Jacob from her bed. "I managed to do everything I planned, I'm so happy."[12] She asked the veteran socialist leader Franz Mehring for critical comments and Clara Zetkin for contributions: "Write something about women, it is very important right now and none of us knows much on the subject."[13] She implored Zetkin to be as brief as possible, for the shortage of paper was a constant problem. She planned a supplement for women, another for soldiers, still another for young audiences. The newspaper was to be on a high literary level, but above all it was to enlighten and educate the workers. Within two months Luxemburg wrote more than twenty articles. Penetrating and sober, at times lyrical, they throbbed with life and passion and that peculiar spirit of a Polish fighter who is ready to die but not to compromise.

An article in the 18 November issue of *The Red Flag* called "The Beginning" exemplifies the blend of pragmatism and idealism that was characteristic of Luxemburg's reaction to the revolution in Germany. It was not a time to rejoice or to triumph, she wrote, but a time to mobilize everyone's energy to continue the work that had just begun. The accomplishments were meager, for nothing of substance had changed. A reactionary country cannot turn into a revolutionary republic overnight, she cautioned; the soldiers who yesterday had been killing their brothers from other countries and the workers who calmly looked on would not turn into socialists with a wave of the hand. The creation of the revolution was a formidable task, not to be achieved with a few decrees from above, but by the conscious action of the workers. Free will and spiritual maturity, not orders or force, would bring about social change. She also called for practical measures. She demanded that a world congress of workers be convened promptly in Germany; a proletarian Red Guard and workers' militia were to defend the revolution; the immediate expropriation of dynastic wealth and landed property was to put an end to hunger; new local Workers' and Soldiers' Councils must be elected to replace those that had sprung up in the first chaotic days.

Luxemburg's vision of the working class, based on Marx's theory, reflects its limitations. Under capitalism, human labor, essentially creative, becomes an ordeal and burden for it is used to satisfy artificially generated needs—in a socialist society, people will work with joy for they recover their creativity. But the vision and reality were at odds. Just as Luxemburg disregarded differences springing from divergent cultural and social conditions—as when she equated an East European Jew with a Negro in Africa—she did, like many others, disregard the appeal that "bourgeois" values—property, nationalism, religion—might have for the workers. Genuinely cosmopolitan, she rejected the barriers of language, nationality, and religion, and she projected her experience onto the workers' day-to-day existence.

While Luxemburg was fighting for the soul of the German worker, the government was busy arming its divisions. About three thousand sailors ordered to Berlin by the chancellor were joined by the Republic Soldiers' Guard, the People's Guard, the Iron Division, and the paramilitary Volunteer Corps *(Freikorps)*. Composed of demobilized soldiers and officers, unemployed workers, disenchanted junkers, fanatical nationalists, and adventurers, these troops abandoned all badges of rank and elected their own military leaders. The chief of staff, Groener, observed: "Even Soviet Russia has introduced drill into her army, which does not have officers elected by the men."[14] That a member of the old military caste should evoke the authority of Soviet Russia, a bogeyman for all other purposes, reflects the cynicism that was to topple both the revolution and the Republic.

No one was more aware than Luxemburg of the apprehension and fear that the Bolsheviks inspired in the Germans. Nor was she unaware of the Bolsheviks' desire to gain political capital in Germany or of the German government's efforts to lump the Spartacists with the Bolsheviks and thus exploit the fears of the German people. To misrepresent socialist aims was, she wrote, a deliberately planned action. To identify the Spartacus League as Bolsheviks was no doubt a clever and, in the short run, successful move. In the long run it helped to pave the way for Adolf Hitler.

Although Luxemburg abstained from publicly criticizing the Soviet regime, she did not laud it. To emphasize that the Spartacists shared the goals and values of Western socialists, she and Jogiches objected to naming the Spartacists' own party "communist" and opted for "socialist," but they were overruled by the majority of the leadership. To thwart the Bolsheviks' attempts to dominate the future International, she wanted the congress of the international workers' movement to be held in Germany. Eventually she instructed the German delegates to Moscow to vote against the creation of the Third International. Most eloquent, however, were her statements testifying to the differences between Lenin's concept of the revolution and her own. In her opinion, the means Lenin employed, especially terror, were worse than the disease his regime was supposed to cure. "The proletarian revolution requires no terror to achieve its aims; it hates and despises mass murder."[15] Terror was to her mind the ultimate perversion of socialism. "We don't need a 'Commissar for Bolshevism,' " Luxemburg greeted Lenin's emissary, Karl Radek. "The Bolsheviks are welcome to keep their tactics for themselves."[16] If in public Luxemburg attributed the rule by terror to the bourgeoisie, friends who knew her views were aware of her thinly disguised criticism of Soviet Russia. Likewise, when she criticized the German government for imagining that socialism could be inaugurated merely by overthrowing the old government and issuing various decrees, she was doubtless alluding to the Bolsheviks. "Socialism will not and

236

cannot be created by decrees; nor can it be established by a socialist government, no matter how excellent. Socialism must be created by the masses, by every proletarian . . . Only that is socialism, and only thus can socialism be created."[17]

For all the uncertainties, the month of November 1918 was a happy time for Luxemburg. She had regained her freedom, had seen the spontaneous outburst of the revolution, and had hoped it would repair the damage the war had dealt to the international workers' movement. With Jogiches at her side, it was as though they were starting over together. Jogiches's one ambition was Luxemburg's success. Now, when he no longer felt threatened by her demanding love and her brilliant mind, he gave her what she needed most—faith. His cool tactician's mind was skeptical about Luxemburg's vision of the spiritual rebirth of the German workers; visions were now being suppressed with machine guns. But he did not discourage her.

They both looked older, much older than their age. Luxemburg was forty-eight, Jogiches fifty-one. Her dark brown hair had turned white, her face was sallow and lined. He had lost his air of power, his shoulders were stooped, his movements heavier. They were filled with a new tenderness for each other, and a tolerance often tinged with humor. "I'm so hungry, why don't you give me something to eat?" Luxemburg once asked Mathilde Jacob in a cab taking them home late at night. "Surely, Leo would say I should control myself better, but I've got to eat something."[18] Jogiches may have suspected that Paul Levi's constant presence at Rosa's side was not necessitated by work alone, and Jogiches's protracted involvement with his landlady may have been no secret to Luxemburg. But their relationship, never conventional, was unaffected.

Unlike Liebknecht or Levi, both staunch supporters of the Bolsheviks, Jogiches understood the depths of Luxemburg's isolation. She was faced with the victorious Lenin, who was now effecting a program she had sharply criticized as far back as 1904, and with the victorious German Social Democrats, who she believed had betrayed socialism. Jogiches knew that she would not make the slightest compromise in either direction and that consequently she was alone and condemned.

Jogiches's support of Luxemburg was not limited to advice. As a member of the Central Committee of the Spartacus League, he took charge of the buildup of Spartacist organizations throughout the country. As always he kept his distance and was rarely seen outside his little room in the Spartacus League's offices, where workers and soldiers came to receive instructions. "The soldiers were let in singly," a witness recalls. "One could not escape the impression that the organization, although legal, considered itself illegal. The atmosphere was heavy with conspiracy."[19] Leo Jogiches had not changed.

Luxemburg's regained freedom was marred by her nomadic existence, moving from hotel to hotel suitcase in hand. The location of her flat hindered contacts with collaborators to whom she had to be available around the clock. Surrounded by people day and night, she craved the privacy of her home and recalled with slightly exaggerated nostalgia the solitude of her prison cell. Finally, on 28 November 1918 she moved back into the apartment she had left on 10 July 1916. It was a short-lived joy. The distance from the editorial office proved too big an obstacle in her work, so a new round of hotels followed. "If you knew how much I have to tell you and how I live here—a veritable hell!" she wrote to Clara Zetkin. "Karl [Liebknecht] and I have been expelled from all the hotels in the vicinity of Potsdam Square."[20] Sometimes a hotel owner would merely look at Luxemburg and show her the door. Annoying as she found the vagrant life and the rejections, "veritable hell" meant more than that. On street corners and billboards, in newspapers and leaflets, everywhere she found herself denounced as a Jewess, a devil, bent on destroying the God-fearing German people. Anti-Semitism was on the loose, and Luxemburg had now become an ideal target. Like other Jewish socialists, she was convinced that revolution would put an end to anti-Semitism. "As to the pogroms against the Jews," she wrote to Sonja Liebknecht, "all the rumors are simply *lies*. In Russia the era of pogroms is finished for once and for all. The power of the workers and of socialism is much too strong. The revolution purified the atmosphere . . . so that Kishinev is forever passé. Rather, I can imagine pogroms against Jews in Germany."[21]

In the ocean of hatred, her small group of friends created an island where she could breathe freely. But Luise Kautsky, her oldest and closest German friend, now refused to see her out of loyalty to her husband. Yet when Luxemburg was dead, Luise Kautsky wrote poignant reminiscences and glorified the friend she had failed.

Another disappointment, unpleasant and surprising, came from Mathilde Jacob. Luxemburg invited a young woman of Diefenbach's acquaintance to stay in her apartment. Jacob, unable to contain her jealousy, moved out. Even seeing Luxemburg occasionally proved to be "such an ordeal," Jacob confided in her memoir, that she avoided Rosa completely and offered her secretarial services to Jogiches. "I'm delighted you have such good taste," Luxemburg, ignorant of Jacob's dilemma, teased her. "I just can't understand that Leo should be more agreeable than I am. He has the most difficult character I know. One can get along with me." "Alas," Jacob sadly commented, "at that point I could not."[22]

The clouds that were gathering throughout November turned into a storm in December. A Bolshevik invasion of Germany was rumored to be imminent, and in one city after another troops tore down the red flags and set them on fire. On 6 December 1918 the press reported that, according to "well-informed sources," the Allies had ordered the German government to disband the Workers' and Soldiers' Councils or face an embargo and invasion. The truth about this day's events will never be known. One version has the Spartacists attempting a *putsch,* provoking the government into occupying the offices of *The Red Flag* and subsequently inciting the government troops to open fire on the Spartacist demonstrators. Another has the government planning the *putsch* as an excuse to wipe out the Spartacists. Whatever the truth, government troops occupied the offices of *The Red Flag* and a Spartacist demonstration was met with machine gun fire, leaving eighteen dead and thirty wounded. It was an ominous signal that there was no united front of soldiers and workers—a signal that Luxemburg ignored.

With the Chausseestrasse massacre, as it became known, the revolution entered a new phase. On 7 December a Spartacist demonstration took place, protected for the first time by armed workers. The next day another gigantic demonstration followed, and on Christmas Day an exchange of fire between government troops and revolutionary sailors entrenched in the royal stables claimed the lives of eleven sailors and fifty-six soldiers.

Clashes between workers and troops erupted all over the country, and a wave of strikes paralyzed its life. The atmosphere was charged with suspicion and suspense. Vying for public support, socialists of the Social Democratic Party and of the Spartacus League accused each other of betraying the revolution. Amid tumultuous street demonstrations, the first Congress of Workers' and Soldiers' Councils opened in Berlin on 16 December. It left the Spartacists deeply disappointed; Luxemburg and Liebknecht were not even elected to the Congress. The great majority of the 489 delegates supported the Social Democrats.

The first Christmas after the war brought a temporary lull. The city took on a festive air, with street vendors, brightly lit shop windows, and candlelight glittering on Christmas trees. Crowds filled the stores, and few soldiers were in sight.

For Chief of Staff General Groener, this interval was the "worst time." The ten divisions he had ordered into Berlin "got out of hand," he admitted in the 1925 stab-in-the-back trial, and if the Spartacists had chosen to use this opportunity to topple the government, "no one could have hindered them." But "miraculously" the Spartacists did not. "Herr Liebknecht and his comrades were celebrating Christmas and were completely quiet during those days when there were no troops at all in Berlin," the general said.[23] To their credit, or discredit, the Spartacists were preoccupied with an ideological rather than an armed battle: should they split from the SPD and found a separate party and, if so, should it be called "socialist" or "communist"?* On Sunday, 29 December, the very day these debates were taking place, Chancellor Ebert ordered the Volunteer Corps into Berlin; the fight against the Spartacists could now proceed.

Luxemburg could not bear the thought of spending Christmas, her first out of prison, among strangers. She returned to her home, the apartment she had moved to in 1911. From here she had written to Paul Levi in the spring of 1914: "Will you perhaps come on Sunday? . . . I do not want to write, I want to see you."[24] He came to see her then, and he came now to spend Christmas Eve 1918 with her.

Levi rarely left Luxemburg's side during the two hectic months between her release from prison and his arrest in January 1919. "Judah is reaching out for the crown," ran the popular Berlin slogan. "We are ruled by Levi and Rosa Luxemburg."[25] At one of the first open meetings of the Spartacus League, in November, Luxemburg, Liebknecht, and Levi—"the three L's"—each delivered a speech on "The

*Leo Jogiches was one of the three Spartacists who voted against founding a separate party.

Paul Levi

Rosa Luxemburg shared in Levi's rise; Lenin caused his fall.

Rosa Luxemburg with Paul Levi, Berlin, 1914

Moscow 1920. Standing behind Paul Levi are Lenin, Bukharin, and Zinovjev.

Cartoon of the July 1914 trial, with roles reversed: Luxemburg is the judge; the prosecutor is the defendant; rows of uniformed skeletons sit on witness benches.

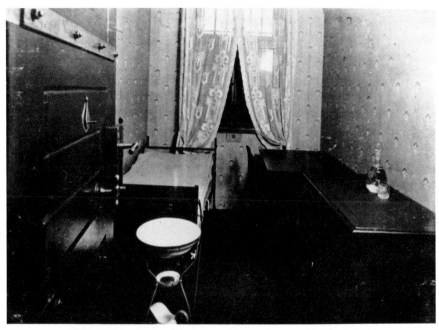

Rosa Luxemburg's prison cell in Wronki, 1916–1917

Leo Jogiches during World War I

Landwehr Canal, where Luxemburg's assassins threw her on the night of
15 January 1919

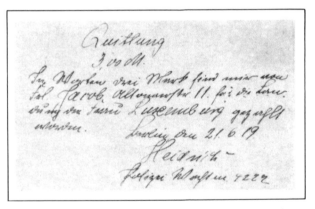

Receipt for three marks paid by Mathilde Jacob for
Rosa Luxemburg's body

Soldier Runge (seated, with drooping mustache) celebrating at the Hotel Eden the day after Luxemburg's assassination. At his trial the presiding judge admonished him: "Defendant Runge, you must behave properly. This is not a laughing matter."

Rosa Luxemburg's funeral on 13 June 1919. Under her picture are the closing words of her last article. The revolution, she wrote, will come back and announce: "I was, I am, I shall be."

Tasks of the Revolution," and subsequently Luxemburg and Levi coauthored the programmatic pamphlet "What Does the Spartacus League Want?"

⎯⎯⎯

She had fifteen more days to live.

On 31 December 1918 Rosa Luxemburg made her last public speech, at the founding Congress of the Communist Party of Germany (KPD). A quarter-century earlier, a 23-year-old, unknown woman from Poland had climbed onto a chair at a meeting in Zurich and created a sensation with her impassioned speech. Since then, she had spoken hundreds of times, in European capitals, at meetings, and at congresses, but never was her heart as heavy as it was that day. Her agreement to split from the SPD was an act of desperation and the most lonely decision of her life. Not even Jogiches supported it. Her speech was clearly designed to expose the chasm dividing Marx from the Social Democrats who falsely claimed his heritage. " 'I do not know whether it is a duty to sacrifice happiness and life to truth,' " she quoted the German philosopher Gotthold Ephraim Lessing. " 'But I know this much: if one desires to teach truth, it is one's duty to teach it wholly or not at all . . . One who brings truth all masked and painted to humanity may well be truth's pimp, but truth's lover he is not.' "[26] The truth was, she said, that the Social Democrats supported the war. They had never cut their ties with the emperor's army and were using it now against the German workers and, jointly with the British Empire, against the Russian workers. The speech asserted that an intensified economic struggle and the workers' participation in a national assembly (should one be created) were means to further the cause of the revolution and warned against the dangerous illusion that the German workers were ready to take over the government. But the warning came too late.

"Ultimately one should accept history as it develops."[27] Luxemburg made this fatalistic statement on 11 January 1919 amidst the blast of grenades, sniper fire, and the pounding of artillery. The battle between the Spartacists and the government troops was in its fifth day, and Luxemburg knew that she and Liebknecht had lost control. "The Spartacists are predominantly a new generation . . . and one must accept this fact with its bright and dark sides," she wrote, vainly trying to justify the bloodshed.[28] What she had most feared had now happened: blind violence turned her vision to shambles. The new generation wanted power now.

The armed confrontation was sparked by the refusal of the president of the Berlin police, Emil Eichhorn, an Independent Socialist, to relinquish his post after the Independents withdrew from the government. Sympathetic to radical workers, he was, the workers claimed, the one man in the government whom they trusted. Deposed by the Minister of the Interior on 4 January 1919, he refused to leave his post and instead began passing out arms to the workers. On Sunday, 5 January, thousands of workers took to the streets, occupied the building of *Vorwärts*, which housed the Social Democrats' newspaper, and invaded other buildings. On the night of 5–6 January the Communist Party of Germany (KPD) and the Independent Social Democrats (USPD) created a Revolutionary Committee; on 6 January they announced the "temporary" takeover of the government. The committee called on the workers to gather at eleven o'clock in the morning in the Siegesallee, which amounted to a call for a general strike. Karl Liebknecht endorsed the takeover without obtaining the consent of the leadership of the KPD. Faced with an accomplished fact, Luxemburg did not conceal her alarm.

On the night of 6 January, the KPD and the USPD started to negotiate a truce with the government. But a truce was not what the government wanted, and it is far from certain that a truce was what the KPD wanted. The government played for time. The immediate and unconditional surrender it demanded was unrealistic in view of the utter chaos in Berlin, the uncontrolled street fights, and the wrath of the people. On 8 January negotiations were broken off and a full-scale offensive against the insurgents began.

It had always been Luxemburg's belief that any split within the socialist ranks was fatal—yet she agreed to the foundation of the Communist Party of Germany; she stated that there is no socialism without the support of the majority of the proletariat—yet its absence did not deter her; she insisted that socialism cannot be implemented by use of force—yet ultimately she supported the January uprising. Events were rolling at such dizzying speed that Luxemburg may have failed to grasp their implications. Of course she was no stranger to the uses and abuses of power in the fight for political survival. But bloodshed she did not want. Loyalty to friends was no doubt an important consideration in her decisions, while terror and intimidation only intensified her rebelliousness. Her theory of spontaneous revolution was being played out in the streets, but not in the way she had conceived of it. In this battle, theory and reality were irreconcilable.

The Spartacist uprising was spontaneous, but it was leaderless, without plan or organization. The Revolutionary Committee voted for the seizure of power, created a number of commissions, and spent most its time debating. "Don't talk! Don't consult! Don't negotiate! *Act!*" Luxemburg urged in an article pointedly entitled "Neglected Duties." "Germany has been the classic country of organization, even of organizational fanaticism, of organizational arrogance," she wrote. "And what are we witnessing today? In the most significant moments of the revolution this renowned 'organizational talent' is the first to fail in the most deplorable way."[29] The following incident bears out her point. The leader of three hundred sailors, dispatched by the Spartacists to occupy the ministry of war, was asked by an official in the invaded building to provide a document authorizing the takeover. The leader left the sailors behind, went to his headquarters, obtained the signed order, and sold it to the government.

If the Spartacists lacked organization, the army did not. Gustav Noske, a former furniture maker and Social Democratic military expert, had been mobilizing forces against the Spartacists for quite some time. Since the regular troops proved undependable, Noske relied on the Volunteer Corps, who could hardly wait to lay their hands on the Spartacists. It is with good reason that the Volunteer Corps is considered the forerunner of Hitler's *Einsatzgruppen,* the mobile killing units of the SS. The Volunteer Corps had one goal: to kill the insurgents. And kill they did, with relish. Anyone bearing a white flag was summarily executed; the workers were savagely beaten and their bodies mutilated beyond recognition. "Where is your Rosa?" jeered the soldiers, ready for a good laugh while doing their grisly job.[30]

The battle ended on 12 January, after the police headquarters, the remaining bulwark of the insurgents, was taken. Their major effort having failed, the Spartacist snipers positioned on rooftops fought hopelessly against heavy artillery and machine guns. Soon it was over, and the troops occupied all Berlin. "At every street crossing stand soldiers in steel helmets, with fixed bayonets and a load of hand grenades . . . The government's convictions may be a little shaky, but at least it has a respectable number of bayonets to stiffen them. Like every government hitherto, it relies on the military force at its disposal," Count Kessler noted in his journal.[31]

Ironically entitled "Order Reigns in Berlin," Luxemburg's last article appeared on 14 January 1919 in *The Red Flag*. An order, she wrote, whose survival depends on ever more bloodshed "inexorably proceeds toward its historical fate—annihilation." She was right. The fighting lasted for another year, was followed by the tormented Weimar Republic, and ended in Hitler's ascent. It was a "matter of honor" for the revolutionaries to fight, she said, expressing the sentiments of such enthusiasts as Bertolt Brecht and Rainer Maria Rilke. And it was the leadership that failed, she stressed, not the masses. The masses had done their duty. They had formed a link in the chain of the revolution, and the revolution will return over and over to proclaim: *"I was, I am, I shall be!"*[32]

She had one more day to live.

She spent that day in hiding. The Marcussohn family, who gave shelter to her and Liebknecht, put her up in a small room at the back of their apartment. She pleaded a headache, for she wanted to be left alone. She lay on her bed, in a sort of slumber, a sort of dream. Was she right in refusing to leave Berlin? Perhaps not; but she could not leave the victims behind and seek safety for herself. Once she had quoted from a legend: "O Adonai, Adonai . . . Let us never speak these words: 'Let us save ourselves and leave the weak to their destiny.' "[33]

She had no premonition of the end. Another prison term would have been a relief. The past ten days had been a nightmare. With each blast of grenades, with each outburst of rifle fire, she had shrunk. Now it was over. The guns fell silent, the carnage stopped.

On 15 January, a little after nine at night, the doorbell rang at the Marcussohn residence at Mannheimer Strasse No. 43. Rosa Luxemburg got up, fully dressed, picked up Goethe's *Faust* from the night table, put it into her handbag, and closed her little suitcase. Then she sat down on the bed and waited. The sound of hobnailed boots and shrill voices reached her through the closed door and she heard her name pronounced. A muffled voice, probably her landlord's, protested, and then the door to her room opened. She did not look up. A man stepped forward, a gun slung over his shoulder. He told her to get her coat, his eyes fixed on her legs. Defiant, she tried to control her limp.

He shot a knowing look at his companions and in a clipped voice ordered her to follow them. She did not ask for an arrest warrant; she knew there was none. She put on her coat and slowly pulled on her gloves, first the left, then the right. It was a relief that Jogiches was not with her. Arrested the day before, he had managed to escape unidentified. Mathilde Jacob and Paul Levi had been arrested a few days earlier. But unlike Luxemburg and Liebknecht, they did not have a price of 100.000 marks on their heads.

Two men marched in front of her, two behind. Her limp had grown more pronounced in the previous weeks and she tried valiantly to walk straight, her head raised.

An automobile was waiting in front of the house. One of the militiamen opened the door and gestured for her to get inside. She gathered the folds of her velvet dress, took a deep breath, and climbed into the car. The man shut the door, sat down next to the driver, and said, "Eden."

The Hotel Eden, located in the center of Berlin, temporarily housed the headquarters of the Garde-Kavallerie-Schützen-Division (Division of Cavalry and Riflemen). The hotel was brightly lit and soldiers were milling about the entrance. Heavily armed, some in half-unbuttoned uniforms with cigarettes stuck in the corners of their mouths, they hardly resembled regular troops. They paid little attention to the civilians, hotel guests, or patrons of the restaurant enjoying a dinner out now that the shooting had stopped. But as the black automobile pulled up, the soldiers, suddenly alert, formed a lane to bar the passersby. Rosa Luxemburg, a militiaman at each side, walked through and entered the building.

In the lobby a rowdy crowd of armed men fell silent as she came in, and then they exploded in boisterous merriment. "Röschen," somebody shouted as she passed, "there goes the old whore." Aloof and distant, she climbed the flight of stairs, conscious of every step, careful not to trip. Staff Captain Pabst waited for her in his office. The identification took no time. "Are you Frau Rosa Luxemburg?" he asked. She looked past him. "That's for you to determine," she answered briskly. "According to the picture it must be you," said Pabst. Her eyes were still fixed on the wall behind him. "If you say so," she retorted.[34]

The captain called in Lieutenant Vogel and ordered him to escort Luxemburg downstairs. She was told to go straight to the car that was to take her to Moabit prison. She buttoned her coat, picked up her suitcase, and without a word left the captain's room.

Meanwhile, the crowd in the lobby grew bigger and rowdier. The news that Red Rosa was on the premises spread quickly, and some guests and servants now mingled with the soldiers. Her face set, Luxemburg descended the stairs and walked toward the exit. Before she reached the revolving door, a soldier tore loose from the crowd and with one quick move clubbed her over the head with his rifle butt. Without a sound she fell on the carpeted floor. Soldier Runge hit her once more, this time in the temple. He raised his rifle to strike again, but a comrade halted him: "Stop it, that'll do."[35] Blood streaming from her mouth and nose, Luxemburg was lifted from the floor. A shoe fell from her foot, and a soldier picked it up—a trophy. She was carried to the car waiting in the street, now cleared of civilians, and put in the back seat between two soldiers. The driver started the engine and drove off.

The shot fired a hundred meters away was heard in the hotel. In all probability it was fired by Lieutenant Vogel, standing on the car's running board. He drew his revolver from its holster, aimed it at Luxemburg's head, and pulled the trigger. Jammed, the revolver fired only on the second try. The bullet went through her left temple. The body jerked once and then lay still. Somebody threw a blanket over her head.

The car drove on. Not far from the bank of the river Spree, the driver was ordered to stop. "Let's take her out here," said Lieutenant Vogel.[36] Helped by one of the soldiers, he dragged the body out of the car and the party headed for the river. On the way a patrol stopped them, but after Vogel identified himself, they were allowed to pass. Once, when Luxemburg's hanging hand caught in the bushes, Vogel touched her body, which, he said later, gave him an unpleasant feeling. When they reached the Landwehr Canal, Vogel ordered the soldiers to throw the body into the river. The order was duly executed. "The old slut is swimming now," somebody remarked.[37]

Epilogue

Her political friends and enemies alike breathed a sigh of relief at Rosa Luxemburg's assassination. Prematurely. Her missing body touched off a controversy, as did her work. It stigmatized the latter-day revolutionaries who had subverted her vision of socialism into a monstrous caricature.

The official version of the murder of Rosa Luxemburg and of Karl Liebknecht was issued on 16 January by the Wolff Telegraph Agency and published in the afternoon and evening newspaper editions. It reported that Liebknecht, en route from the Hotel Eden to Moabit prison, was dealt a heavy blow to the head by an unknown assailant as he sat in a car under military escort. The car had engine trouble and Liebknecht was ordered to proceed on foot. Staggering and profusely bleeding from the head wound, Liebknecht tried to escape and was shot.

The version of Luxemburg's death was even more bizarre. A mob was said to have attacked her while she was leaving the Hotel Eden, but her escort managed to rescue her and put her, unconscious, into the waiting car. When the car pulled out, an unknown person jumped on the running board and fired a pistol at her. The car drove on until a crowd stopped it near the canal. Screaming "This is Rosa!" they dragged her out and vanished in the darkness.[1] There was no body.

"It should not be forgotten," commented one newspaper, "that it was a people's court of justice that meted out the sentence to both terrorist leaders."[2] The people's verdict was cruel, the paper said, but it was just. From the ensuing reports it was apparent that the "treason" of the son of the venerated socialist leader Wilhelm Liebknecht was more shocking than that of Luxemburg, who was after all a Russian, a Pole, and a Jew.

Leo Jogiches took it upon himself to discover the truth. He refused to leave Berlin, aware though he was of his double jeopardy; he was now at the helm of the Communist Party of Germany and, worse, he threatened to demolish the government's flimsy cover-up. The official four-week-long investigation, not surprisingly, was inconclusive; it was conducted by a court-martial determined to obscure the facts. However, on 12 February 1919, after the investigation had come to a virtual standstill, *The Red Flag* carried a long report on the murders committed on the night of 15 January. Meticulously it reconstructed the events and identified the perpetrators, claiming that both murders were planned and executed with the knowledge and cooperation of the military now conducting the investigation. A picture taken at the Hotel Eden on the day after the assassinations, showing soldier Runge in the company of his accomplices celebrating their feat, was also published.

No one doubted who was behind the attempt to put the blame where it belonged. And so Jogiches sealed his fate. Though friends pressed him at least to change his address, he told Mathilde Jacob, "I cannot abandon my landlady just now."[3] It is striking that this man, to whom women never seemed to matter much, should have jeopardized his life in 1906 in Warsaw by staying in the same hotel with Luxemburg and now by staying with his mistress.

As the net tightened around him, Jogiches made a daring expedition reminiscent of his youthful exploits in Wilno—he went to Luxemburg's apartment. "It is beautiful here," he said to Mathilde Jacob, his gaze wandering over the familiar objects. It was a rare admission from the man who always preferred a bivouac to home. "I feel as though Rosa could walk in any moment." Before he departed he asked Mathilde Jacob to do something for him: to keep the apartment.[4]

Early in March the police tracked him down. Brought to police headquarters, he was immediately separated from the other detainees, clearly singled out for special treatment. Only at gunpoint did he identify himself, and then only after his request for an investigating magistrate was jeeringly turned down. He was walked to his last destination—a roomful of officers. For a long time the sounds of the beating reverberated in the corridors. Officially, Jogiches was shot in the back by a sergeant major Ernst Tamschick "while attempting to escape." In the morgue, where Mathilde Jacob went to identify his body, a watchman who had seen the massacred remains stopped her. "Don't go inside," he said. "You will never get rid of that sight, never."[5]

Once the facts about the murders of Luxemburg and Liebknecht had become public, the government was forced to try the perpetrators. The court-martial took place on 8–14 May 1919. Speaking for the prosecution, the magistrate, Paul Jorns (Jorns was promoted to Reichsanwalt in the Weimar Republic and later in Nazi People's Court), stated in his closing speech that Lieutenant Vogel and soldier Runge had "severely mistreated" the culprits. There were extenuating circumstances, however: the defendants' previous excellent records and their participation in the war. Also, there was Runge's diminished responsibility; the "fury" which the mere sight of Luxemburg and Liebknecht provoked in him was, after all, "hardly surprising." As for the picture taken at the Hotel Eden, the gathering that had been ostensibly celebrating the assassinations was entirely accidental; Runge just happened to be sitting at the table, quietly eating his dinner. There was indeed a wine bottle on the tray, but it was empty; nothing but beer and pastries had been consumed. There was no way of proving, Jorns asserted, that Runge's blows or Vogel's bullet had caused Rosa Luxemburg's death. Accordingly, Lieutenant Vogel was sentenced to two years and four months' imprisonment for committing a misdemeanor while on guard duty, for illegally disposing of a corpse, and for filing an incorrect report. Soldier Runge was sentenced to two years and two weeks imprisonment for attempted manslaughter.[6]

Runge declared shortly afterward: "The investigation was a farce . . . Jorns told me in private, 'You take the whole blame upon yourself, you will get at most four months, and you can always count on us should you be in trouble.' "[7] Whether he was ordered or bribed to strike Luxemburg with his rifle butt remained unclear, but it was clear that his actions had been prompted by others. In 1933, invoking his early contribution to the cause of Nazi Germany, soldier Runge requested financial compensation for being unjustly punished. "My noble Führer, the people's Chancellor, Adolf Hitler," he wrote to the Ministry of Justice, "has also paid for his ideals with prison."[8] The government granted him a lump sum of 6,000 marks.

Captain Waldemar Pabst, who identified Luxemburg and Lieb-knecht at the Hotel Eden and sent them to their deaths, provided some details in an interview he granted in 1959. The two were dangerous, he said, and had to be killed, despite the lack of evidence against them. Liebknecht was to be shot while attempting to escape, Luxemburg was to be murdered by a furious crowd. In Liebknecht's case the plan worked, more or less; with Luxemburg it failed. For unknown reasons the "crowd" did not materialize. Commenting officially on Pabst's statement in 1962, the government of the German Federal Republic referred to the murders as "executions in accordance with martial law."[9]

The manner of death chosen for the offenders was, it seems, in keeping with their station. Liebknecht was to be shot—he was a German. The mob murder was reserved for Luxemburg—she, a Jew, should perish in a pogrom.

The statute of limitation for Luxemburg's murder would run out in ten years. Levi was determined to prevent this. In 1928, the public prosecutor, Paul Jorns, sued an editor, Josef Bornstein, for publishing an article accusing Jorns of mishandling the Luxemburg-Liebknecht investigation. Paul Levi, acting as the editor's attorney, revealed Jorns's complicity in the cover-up. In a four-hour-long speech, which the eminent writer, Carl von Ossietzky, described as the "most powerful speech in German after Ferdinand Lassalle," Levi proved that Jorns had suppressed evidence in both murders.[10] Jorns, at the time of the trial a public prosecutor in the Supreme Court of the Weimar Republic, was found guilty of abetting the assassins. Levi asked in the courtroom how Jorns, a disgrace to his profession, could have been appointed to one of the nation's highest judicial positions. It confirmed his gravest doubts about the future of his country.

Albert Einstein wrote to Levi that it was "uplifting to see a man, all alone, with no support other than his love of justice and his sagacity, cleanse the atmosphere—a wonderful parallel to Zola. Among the best of us Jews," Einstein said, "some of the social justice of the Old Testament is still alive."[11] Jorns appealed the verdict—the Nazis later compensated him for his ordeal. During the protracted court battle Levi was stricken in 1930 with a pernicious fever that ended in his tragic death. "Suicide of a traitor to his country," screamed the newspaper headlines. "He couldn't stand the stench of his own race so he jumped out the window." "A renegade from conviction," wrote *The Red Flag*, founded by Rosa Luxemburg.[12]

On Saturday, 31 May 1919, a female body was spotted in one of the locks of the Landwehr Canal and taken to the city morgue. Later that night the minister of the interior, accompanied by Berlin's police president, disrupted a dinner party attended by the minister of defense, Gustav Noske. "She has been found," they whispered when Noske joined them in a secluded study. "Who?" asked the surprised Noske. "Rosa," came the answer.[13] They pleaded with Noske to remove the corpse from the morgue immediately lest the easily excitable Sunday crowds stage a demonstration.

Under cover of night, the body was taken by car to a military camp in Zossen, about 40 kilometers outside Berlin, for secret burial. But the plan failed. The press was quick to pick up the news, sensational as it was in view of the recent verdicts. Paul Levi, who took over the leadership of the Communist Party of Germany after Jogiches's murder, demanded an independent identification and postmortem examination. Three physicians refused to perform it, fearing for their lives. The postmortem was finally performed, and the police took photographs of the body. Dr. Maxim Zetkin, Costia's older brother, agreed to identify the photographs and the body in the presence of Mathilde Jacob. The cause of Luxemburg's death remained unknown. The skull showed no injuries despite the blows she had received, and the effect of the gunshot wound in the left temple could not be established because of advanced decomposition. She might have been tossed into the water still alive.

Mathilde Jacob identified the belongings. The gloves, which she herself had bought, were still on Rosa's hands. She recognized the shreds of the velvet dress and the golden amulet. The body was released in her care on payment of a 3-mark fee. A receipt, duly signed, was handed to her.

Rosa Luxemburg was buried in the Friedrichsfelde cemetery on 13 June 1919.

Twenty years earlier, meditating on the death of Leo Jogiches's mother, she had written to him, "The thought that gnaws at me is, what was that life about? What was it for? Was it *worth living?*"[14]

Driven by an urge to live a complete life, Rosa Luxemburg left her country, her home, her family. She sought to make the lives of all people complete, worth living, even though she knew that we are "like the Jews, being led by Moses through the desert."

Acknowledgments

My principal thanks go to Krystyna Pomorska Jakobson.

A special debt of gratitude is due to Feliks Tych.

My sincere thanks are offered to Maia Ettinger.

I am grateful to Maria Chodakowska, Bert Hartry, Artur Eisenbach, Diana H. Green, Przemysław Ogrodziński, and Tadeusz Perl.

For sharing memories with me and giving inestimable assistance I am indebted to Halina Luxemburg-Więckowska, Gertrud Zetkin, Konstantin Zetkin, Karl Kautsky, Jr., Charlotte Beradt, Rose Frölich, Zofia Marchlewska, and many people who wish to remain anonymous.

I wish to thank Hannah Arendt, Abraham Bick, Anette Petersen-Brandhorst, Milorad M. Drachkovitch, Janusz Durko, Shmuel Ettinger, Dawid Fajnhauz, Walter Grossmann, Harold J. Hanham, Sarah Hartry, Roman Kaufmann, Alfons Klafkowski, Paweł Korzec, Verena Stadler-Labhart, Manfred Lachs, Jerzy Stahl, Mieczysław Maneli, Kenneth R. Manning, Marietta Nettl-Meltzer, Moshe Mishkinski,

253

Ladislav Mysyrowicz, Sybille Quack, Emma Rothschild, Gershom Scholem, Annette Silbert, Janna Malamud Smith, David Smith, Fritz Stern, and J. L. Talmon.

I offer special thanks to my agent, Georges Borchardt, for his unfailing enthusiasm and encouragement. Particular appreciation must go to my editor at Beacon Press, Joanne Wyckoff, to Pam Pokorney, Beacon's production manager, and to Barbara Flanagan for her careful and inventive copyediting.

Maria Sachs and Marilyn Henry worked helpfully on the manuscript.

Note on Transliteration and Translation

Transliteration from the Cyrillic alphabet follows the modified international scientific system (see J. Thomas Shaw, *The Transliteration of Modern Russian for English-Language Publications*, Madison, Milwaukee, and London: University of Wisconsin Press: 1967). The only exceptions are cases of widely accepted English spelling of names, such as *Tolstoy* and *Dostoevsky* rather than *Tolstoj* and *Dostoevskij*.

All translations are by the author unless otherwise indicated.

Abbreviations

Political parties mentioned in the text are abbreviated as follows:

KPD	Communist Party of Germany
PPS	Polish Socialist Party
RSDRP	Russian Social Democratic Workers' Party
SDKP	Social Democracy of the Kingdom of Poland
SDKPiL	Social Democracy of the Kingdom of Poland and Lithuania (also referred to as Polish Social Democracy and Polish Social Democrats)
SPD	German Social Democratic Party
USPD	Independent Social Democratic Party of Germany

Notes

Preface

1. Rosa Luxemburg, *J'étais, je suis, je serai! Correspondance 1914–1919*, ed. Georges Haupt (Paris: Francois Maspero, 1977), 306.

Chapter 1   *Zamość: The Native Town* · 1870–1873

1. Bogumiła Sawa, "Przyczynek do sytuacji prawnej Żydów zamojskich od II połowy XVI do XIX w." (The legal status of the Jews in Zamość from the second half of the sixteenth century until the nineteenth century), *Biuletyn Żydowskiego Instytutu Historycznego* 3(99); 29 (Warsaw, 1976).

2. Ibid., 35.

3. Rabbi Abraham Bick of Jerusalem kindly provided me with exhaustive information about the ancestors of Lina Luksenburg née Löwenstein.

Chapter 2   *Warsaw: The Drastic Change* · 1874–1882

1. Many details about Rosa Luxemburg's childhood and adolescence are based on personal interviews with Mrs. Zofia Marchlewska in 1977–1979 and Dr. Gertrud Zetkin in 1980.

2. Feliks Kon, *Narodziny Wieku* (Warsaw: Książka i Wiedza, 1969), 12–13.

3. Rosa Luxemburg, *Briefe an Karl und Luise Kautsky*, ed. Luise Kautsky (Berlin: E. Laub'sche Verlagsbuchhandlung GmbH, 1923), 181.

4. *Czerwony Sztandar*, Warsaw, February 1911, no. 180, p. 2.

Chapter 3   *Warsaw: The Adolescent Quest* · 1882–1889

1. Adam Mickiewicz, *Dzieła*, 16 vols. (Warsaw: Czytelnik, 1955), 3:307–8.

2. Mickiewicz, *Dzieła*, 12:121–22.

3. Alina Witkowska, *Mickiewicz, Słowo i Czyn* (Warsaw: Państwowe Wydawnictwo Naukowe, 1975), 266.

4. Mickiewicz, *Dzieła*, 6:18.

5. Ibid., 47.

6. Jakub Szacki, "Rola Żydów w życiu ekonomicznym Warszawy w latach 1863–1896" (The role of the Jews in the economic life of Warsaw in 1863–1896), *Biuletyn Żydowskiego Instytutu Historycznego* 29:12–49 (Warsaw, 1959).

7. A. I. Gercen, *Sochinenija v devjati tomakh*, 9 vols. (Moscow: Goslitisdat, 1956), 5:606.

8. Helene Deutsch, *Confrontations with Myself* (New York: Norton, 1972), 98.

9. Personal interview with Zofia Marchlewska, 1978.

10. Maria Żmigrodzka, *Orzeszkowa* (Warsaw: Państwowy Instytut Wydawniczy, 1965), 54. See also Franciszek L. von Erlach, *Partyzantka w Polsce w roku 1863* (Warsaw: Wydawnictwo Ministerstwa Obrony Narodowej, 1960), 148.

Chapter 4   *Wilno: Leo Jogiches, the Young Conspirator* · 1867–1890

1. Z. Rejzin, "L. Jogiches and the Beginning of the Jewish Labor Movement" (in Yiddish), *YIWO* 3:432–48 (Wilno, 1939). I am indebted to Mr. Leo L. Wolfe for the English translation.

2. Róża Luksemburg, *Listy do Leona Jogichesa-Tyszki*, ed. Feliks Tych, 3 vols. (Warsaw: Książka i Wiedza, 1968–1971), 1:141.

3. Ibid. 1:xxiv.

4. Cited in Franco Venturi, *Roots of Revolution* (New York: Grosset & Dunlap, 1966), 359.

5. Zdzisław Leder (Władysław Feinstein), "Leon Jogiches-Tyszka," in *Archiwum Ruchu Robotniczego* (Warsaw: Książka i Wiedza, 1976), 215.

6. Ibid., 207.

7. Rejzin, "Jogiches," 445–46.

8. Charles Rappaport, "The Life of a Revolutionary Emigré," *YIVO Annual*, 213 (New York, 1951).

9. Luksemburg, *Listy* 1:578.

10. Ibid. 1:xxiv.

11. Rappaport, "Life," 214.

Chapter 5   *Rosa Luxemburg and Leo Jogiches* · 1889–1894

1. Róża Luksemburg, *Listy do Leona Jogichesa-Tyszki*, ed. Feliks Tych, 3 vols. (Warsaw: Książka i Wiedza, 1968–1971), 1:7.

2. Zdzisław Leder (Władysław Feinstein), "Leon Jogiches-Tyszka," in *Archiwum Ruchu Robotniczego* (Warsaw: Książka i Wiedza, 1976), 222–27.

3. G. Plekhanov's letter to F. Engels, 16 May 1894, in *Pod Znamenem Marksizma* no. 11–12:17 (Moscow, 1928).

4. Luksemburg, *Listy* 1:xxvii.

5. Ibid.

6. Ibid. 2:50.

7. Ibid. 1:360.

8. Róża Luksemburg, *Wybór Pism*, ed. Bronisław Krauze, 2 vols. (Warsaw: Książka i Wiedza, 1959), 1:374.

9. Ibid., 2:130.

10. John Mill, *Pioneers and Builders* (in Yiddish) (New York: Der Wecker, 1943),

167. I am indebted to Professor Moshe Mishkinski for the English translation.
    11. Cited in Paul Frölich, *Rosa Luxemburg, Gedanke und Tat* (Paris: Editions Nouvelles Internationales, 1939), 38–39.
    12. Feliks Tych, *Polskie Programy Socjalistyczne, 1878–1918* (Warsaw: Książka i Wiedza, 1975), 241.
    13. *Pod Znamenem*, 17.
    14. Luksemburg, *Listy* 1:3.
    15. Ibid., 21.
    16. Ibid., 403.
    17. Ibid., 77.
    18. Ibid., 77.
    19. Ibid., 2:94.
    20. *Pis'ma M. A. Bakunina k A. I. Gercenu i N. P. Ogarevu*, ed. M. P. Dragomanov (Geneva: Georg & Co. Libraires Editeurs, 1896), 493.

Chapter 6   The Uphill Struggle · 1895–1898

1. Róża Luksemburg, *Listy do Leona Jogichesa-Tyszki*, ed. Feliks Tych, 3 vols. (Warsaw: Książka i Wiedza, 1968–1971), 1:267.
    2. Ibid., 189.
    3. Ibid., 74.
    4. Ibid., 2:146.
    5. Ibid., 1:244.
    6. Ibid., 2:101.
    7. Ibid., 42–44.
    8. Ibid., 1:400.
    9. Ibid., 349.
    10. Ibid., 2:474.
    11. Ibid., 1:84.
    12. Ibid., 554.
    13. Ibid., 537.
    14. Ibid., 485.
    15. Róża Luksemburg, "Nieznane listy Róży Luksemburg do działaczy SDKPiL," ed. Feliks Tych, in *Archiwum Ruchu Robotniczego* (Warsaw: Książka i Wiedza, 1976), 179.
    16. Luksemburg, *Listy* 1:31.
    17. Ibid., 2:472.
    18. Ibid., 17.
    19. Ibid., 1:401–2.
    20. Ibid., 401.
    21. Ibid., 579.
    22. Luksemburg, "Nieznane listy," 177.
    23. Luksemburg, *Listy* 1:31–32.
    24. Ibid., 31–38.
    25. Ibid., 136–40.
    26. Ibid., 49.
    27. Ibid., 65.
    28. Ibid., 102.
    29. Ibid., 47.
    30. Ibid., 56–57.
    31. Ibid., 55.

32. Ibid., 93.
33. Ibid., 2:501.
34. Anna Luksenburg (AL), postmark 2 November 1897. The unpublished Polish originals of the letters written to Rosa Luxemburg by her father and siblings from Warsaw are at the Hoover Institution on War, Revolution and Peace, Stanford, Calif., Folder, XI.
35. AL, 4 May and 9 May 1897.
36. AL, 29 July 1897.
37. AL, 30 October 1897.
38. Elias Luksenburg, 30 October 1897.
39. AL, undated (after 30 September 1897).
40. Luksemburg, *Listy* 2:501.
41. AL, postmark 2 November 1897.
42. Elias Luksenburg, 30 October 1897.
43. AL, undated (after 30 September 1897).
44. Luksemburg, *Listy* 1:93.
45. Ibid., 94.
46. Ibid., 115.
47. Ibid., 179.

Chapter 7   The German Conquests · 1898–1900

1. Róża Luksemburg, *Listy do Leona Jogichesa-Tyszki*, ed. Feliks Tych, 3 vols. (Warsaw: Książka i Wiedza, 1968–1971), 1:150.
2. Ibid., 156–57.
3. Ibid., 167.
4. Ibid., 180, 166–67, 213.
5. Ibid., 181.
6. Ibid., 190.
7. Ibid., 197.
8. Ibid., 207, 211.
9. Ibid., 194.
10. Ibid., 213.
11. Ibid.
12. Ibid., 149.
13. Ibid., 220.
14. Ibid., 236.
15. Ibid., 217.
16. Ibid., 200.
17. Ibid., 226.
18. Ibid., 218.
19. Ibid., 173, 185.
20. Arno Herzig, "Paul Singer—Heinrich Braun, zum Revisionismusstreit der deutschen Sozialdemokratie vor dem I. Weltkreig," in *Jahrbuch des Institut für Deutsche Geschichte, Beiheft* 6:127 (Tel-Aviv, 1983).
21. Luksemburg, *Listy* 1:225.
22. Ibid., 218.
23. Shulamit Volkov, "Social Democracy Against Anti-Semitism in Imperial Germany," in *Jahrbuch des Institut für Deutsche Geschichte, Beiheft* 2: 70 (Tel Aviv, 1976).
24. Luise Kautsky, *Rosa Luxemburg, ein Gedenkbuch* (Berlin: E. Laub'sche Verlagsbuchhandlung, 1929), 23–24.

25. Luksemburg, *Listy* 2:304–5.
26. Ibid., 24.
27. Ibid., 1:230.
28. Ibid., 229.
29. Ibid., 220.
30. Ibid., 287–88.
31. Ibid., 397.
32. Ibid., 446–47.
33. Ibid., 448.
34. *Z Pola Walki* 1(5):69 (Warsaw, 1959).
35. Luksemburg, *Listy* 1:328.
36. Werner Blumenberg, ed., "Einige Briefe Rosa Luxemburgs und andere Dokumente," *Bulletin of the International Institute of Social History* 2:16–18 (Amsterdam, 1952).
37. Luksemburg, *Listy* 1:466, 469.
38. Róża Luksemburg, "Nieznane listy Róży Luksemburg do działaczy SDKPiL," ed. Feliks Tych, in *Archiwum Ruchu Robotniczego* (Warsaw: Książka i Wiedza, 1976), 177.
39. Luksemburg, *Listy* 1:36.
40. Ibid., 92.
41. Ibid., 457, 369, 466.
42. Ibid., 2:24.
43. Ibid., 1:331.
44. Ibid., 2:520.
45. Ibid., 1:240.
46. Ibid., 2:42.
47. Ibid., 60.
48. Ibid., 102.
49. Ibid., 1:238.
50. Ibid., 2:53.
51. Ibid., 39–42.
52. Ibid., 49.
53. Ibid., 43.
54. Ibid., 50.
55. Ibid., 100.
56. Ibid., 50.
57. Ibid., 1:268–69.
58. Ibid., 578–79.
59. Ibid., 334.

Chapter 8   *"Love and Work Together"* · 1900–1902

1. Róża Luksemburg, *Listy do Leona Jogichesa-Tyszki*, ed. Feliks Tych, 3 vols. (Warsaw: Książka i Wiedza, 1968–1971), 2:102.
2. Ibid., 62.
3. Ibid., 85.
4. Ibid., 104.
5. Ibid., 51.
6. Ibid., 1:577–78.
7. Ibid., 2:72.
8. Ibid., 102–3.

9. Ibid., 78–79.
10. Ibid., 78.
11. Ibid., 46.
12. Rosa Luxemburg, *Briefe an Karl und Luise Kautsky*, ed. Luise Kautsky (Berlin: E. Laub'sche Verlagsbuchhandlung GmbH, 1923), 13–17.
13. Ibid., 18–19.
14. Luksemburg, *Listy* 1:438.
15. Ibid., 481.
16. Ibid., 434–35.
17. Ibid., 2:107.
18. Ibid., 110–11.
19. Ibid., 115.
20. Rosa Luxemburg, *Briefe an Freunde*, ed. Benedikt Kautsky (Hamburg: Europäische Verlagsanstalt, 1950), 129.
21. Róża Luksemburg, "Nieznane listy Róży Luksemburg do działaczy SDKPiL," ed. Feliks Tych, in *Archiwum Ruchu Robotniczego* (Warsaw: Książka i Wiedza, 1976), 179.
22. Elias Luksenburg (EL), 25 January 1900.
23. EL, 2 November 1899.
24. Anna Luksenburg, 9 May 1897.
25. EL, 11 April 1900.
26. EL, 20 April 1900.
27. Luksemburg, *Listy* 2:118.
28. Ibid., 1:142.
29. Ibid., 463.
30. Władysław Feinstein, alias Zdzisław Leder, Jogiches's disciple and collaborator, wrote the one existing biography of Jogiches in 1929 in Moscow. It was first published by Feliks Tych in *Archiwum Ruchu Robotniczego*, vol. 3 (Warsaw: Książka i Wiedza, 1956), 193–339.
31. Luksemburg, *Listy* 2:165.
32. Ibid., 143–44.
33. Ibid., 195–96.
34. Ibid., 122.
35. Ibid., 213–14.
36. Ibid., 214, 244.
37. Ibid., 125.
38. Ibid., 191, 185.
39. Ibid., 155.
40. Ibid., 166–69.
41. Ibid., 184.
42. Ibid., 210.
43. Ibid., 135.
44. Ibid., 145.
45. Ibid., 159.
46. Ibid., 233.
47. Ibid., 130.
48. Ibid., 136.
49. Ibid., 147.

Chapter 9   Prison: The Real Initiation · 1902–1904

1. Róża Luksemburg, *Listy do Leona Jogichesa-Tyszki*, ed. Feliks Tych, 3 vols. (Warsaw: Książka i Wiedza, 1968–1971), 2:254.
2. *Gazeta Ludowa*, Poznań, 16 June 1904, 1.
3. Luksemburg, *Listy* 2:266–67.
4. Ibid., 257.
5. Ibid., 267–77.
6. Ibid., 274.
7. Zdzisław Leder (Władysław Feinstein), "Leon Jogiches-Tyszka," in *Archiwum Ruchu Robotniczego* (Warsaw: Książka i Wiedza, 1976), 258.
8. Ibid., 253.
9. Ibid., 258.
10. James Joll, *The Second International: 1889–1914* (London: Routledge & Kegan Paul Ltd., 1974), 102.
11. Luksemburg, *Listy* 2:297.
12. Ibid., 293–95.
13. Rosa Luxemburg, *Briefe an Karl und Luise Kautsky*, ed. Luise Kautsky (Berlin: E. Laub'sche Verlagsbuchhandlung GmbH, 1923), 60–62.
14. Luksemburg, *Listy* 2:299–300.
15. Ibid., 295.
16. Ibid., 301.
17. Róża Luksemburg, *Wybór Pism*, ed. Bronisław Krauze, 2 vols. (Warsaw: Książka i Wiedza, 1959), 1:331.
18. Ibid., 340–47.
19. Feliks Tych, ed., *Socjaldemokracja Królestwa Polskiego i Litwy, Materiały i Dokumenty*, 2 vols. (Warsaw: Książka i Wiedza, 1957–1962), 2:229.
20. Feliks Tych and Horst Schumacher, *Julian Marchlewski* (Warsaw: Książka i Wiedza, 1966), 120.
21. Luksemburg, *Listy* 2:495.

Chapter 10   Back in Warsaw · 1905–1906

1. Róża Luksemburg, *Listy do Leona Jogichesa-Tyszki*, ed. Feliks Tych (Warsaw: Książka i Wiedza, 1968–1971), 2:60.
2. Ibid., 225–26.
3. Ibid., 312.
4. Zdzisław Leder (Władysław Feinstein), "Leon Jogiches-Tyszka," in *Archiwum Ruchu Robotniczego* (Warsaw: Książka i Wiedza, 1976), 268–81.
5. Ibid., 277–78.
6. Luksemburg, *Listy* 2:321.
7. Ibid., 325.
8. Ibid., 360.
9. Ibid., 367.
10. Ibid., 518–19.
11. Ibid., 397.
12. Leder, "Leon Jogiches-Tyszka," 269.
13. *Z Pola Walki*, 11–12:173–74 (Moscow, 1931).
14. Luksemburg, *Listy* 2:443–45.
15. Ibid., 459.
16. Ibid., 465.
17. Ibid., 472.

18. Ibid., 509.
19. Ibid., 464.
20. Ibid., 452.
21. Ibid., 474.
22. Ibid., 541.
23. Rosa Luxemburg, *Briefe an Karl und Luise Kautsky*, ed. Luise Kautsky (Berlin: E. Laub'sche Verlagsbuchhandlung GmbH, 1923), 86–87.
24. Ibid., 79.
25. Ibid., 81.
26. Ibid., 93.
27. Ibid., 96–97.
28. Feliks Tych, "Ostatni pobyt Róży Luksemburg w Warszawie," in *Warszawa popowstaniowa* 1864–1918 (Warsaw: Państwowe Wydawnictwo Naukowe, 1968), 243. See also W. Bystrjański, "Róża Luksemburg i Leon Tyszka w obliczu carskiej sprawiedliwości," in *Z Pola Walki* 2:116–27 (Moscow, 1927).
29. Tych, "Ostatni pobyt," 247.
30. Luxemburg, *Briefe Kautsky*, 102.
31. Ibid., 101–2.
32. Ibid., 99, 114.
33. Rosa Luxemburg, *Briefe an Freunde*, ed. Benedikt Kautsky (Hamburg: Europäische Verlagsanstalt GmbH, 1950), 43.
34. Luxemburg, *Briefe Kautsky*, 95.
35. Ibid., 116.
36. Rosa Luxemburg, *Ausgewählte Reden und Schriften*, 2 vols. (Berlin: Dietz Verlag, 1951), 1:208.
37. Luxemburg, *Briefe Kautsky*, 107.
38. Ibid., 116.
39. Luksemburg, *Listy* 3:265.
40. Luxemburg, *Ausgewählte* 1:165.
41. Ibid., 222.
42. Ibid., 212.
43. Ibid., 230.

Chapter II   Costia Zetkin · 1907–1912

1. Karl Kautsky, Jr., ed., *August Bebels Briefwechsel mit Karl Kautsky* (Assen: Van Gorcum & Co., 1971), 184.
2. Rosa Luxemburg, *Briefe an Freunde*, ed. Benedikt Kautsky (Hamburg: Europäische Verlagsanstalt GmbH, 1950), 16.
3. Kautsky, *Bebels*, 227.
4. Rosa Luxemburg, *Gesammelte Briefe*, ed. Annelies Laschitza and Günter Radczun, 5 vols. (Berlin: Dietz Verlag, 1982–1984), 3:229.
5. Ibid., 74.
6. Ibid., 50.
7. Ibid., 63.
8. Ibid., 2:378, 3:151.
9. Ibid., 3:53.
10. Ibid., 2:373.
11. Ibid., 4:205.
12. Ibid., 2:289.
13. The quotes from Luxemburg's letters to Konstantin Zetkin, referred to as

Zetkin, are from Zetkin's papers to which his wife, Dr. Gertrud Zetkin, kindly gave me access. The page numbers refer to my transcript of these papers. Zetkin, 4.

14. Luxemburg, *Gesammelte Briefe* 2:291.
15. Róża Luksemburg, *Wybór Pism*, ed. Bronisław Krauze, 2 vols. (Warsaw: Książka i Wiedza, 1959), 1:589–603.
16. Luxemburg, *Gesammelte Briefe* 2:289.
17. Ibid., 2:282.
18. Zetkin, 12.
19. Rosa Luxemburg, *Briefe an Karl und Luise Kautsky*, ed. Luise Kautsky (Berlin: E. Laub'sche Verlagsbuchhandlung GmbH, 1923), 121.
20. Róża Luksemburg, *Listy do Leona Jogichesa-Tyszki*, ed. Feliks Tych, 3 vols. (Warsaw: Książka i Wiedza, 1968–1971), 3:12.
21. Ibid., 72–73.
22. Luxemburg, *Gesammelte Briefe* 2:290.
23. Ibid., 284.
24. Zetkin, 6.
25. Zetkin, 18.
26. Luxemburg, *Gesammelte Briefe* 3:69.
27. Ibid., 88.
28. Ibid., 223.
29. Luksemburg, *Listy* 3:179–80.
30. Luxemburg, *Gesammelte Briefe* 3:151.
31. Ibid., 4:72.
32. Ibid., 3:271–72.
33. Ibid., 230.
34. Luise Kautsky, *Rosa Luxemburg, ein Gedenkbuch* (Berlin: E. Laub'sche Verlagsbuchhandlung, 1929), 14.
35. Luxemburg, *Gesammelte Briefe* 4:239.
36. Ibid., 5:37, 54.
37. Ibid., 4:106, 188.
38. Ibid., 3:77.
39. Ibid., 149.
40. Ibid., 4:75.

Chapter 12   Other Fires, Other Fights · 1908–1913

1. Róża Luksemburg, *Listy do Leona Jogichesa-Tyszki*, ed. Feliks Tych, 3 vols. (Warsaw: Książka i Wiedza, 1968–1971), 3:32, 66.
2. Ibid., 177.
3. Personal interview with Halina Luxemburg-Więckowska, 1977.
4. Luksemburg, *Listy* 3:215, 187, 174.
5. Ibid., 196–97.
6. Ibid., 156; 156 note a.
7. Ibid., 87–88.
8. Ibid., 50.
9. Ibid., 46–48.
10. Rosa Luxemburg, *Ausgewählte Reden und Schriften*, 2 vols. (Berlin: Dietz Verlag, 1951), 1:203.
11. Róża Luksemburg, *Wybór Pism*, ed. Bronisław Krauze, 2 vols. (Warsaw: Książka i Wiedza, 1959), 1:600–609.
12. György Lukács, *Geschichte und Klassenbewustsein* (Berlin: Malik-Verlag, 1923), 5–6.

13. Isaiah Berlin, *Against the Current* (New York: Viking Press, 1980), 337.

14. Rosa Luxemburg, *The National Question*, ed. Horace B. Davis (New York Monthly Review Press, 1976), 135.

15. Ibid., 140.

16. Ibid., 139–40.

17. Ibid., 117.

18. Ibid., 141–43.

19. Ibid., 195.

20. J. V. Stalin, *Sochinenija*, 13 vols. (Moscow, 1946–1952), 4:31–32.

21. Rosa Luxemburg, *Gesammelte Briefe*, ed. Annelies Laschitza and Günter Radczun, 5 vols. (Berlin: Dietz Verlag, 1982–1984), 4:197.

22. Ibid., 3:268.

23. Karl Marx, *Interviews and Recollections*, ed. David McLellan (Totowa, N.J.: Barnes & Noble Books, 1981), 153.

24. Werner Blumenberg, ed., "Einige Briefe Rosa Luxemburgs und andere Dokumente," in *Bulletin of the International Institute of Social History* 7:39 (Amsterdam, 1952).

25. Luksemburg, *Listy* 3:157–58.

26. Victor Adler, *Briefwechsel mit August Bebel und Karl Kautsky*, ed. Friedrich Adler (Vienna: Verlag der Wiener Volksbuchhandlung, 1954), 510.

27. Karl Kautsky, Jr., ed., *August Bebels Briefwechsel mit Karl Kautsky* (Assen: Van Gorcum & Co., 1971), 221 note 3, 226.

28. Adler, *Briefwechsel*, 513.

29. Luksemburg, *Listy* 3:167.

30. Luxemburg, *Gesammelte Briefe* 4:139.

31. Luksemburg, *Listy* 2:406.

32. Ibid., 503, 524.

33. Ibid., 3:167, 169.

34. Zdzisław Leder (Władysław Feinstein), "Leon Jogiches-Tyszka," in *Archiwum Ruchu Robotniczego* (Warsaw: Książka i Wiedza, 1976), 292.

35. Feliks Tych and Horst Schumacher, *Julian Marchlewski* (Warsaw: Książka i Wiedza, 1966), 202.

36. Luksemburg, *Listy* 3:273.

37. Ibid., 302–3, 309, 357, 369.

38. Karl Radek, "Noiabr," in *Krasnaia Nov'* 10:150 (Moscow, 1926).

39. Luksemburg, *Listy* 3:280.

40. Ibid., 314 note 10.

41. *Czerwony Sztandar*, Warsaw, July 1912, no. 188, p. 2.

42. Luxemburg, *Gesammelte Briefe* 4:107.

43. Luksemburg, *Listy* 3:216–17.

44. *Myśl Niepodległa*, Warsaw, September 1910, no. 146, p. 1258. See also G. Haupt and P. Korzec, "Les socialistes et la campagne antisémite en Pologne en 1910: un épisode inédit," *Revue du Nord*, (Lille: April–June 1975): 185–91.

45. *Myśl Niepodległa*, no. 148, p. 1348.

46. Ibid., no. 146, pp. 1264–72.

47. "Protokoll über die Verhandlungen des Parteitages der S.D. Partei," 22–28 September 1901 (Lübeck), 191–95.

48. Luksemburg, *Listy* 3:177.

49. Ibid., 179–80.

50. *Młot*, Warsaw, 22 October 1910, no. 12, pp. 5–6.

51. Personal interview with Mrs. Rose Frölich, 1978.

52. Luksemburg, *Listy* 3:251–53 note 1.

53. Rosa Luxemburg, *Briefe an Freunde*, ed. Benedikt Kautsky (Hamburg: Europäische Verlagsanstalt GmbH, 1950), 105.

54. *Z Pola Walki*, 1(45):165 (Warsaw, 1969).

55. Luksemburg, *Listy* 3:318–19.

56. Both *Introduction to Political Economy* and *Anti-Critique* were posthumously edited and published by Paul Levi in 1925 and 1921, respectively. The full title of the latter is *The Accumulation of Capital or What the Epigones Have Made of Marxist Theory: An Anti-Critique.*

57. Luxemburg, *Briefe an Freunde*, 85.

58. Rosa Luxemburg, *The Accumulation of Capital: An Anti-Critique*, ed. Kenneth J. Tarbuck (New York: Monthly Review Press, 1972), 62.

59. Ibid., 74–75.

Chapter 13   War on War · 1914

1. Róża Luksemburg, *Listy do Leona Jogichesa-Tyszki*, ed. Feliks Tych, 3 vols. (Warsaw: Książka i Wiedza, 1968–1971), 3:141.

2. Ibid., 346.

3. Ibid., 387–90.

4. Rosa Luxemburg, *Ausgewählte Reden und Schriften*, 2 vols. (Berlin: Dietz Verlag, 1951), 2:491–504.

5. Charlotte Beradt, *Paul Levi* (Frankfurt/Main: Europäische Verlagsanstalt, 1969), 12.

6. Luksemburg, *Listy* 3:318.

7. Rosa Luxemburg, *Gesammelte Briefe*, ed. Annelies Laschitza and Günter Radczun, 5 vols. (Berlin: Dietz Verlag, 1982–1984), 4:62.

8. Luksemburg, *Listy* 3:405.

9. Luxemburg, *Gesammelte Briefe* 3:224.

10. James Joll, *The Second International:* 1889–1914 (London: Routledge & Kegan Paul Ltd., 1974), 146.

11. Luxemburg, *Ausgewählte* 1:208.

12. *Krieg dem Kriege* (Berlin: Buchhandlung Vorwärts, 1912), 9.

13. Luksemburg, *Listy* 3:402.

14. Rosa Luxemburg, *Briefe an Karl und Luise Kautsky*, ed. Luise Kautsky (Berlin: E. Laub'sche Verlagsbuchhandlung GmbH, 1923), 153.

15. Angelica Balabanoff, *My Life as a Rebel* (Bloomington: Indiana University Press, 1973), 114–15.

16. Ibid., 116.

17. Rosa Luxemburg, *Briefe an Freunde*, ed. Benedikt Kautsky (Hamburg: Verlagsanstalt GmbH, 1950), 115–16.

18. Ibid., 75.

19. Victor Adler, *Briefwechsel mit August Bebel und Karl Kautsky*, ed. Friedrich Adler (Vienna: Verlag der Wiener Volksbuchhandlung, 1954), 606–7.

20. Luxemburg, *Gesammelte Briefe*, 5:28–29.

21. Ibid., 18.

22. Luxemburg, *Briefe an Freunde*, 67.

23. Ibid., 70.

24. Ibid., 137.

25. Rosa Luxemburg, *Gesammelte Werke*, ed. G. Radczun, 5 vols. (Berlin: Dietz Verlag, 1972–1975), 4:25.

Chapter 14   In and Out of Prison · 1915–1918

1. VIIe Congrès Socialiste, Compte Rendu Analitique, Brussels, 1908, p. 123.
2. Rosa Luxemburg, *Briefe an Freunde,* ed. Benedikt Kautsky (Hamburg: Europäische Verlagsanstalt GmbH, 1950), 155.
3. Mathilde Jacob, "Von Rosa Luxemburg und ihren Freunden in Krieg und Revolution: 1914–1919," unpublished manuscript, Hoover Institution on War, Revolution and Peace, Stanford, Calif., MS 276, L98TZZ, p. 14.
4. Charlotte Beradt, ed., *Rosa Luxemburg im Gefängnis* (Frankfurt/Main: Fischer Verlag, 1973), 17.
5. Ibid., 32.
6. Ibid., 107, 84, 79.
7. Ibid., 22.
8. Ibid., 87.
9. Ibid., 16.
10. Ibid., 19.
11. Rosa Luxemburg, *Briefe an Karl und Luise Kautsky,* ed. Luise Kautsky (Berlin: E. Laub'sche Verlagsbuchhandlung GmbH, 1923), 155.
12. Beradt, *Luxemburg im Gefängnis,* 34.
13. Rosa Luxemburg, "Die Krise der Sozialdemokratie" (*Juniusbroschüre*) (Berlin: Verlag Rote Fahne, 1919), 1–2.
14. Ibid., 3–4.
15. Henriette Roland Holst-van der Schalk, *Rosa Luxemburg, Ihr Leben und Wirken* (Zurich: Jean Christoph Verlag, 1937), 221.
16. Luxemburg, "Die Krise," 98.
17. Zdzisław Leder (Władysław Feinstein), "Leon Jogiches-Tyszka," in *Archiwum Ruchu Robotniczego* (Warsaw: Książka i Wiedza, 1976), 306.
18. Ibid., 310.
19. Jacob, *Luxemburg,* 81.
20. Ibid., 81–83.
21. Beradt, *Luxemburg im Gefängnis,* 39.
22. Rosa Luxemburg, *Gesammelte Briefe,* ed. Annelies Laschitza and Günter Radczun, 5 vols. (Berlin: Dietz Verlag, 1982–1984), 5:13.
23. Beradt, *Luxemburg im Gefängnis,* 40.
24. Luxemburg, *Briefe an Freunde,* 120.
25. Beradt, *Luxemburg im Gefängnis,* 50.
26. Ibid., 51.
27. Ibid., 68, 62.
28. Luxemburg, *Briefe Kautsky,* 203.
29. Beradt, *Luxemburg im Gefängnis,* 96.
30. Ibid., 68.
31. Luxemburg, *Briefe an Freunde,* 150.
32. Luxemburg, *Briefe Kautsky,* 172.
33. Luxemburg, *Briefe an Freunde,* 159.
34. Ibid., 76.
35. Ibid., 100.
36. Ibid., 123.
37. Ibid., 112.
38. Ibid., 113.
39. Ibid., 106.
40. Ibid.

41. Ibid., 130.
42. Luxemburg, *Briefe Kautsky,* 198.
43. Luxemburg, *Briefe an Freunde,* 95.
44. Ibid., 78.
45. Ibid., 114.
46. Ibid., 80.
47. Ibid., 112.
48. Luxemburg, *Briefe Kautsky,* 191.
49. Ibid., 176.
50. Ibid.
51. Luise Kautsky, *Rosa Luxemburg, ein Gedenkbuch* (Berlin: E. Laub'sche Verlagsbuchhandlung, 1929), 12.
52. W. Blumenberg, ed., "Einige Briefe Rosa Luxemburgs," *International Review of Social History* 8:106 (Amsterdam, 1963).
53. Luxemburg, *Briefe Kautsky,* 156.
54. Ibid., 209.
55. Rosa Luxemburg, *Briefe aus dem Gefängnis* (Berlin: Verlag der Jugendinternationale, 1927), 59.
56. Ibid., 61, 53.
57. Ibid., 22–23.
58. Ibid., 23.
59. Rosa Luxemburg, *J'étais, je suis, je serai! Correspondance* 1914–1919, ed. Georges Haupt (Paris: François Maspero, 1977), 184.
60. Beradt, *Luxemburg im Gefängnis,* 73.
61. Ibid., 76.
62. Ibid., 81.
63. Luxemburg, *Briefe an Freunde,* 48–49.
64. Ibid., 45.
65. Tadeusz Radwański, "Wspomnienia działacza SDKPiL, 1900–1905," *Z Pola Walki* 1(5):99 (Warsaw: Książka i Wiedza, 1959).
66. Vladimir Korolenko, *Die Geschichte meines Zeitgenossen,* Preface by Rosa Luxemburg (Berlin: Verlag P. Cassirer, 1919), xi–liii, xxiv.
67. Ibid., vil–ivl.
68. Ibid., xii.
69. Beradt, *Luxemburg im Gefängnis,* 85–86.
70. Ibid., 97.
71. Leder, "Leon Jogiches-Tyszka," 322.
72. Luxemburg, *Briefe an Freunde,* 88.
73. Ibid., 157–61.
74. Luxemburg, *Briefe Kautsky,* 193.
75. Ibid., 209.
76. Leder, "Leder Jogiches-Tyszka," 319–20.
77. Rosa Luxemburg, *Gesammelte Werke,* ed. G. Radczun, 5 vols. (Berlin: Dietz Verlag, 1972–1975), 4:385–92.
78. Paul Levi, *Zwischen Spartakus und Sozialdemokratie,* ed. Charlotte Beradt (Frankfurt/Main: Europäische Verlagsanstalt, 1969), 96.
79. Rosa Luxemburg, *Die Russische Revolution,* edited and introduced by P. Levi (Berlin: Verlag Gesellschaft und Erziehung GmbH, 1922), 67ff.
80. Levi, *Zwischen Spartakus,* 136–38.
81. Ibid., 96–97.

82. Ibid., 122.
83. Beradt, *Luxemburg im Gefängnis*, 121.
84. Ibid., 123.

Chapter 15   The End and the Beginning · 1919

1. Joseph Goebbels, *Die Verfluchten Hakenkreuzler* (Munich: Verlag Frz. Eher Nachf., 1932), 15–16.
2. *Illustrierte Geschichte der Deutschen Revolution* (Berlin: Internationaler Arbeiterverlag, 1929), 201.
3. Hajo Holborn, *A History of Modern Germany: 1840–1945* (New York: Knopf, 1970), 514.
4. *Illustrierte*, 209. See also Arnold Brecht, *Aus Nächster Nähe, Lebenserinnerungen 1884–1927* (Stuttgart: Deutsche Verlags–Anstalt, 1966), 188–91; Philipp Scheidemann, *Memoiren eines Sozialdemokraten* (Dresden: Carl Reissner Verlag, 1930), part 2, 309–13.
5. Harry Graf Kessler, *Tagebücher: 1918–1937*, ed. Wolfgang Pfeiffer-Belli (Frankfurt/Main: Im Insel Verlag, 1961), 24.
6. *Illustrierte*, 236.
7. *Illustrierte*, 232–33. See also Brecht, *Aus Nächster*, 194–95.
8. Brecht, *Aus Nächster*, 194.
9. Mathilde Jacob, "Von Rosa Luxemburg und ihren Freunden in Krieg und Revolution: 1914–1919," unpublished manuscript, Hoover Institution on War, Revolution and Peace, Stanford, Calif., MS 276, L98TZZ, p. 95.
10. Rosa Luxemburg, *J'étais, je suis, je serai! Correspondance 1914–1919*, ed. Georges Haupt (Paris: François Maspero, 1977), 359.
11. Ibid., 363.
12. Jacob, "Luxemburg," 96.
13. *Correspondance*, 360.
14. Brecht, *Aus Nächster*, 240.
15. Rosa Luxemburg, *Gesammelte Werke*, ed. G. Radczun, 5 vols. (Berlin: Dietz Verlag, 1972–1975), 4:445.
16. *Unser Weg*, 15 January 1922, p. 45.
17. Luxemburg, *Gesammelte Werke*, 4:504.
18. Jacob, "Luxemburg," 97.
19. J. Ciszewski, "Z Warszawy do Berlina," *Z Pola Walki* 7–8:297 (Moscow, 1929).
20. Luxemburg, *Correspondance*, 365.
21. Ibid., 311.
22. Jacob, "Luxemburg," 84–85.
23. *Illustrierte*, 272.
24. Rosa Luxemburg to Paul Levi, 24 March 1914. I am indebted to Dr. Sibylle Quack for access to the transcript. See also Sibylle Quack, *Geistig frei und niemandes Knecht* (Cologne: Kiepenheuer & Witsch, 1983), 198.
25. Charlotte Beradt, *Paul Levi* (Frankfurt/Main: Europäische Verlagsanstalt, 1969), 22.
26. Luxemburg, *Gesammelte Werke*, 4:501.
27. Luxemburg, *Correspondance*, 373.
28. Ibid., 372.
29. Luxemburg, *Gesammelte Werke*, 4:524.
30. *Illustrierte*, 289.
31. Kessler, *Tagebücher*, 105–6.
32. Luxemburg, *Gesammelte Werke*, 538.

33. Vladimir Korolenko, "Legende vom Florus," quoted by Rosa Luxemburg in preface to Korolenko's *Die Geschichte meines Zeitgenossen,* p. il.

34. Elisabeth Hannover-Drück and Heinrich Hannover, eds., *Der Mord an Rosa Luxemburg und Karl Liebknecht* (Frankfurt/Main: Suhrkamp Verlag, 1967), 141, 67.

35. Ibid., 72.

36. Ibid., 86.

37. Ibid., 129.

Epilogue

1. Elisabeth Hannover-Drück and Heinrich Hannover, eds., *Der Mord an Rosa Luxemburg und Karl Liebknecht* (Frankfurt/Main: Suhrkamp Verlag, 1967), 39.

2. Ibid., 41.

3. Mathilde Jacob, "Von Rosa Luxemburg und ihren Freunden in Krieg und Revolution: 1914–1919," unpublished manuscript, Hoover Institution on War, Revolution and Peace, Stanford, Calif., MS 276, L98TZZ, 104–5.

4. Ibid., 107.

5. Ibid., 109.

6. *Mord,* 112–119.

7. Ibid., 135.

8. Ibid., 180.

9. *Der Spiegel,* 18 April 1962, p. 38. See also "Bulletin des Presse-und Informationsamtes der Bundesregierung," 8 February 1962, 223.

10. Charlotte Beradt, *Paul Levi* (Frankfurt/Main: Europäische Verlagsanstalt, 1969), 122.

11. Ibid., 126.

12. Ibid., 148–49.

13. Gustav Noske, *Aufstieg und Niedergang der deutschen Sozialdemokratie* (Zurich: Air-Edition, 1947), 85.

14. Róża Luksemburg, *Listy do Leona Jogichesa-Tyszki,* ed. Feliks Tych, 3 vols. (Warsaw: Książka i Wiedza, 1968–1971), I:218.

Sources

Published

Luksemburg, Róża. *Listy do Leona Jogichesa-Tyszki*. Edited by Feliks Tych. 3 vols. Warsaw: Książka i Wiedza, 1968–1971.

Luxemburg, Rosa. *Briefe an Karl und Luise Kautsky*. Edited by Luise Kautsky. Berlin: E. Laub'sche Verlagsbuchhandlung GmbH, 1923.

Luxemburg, Rosa. *Briefe an Freunde*. Edited by Benedikt Kautsky. Hamburg: Europäische Verlagsanstalt GmbH, 1950.

Luxemburg, Rosa. *Vive la lutte! Correspondance 1891–1914*. Edited by Georges Haupt. Paris: François Maspero, 1975.

Luxemburg, Rosa. *J'étais, je suis, je serai! Correspondance 1914–1919*. Edited by Georges Haupt. Paris: François Maspero, 1977.

Luxemburg, Rosa. *Gesammelte Briefe*. Edited by Annelies Laschitza and Günter Radczun. 5 vols. Berlin: Dietz Verlag, 1982–1984.

Luksemburg, Róża. *Wybór Pism*. Edited by Bronisław Krauze. 2 vols. Warsaw: Książka i Wiedza, 1959.

Luxemburg, Rosa. *Ausgewählte Reden und Schriften*. 2 vols. Berlin: Dietz Verlag, 1951.

Luxemburg, Rosa. *Gesammelte Werke*. Edited by G. Radczun. 5 vols. Berlin: Dietz Verlag, 1972–1975.

Rosa Luxemburg's letters to Paul Levi, courtesy of Dr. Sibylle Quack.

Unpublished

Papers of Konstantin Zetkin, courtesy of Dr. Gertrud Zetkin.

Papers of Halina Luxemburg-Więckowska, courtesy of owner.

Papers of Charlotte Beradt, courtesy of owner.

Memoir of Mathilde Jacob, courtesy of the Hoover Institution on War, Revolution and Peace at Stanford University, California.

Letters to Rosa Luxemburg from her father, Elias Luksenburg, and from her siblings, Anna, Maksymilian, Natan, and Józef, courtesy of the Hoover Institution on War, Revolution and Peace at Stanford University, California.

Letters of Luise Kautsky to Karl Kautsky, courtesy of the International Institute of Social History, Amsterdam.

Materials in private possession.

Personal interviews with persons listed in "Acknowledgments" and with persons who wished to remain anonymous.

The bibliography of Rosa Luxemburg's works is published in "Biblioteka pierwodruków Róży Luksemburg," Jadwiga Kaczanowska przy konsultacji i współpracy Feliksa Tycha, *Z Pola Walki* 3(19) (Warsaw: Książka i Wiedza, 1962), and "Uzupełnienia do bibliografii prac (pierwodruków) Róży Luksemburg," ed. Feliks Tych, *Z Pola Walki* 1(53) (Warsaw: Książka i Wiedza, 1971).

Credits

Grateful acknowledgment is made to archives and libraries for permission to use material in their collections:

Centralne Archiwum KC PZPR, Warsaw

Żydowski Instytut Historyczny, Warsaw

Archiwum Główne Akt Dawnych, Warsaw

Naczelna Dyrekcja Archiwów Państwowych, Warsaw

Muzeum Historyczne m.st.Warszawy, Warsaw

Urząd Stanu Cywilnego, Zamość

Archiwum w Zamościu, Zamość

Archive of J. P. Nettl courtesy of Marietta Nettl-Meltzer

Archive of Konstantin Zetkin courtesy of Gertrud Zetkin

International Institute of Social History, Amsterdam

Archives and Library of the Swedish Labour Movement, Stockholm

Stadtarchiv, Zurich

Sozialarchiv, Zurich

Zentralbibliothek, Zurich

Staatsarchiv, Zurich

Universitätsarchiv, Zurich

275

Archives d'État, Geneva

Friedrich–Ebert–Stiftung, Archiv der sozialen Demokratie, Bonn

Hebrew University Archive, Jerusalem

Bibliothéque National, Paris

Alliance Israélite Universelle, Paris

YIVO Institute for Jewish Research, New York

Widener Library, Harvard University, Cambridge, Massachusetts

To the Hoover Institution on War, Revolution and Peace at Stanford University, California, special acknowledgment for permission to use previously unpublished material.

To the MIT Press for permission to reprint from *Comrade and Lover, Rosa Luxemburg's Letters to Leo Jogiches*. Translated and edited by Elżbieta Ettinger (Cambridge, Massachusetts, and London, England: 1979).

Photographs are reprinted courtesy of: Centralne Archiwum KC PZPR, Warsaw; Archive of J. P. Nettl; SPD Archive, Bonn; The Hoover Institution on War, Revolution and Peace, Stanford, California; Gertrud Zetkin; Charlotte Beradt, Halina Luxemburg Więckowska.

Name Index

Subject Index

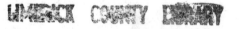